OLYMPIC GANGSTER

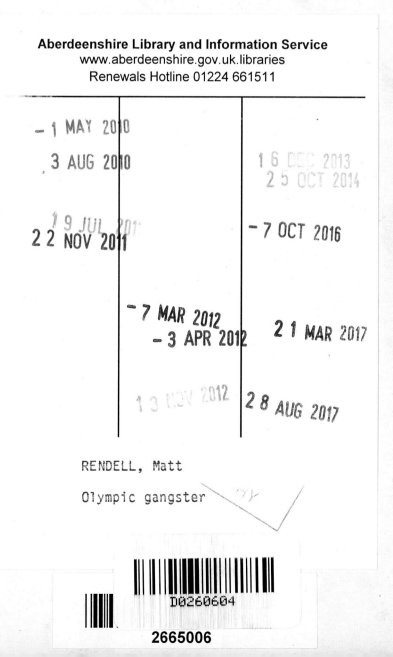

OLYMPIC GANGSTER

The Legend of José Beyaert
– Cycling Champion,
Fortune Hunter and Outlaw

Matt Rendell

MAINSTREAM
PUBLISHING

EDINBURGH AND LONDON

First published in Great Britain in 2009 by
MAINSTREAM PUBLISHING COMPANY
(EDINBURGH) LTD
7 Albany Street
Edinburgh EH1 3UG

ISBN 9781845963989

Grateful acknowledgement is made to *L'Équipe*
for permission to reproduce extracts here

A catalogue record for this book is available
from the British Library

Typeset in Caslon and He

Printed in Great Britain b
CPI Mackays of Chatham

To Vivi and to my father

CONTENTS

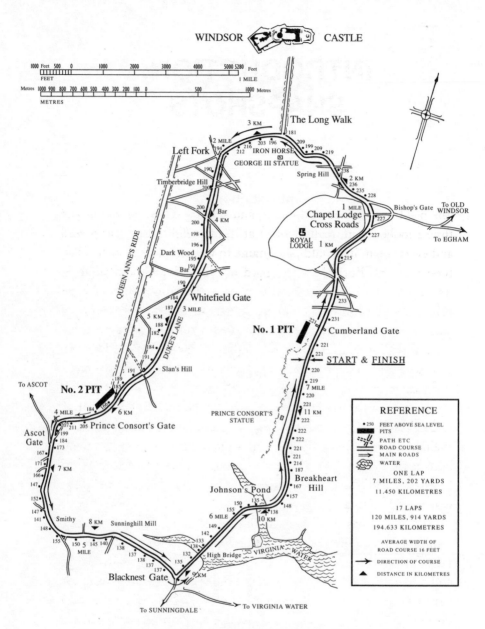

PLAN OF THE OLYMPIC ROAD COURSE,
WINDSOR GREAT PARK

INTRODUCTION: SNAPSHOTS

The print was stained and fading and slightly scratched and by the time I looked at it, really looked at it, fifty-eight years had passed and everyone in it I could put a name to was either dead or had lost their memory. But it was still hard not to look at it and smile. It was one of those black-and-white photographs you somehow see in colour. The sun is shining, that much you can tell. Three or four rows back people are squinting between the bodies in front or craning their necks to see over them, and although the crowd is a blur you can make out enough to see that everyone is looking at the same thing, an item whose momentary loss an instant ago caused the kind of anxiety that starts people scanning the area with the uncanny feeling that some sort of collective inattention is blinding them to the mislaid object, as if the problem were not any absence 'out there' but a pathology of the will and that greater clarity or purpose would be enough to make it visible again. Or catch the thief before he can make good his escape.

And now it has been found. The leader of the Tour de France, soon to be the winner of the Tour de France, has found the missing yellow jersey. You can tell it's yellow because it has a stylised logo embroidered on the breast pocket: 'HD' for Henri Desgrange, the man who created the yellow jersey, the man who created the Tour de France. In 1950 cycling shirts still had a button-pocket across the chest and it is by the flap of that breast pocket that Ferdinand Kübler has caught the thief, who isn't even trying to get away. And there he is, centre-right, the practical joker with the famous black-rimmed glasses and a mischievous grin: José Beyaert.

Bay. Are. Air. The 't' no one was ever quite sure whether to pronounce or not, which was Marie Legrand's fault. Or, rather, it was the fault of the German soldiers who had raped her mother and sister during the '14–'18 war. Since Marie couldn't tell the German they spoke from her husband's native Flemish, she banned both languages from the house, permanently detaching those three distinctly foreign syllables, bay, are and air, with a debatable 't', from their native tongue and leaving her sons José and Georges with a name more or less unpronounceable anywhere in the world beyond the land and language their father had long ago abandoned.

As for the forename José, Marie's eldest son didn't know where it came from, although he did say, seventy-nine years after he had received it, speaking Spanish now, 'Flanders was occupied by Spain for a few hundred years, Charles V and so on, but who knows?

'The "Be" in Beyaert,' he added, 'is supposed to mean "ruddy", but there's a black line in the family – skin, hair, all that. Everyone else was big and blond. When people wanted to insult us, they called us "Sidis" as if we were Moroccan. And when they said "Sidi", it meant there was going to be a fight.'

And there, perhaps, are the beginnings of this story, or some of them. The name José Beyaert was something like a prophecy.

I had always looked at the photograph and seen Kübler and the two men beside him, and the gendarme and everyone in the crowd, all looking at José and smiling. It seemed to me a magical scene, one of those memories you never forget as long as you have memory itself. But I had been missing something. Ferdinand Kübler, whom everyone called Ferdi and who spoke French with a comical accent and was for a few years one of the finest athletes alive, is pulling down the lip of the breast pocket and looking inside. José is looking inside too, and so is the smiling figure standing between them (José's team director, Jean Maréchal) and the other one looking over Ferdi's shoulder (possibly the *France-Soir* reporter Jean Coussy). The joke had two parts. The first part was the stealing of the yellow jersey. The second part was whatever was in the pocket. But no one can remember what it was.

On the back of the print José had written, with a number of grammatical errors and spelling mistakes and commas instead of full stops, 'When I put on Kübler's yellow jersey. Everyone was looking for the jersey, me with them. They all laughed, José Beyaert'.

I never found out what was in the pocket. I could never even put a date to it because José remembered it was in Montpellier, but the Tour didn't go to Montpellier that year so he remembered it wrong and none of the press reports from the 1950 Tour de France mentioned José's practical joke at all: the theft of the yellow jersey, even the temporary theft, in jest and quickly restored to the delight and laughter of everyone who saw it, was not something the race organisers either approved of or wanted to publicise. But when they tell you José Beyaert never wore the yellow jersey you'll know what to say.

He was a natural storyteller. He had the gift of gathering his experiences into quick narratives. These he used to conjure up acquaintances and lasting friendships. He fascinated people and during his cycling career his enormous spirit of fun made him a favourite with journalists who needed a comment or an anecdote to fill a column inch. Of his many gifts the two they valued most were the relentless optimism that continually persuaded him to look on the fair side of things and the sanguine turn of mind that allowed him to encapsulate his experiences in pithy, structured tales.

It was much more than just a knack, of course. The very act of telling our lives redefines the way we live them. José was one of those people who largely live to tell the tale. In other words he constructed his existence according to the rules of fiction, in which (unlike in life) something always has to happen. He was never one to sit and read when life was out there, waiting to be lived, but it did seem to me that he had something of that fictional character with 'an odd autobiographical habit which led him to compose in his mind from time to time a short sentence about himself containing a subject in the third person and a predicate in the past tense'. Which, it goes without saying, made the prospect of writing his story irresistible.

Optimistic and media friendly, José was also instantly recognisable thanks to the thick spectacles he wore with theatrical aplomb. In the years immediately after the end of the Second World War, the period known as the Reconstruction, he was one of several well-known national figures in France famous for their ostentatious round-rimmed glasses. Others included the President of the Republic, Vincent Auriol, and the intellectual Jean-Paul Sartre.

The day before José travelled to the French colony of Algeria to make his debut as a professional cyclist in January 1949, the leading French sports daily, *L'Équipe*, wrote:

JOSÉ BEYAERT HAS LEARNED THE MANUAL OF THE PERFECT ROAD RACER

He will start his first 'pro' season at Oran with three thousand kilometres of training, plenty of ambition and . . . ten pairs of glasses.

'Each pair has different coloured lenses,' he told his interviewer, *L'Équipe*'s cycling correspondent Albert De Wetter:

'I have special frames for competition. And believe me, rain and fog don't bother me. I coat my lenses with a covering so that water and humidity don't fog them up.'

A special covering?

'Not really. It was what we used to have on the gas masks at the beginning of the war.'

De Wetter even considered José something of an intellectual. 'Beyaert's replies always follow a clear logic,' he wrote. When asked how he expected to make the leap from amateur to professional cycling,

He pursed his lips and gave one of his customary acute replies:
'I hope I'll take the fast route to success, but you never know. I couldn't wait any longer, in any case. I'm twenty-three, I've seven years of racing behind me as an amateur. I've ridden all types of

race, mass start, time trials, climbing, stage races . . . So [as an amateur] I didn't have much more to learn.' . . . Like all riders he dreams of the Tour, but he knows that his Olympic title won't be enough to get him there. He'll have to earn his place.

L'Équipe had already named José its 'Rider to Watch in 1949'. Days later José won 'his first major race as a professional', the Critérium de l'Écho d'Alger. He was eulogised in the press. Great things were expected.

All this made him a rather natural celebrity, especially in that less cynical age when people's versions of themselves were still broadly being taken at face value. But it could get him into trouble too.

'I stopped the Tour de France,' he announced on day three of the six or seven I planned to spend interviewing him at his last home, in the tiny village of La Grève-sur-Mignon in the arrondissement of La Rochelle, the historic port town on France's Atlantic coast, in November 2004.

'You stopped the Tour de France?'

'In the middle of a stage. To go for a swim in the sea. At Sainte-Maxime.'

José was seventy-nine and gravely ill and I didn't spend seven days with him but four, after which he had to be taken to hospital. I waited out my empty mornings on long bicycle rides, hoping he'd be well enough to see me later on. The empty afternoons I sat around in my hostel at La Rochelle, or a café, reading and hoping he'd be well enough the next day or the day after that.

'We were riding gently along the shore in a bunch, and people were complaining: "It's hot! It's hot!" So I rode to the front and said, "Why don't you stop so I can have a quick paddle?"'

Of course! The famous photograph of riders at the shoreline, some splashing water over their heads, others immersing themselves bodily into the Gulf of Saint-Tropez.

'Everyone stopped and a few of us went down to the water's edge. We doused ourselves in water, went back up and set off again.'

I did go back a couple of days later for an hour at most but it was only when I had left José and returned home that I had a chance to look again at the famous image. No more than five or six race numbers are legible, none of them José's, and the riders' faces are mostly obscured by spray or turned away from the camera. But further out, twenty or thirty feet from the shore, someone is swimming backwards, away from the camera but facing the beach and observing the scene through black-rimmed glasses. Could it be . . . ? Well, yes, I thought it could. Conceivably. But I never had the chance to ask.

I had looked for him, on and off, for six years. I had done so because of three things I knew, or thought I knew, about him. I knew José had been a champion cyclist. He remains the last Frenchman to have won, at the Frenchman de Coubertin's revived, modernised Olympics, in that utterly French invention, bicycle racing – more than that, bicycle racing on the road – the quintessentially French title of Olympic road-race champion.

I also knew he had gone to South America to open the velodrome in the Colombian capital, Bogotá, and that he had intended to stay a month but instead he had stayed fifty years. And I knew that in Colombia he had entered dangerous professions: he had been an emerald trader at a time when the emerald mines were killing fields and there were shoot-outs on the streets of Bogotá, and he had been a logger in the rainforest, where the only law was the strength of a man's personality and his speed with a gun.

And that was all I knew about the white-haired old man I met near La Rochelle that cold Atlantic November.

The Olympic champion had spurned his celebrity so completely that no one seemed to know where to look for him. In Colombia, where José Beyaert had been a champion cyclist, then the national cycling coach and later on a sports commentator on national television, he remains a household name. Even so, I heard the same thing time and again:

'José Beyaert? I think he died.'

I soon learnt that people had been saying so since the '50s. José had something like a craving to disappear. He'd always turn up somewhere else in a new guise.

By 1999, when he finally returned to the place he had once called home, home was somewhere else. France, the country he had represented at the Olympic Games – the country he felt had abandoned him – was merely the place he had chosen to die.

Then, in November 2004, I found him, not dead, just forgotten. I flew to La Rochelle to spend a week with him. On the recordings of those interviews José's voice is often lost in the gasping of a sick old man who knows he is living his final months. He made it clear to me he had no further interest in life. And yet, seven months before his death, he told me, 'I've not lived long, but I've lived more than other people of my age.' The more I learnt about his life the more I felt he was right. 'I've had an incredible life,' he said, 'a life that was special.' But he had other leitmotivs: 'There are things I can't tell you,' he repeated, several times a day. Which made him more irresistible still.

However, with no clear idea whether José would recover or when, I flew back to England. There I managed to interest no publisher in the adventurous but distant life of a partly forgotten champion. Hell, I couldn't find a magazine prepared to give some space to José's story. There was a temporary improvement in his condition but with no funding to pay for research – no money to pay the rent – I never went back to see him. Within seven months José was dead. I'd found him too late.

I was left with eight hours of interviews: a miserly time in which to tell a life although at least I now had some of his stories, told, admittedly, with an indomitable Munchausenism that was as exasperating as it was promising. His anecdotes were darkly humorous, often untruthful, moving in places despite repeated acts of violence and revenge and the occasional bawdy episode. Some had obviously been told so often they had become opaque, masking rather than revealing the reality that lay behind them. There were monologues and sermons on subjects that obsessed or annoyed him, and the occasional stepping too far followed by an instinctive covering of tracks: 'I don't give a damn about my life. It's of no concern to anyone else. It's my affair, no one else's. I have done things that only have to do with me.' All the same, I found myself falling into the trance that comes when a story that has ensnared you demands to be fashioned into a book.

At one time he was a figure of fascination for a variety of French writers. Such and such an author, José told me, 'asked if he could write a book about me because I've done things, understand? I said, "No, you can't."

'And he said, "Well, think about it. If you do it, do it with me."

'So we put it down on paper. I can't remember exactly what it said but if I was going to have a book about my life within the next twenty years, we agreed he would be the one to write it. I thought I'd be dead by then anyway, so why not? And afterwards he left me in peace.'

I later discovered José was a known associate of a variety of French criminals. However French he was, and however famous – and he had been a personality as well as a name in several nations – he belonged nowhere and was forever changing countries and regions, disappearing from one wilderness into another, all the time leaving others supposing him deceased. Perhaps that was what made him so attractive.

Happily, and for reasons I only began to understand some years later, he agreed to let me write about him. He even allowed me to take away a box full of press cuttings, expired passports and photos ('My wife kept everything. I kept nothing. When it's done, it's done.'), among them the stained, fading, slightly scratched print of José in the yellow jersey, which, of course, he never wore.

I say happily because something then happened that changed things. A decision that had been taken in 1946 and had ended up supplying José with the reputation and entitlement that had made possible his unusual existence was taken again in 2005, and this time it made it possible to examine his uncommon life in the form of a book. The International Olympic Committee decided to take the Games to London. By touching on the 1948 London Games, however tangentially, it became feasible to delve into the past and set about recovering fragments, histories, a life, that would otherwise be lost. I didn't need to be asked twice. I retouched the proposal that had done the rounds in 2004 and as the Beijing Games approached in 2008 a publisher appeared. I tidied up my affairs, packed my bags and set off, initially for Paris, Nice and Corsica, and then for a couple of four-month sojourns at my other home in Medellín, Colombia, which became the base from which I followed José's footsteps into regions where, without his guidance and company, imagined, of course, not real – although real enough to me – I would probably never have gone.

There were other difficulties. For long periods of José's life there were no newspaper reports or published memoirs, no sheaves of letters or private diaries with which to corroborate his enchanted version of events. It wasn't just the personal, the innermost level of thoughts that was lost; even the broader structure of names, dates and places, the easy pickings of official records, had gone. José's stories either had no date or biographical context, or these things changed with each telling. In some cases they had been told so many times that they had an opaqueness that seemed to mask out much of the sheer richness of lived reality and reveal only a meagre, schematic abstraction that perfectly illustrated Milan Kundera's observation, 'The present moment is unlike the memory of it. Remembering is not the negative of forgetting. Remembering is a form of forgetting.'

To make things even thornier many of the people who associated with José had every reason either not to speak to me at all or to distort the truth about their activities together. I'd made some effort to get José's biography commissioned but the more I worked on it the less certain I was that my discoveries amounted to anything other than fiction. So, for instance, when I went to the newspaper archives I found no mention of the Sainte-Maxime dip either. I could not positively identify José in the photograph, which was only published later, with a comment by the Tour de France director Jacques Goddet, who fumed: 'Would it not be preferable for the cyclists to learn their gruelling metier, or reschool themselves in its lore, instead of indulging in the carnival antics that put half the peloton in the waters of the Gulf of Saint-Tropez?'

At the time Goddet had his driver pull alongside José to voice his disapproval. 'Beyaert,' he raged, 'you're always up to something, aren't you?'

José smiled and carried on pedalling. That was his story, anyway.

ONE

EUROPE / AFRICA

1

Marie Legrand's eldest son came into the world at 11 p.m. on 1 October 1925 at 134 Rue du Bois, Lens, a street that no longer exists in a city that had changed beyond all recognition during the previous conflict and would do so again in the next. During the First World War north-eastern France had been shelled into oblivion. In areas overrun by the Germans more than a million people had been forced from their homes. Thousands of buildings had been partially or totally destroyed, livestock all but wiped out and factory machinery systematically disassembled and shipped to Germany. The new town built by a workforce of citizens, convicts and Chinese workers to replace the old Lens would in turn be devastated in the war to come. You didn't say Rue du Bois anyway, or even the du Bois Terrace, it was Pit Four, although the mines are closed now and the argot dead.

They had found coal in 1849. Thanks to the deposits a hundred and fifty metres underground many worlds met in the town that squatted on the surface. Algerian Berbers arrived as the twentieth century began. In 1908, after the Courrières catastrophe – Europe's worst mining accident, one thousand two hundred lives lost underground – ethnic Poles, many of whose families had already migrated to Germany's industrialised Ruhr region, flooded in. Then between 1914 and 1918 nearly a million and a half French soldiers, 10.5 per cent of France's economically active male population, died in battle. Another 1.1 million were permanently disabled. At the start of the '20s, Italian workers arrived.

Flemish-speaking Belgians, of course, had always border-hopped. José's father, also José Beyaert, had arrived from the tiny Flanders village of Nazareth after the First World War, aged twenty or twenty-one, bringing his mother. He had learnt the Lens argot and believed it the national language until he moved his family to Paris and had to start again.

José, then, arrived in 1925. His brother Georges was born two years later. José told me, 'Georges was inclined to be ill. When he was four, he suffered double-bronchial pneumonia. It looked like it was all over. The priest came to the house. My grandmother gave him hot mustard baths. He was all red in the hot water; I can still see him. These are things you remember all your life. And even when he was a young man, you had to be careful with him.'

Even for families too poor to travel daily life in Lens entailed unavoidable exposure to very different ways of seeing the world. Friction between the communities was inevitable but the Poles and Italians were Catholics like the Flemish and on Sundays they all worshipped together. Georges Beyaert remembered the Polish marriages: 'Children were always welcome. We would swarm around the sweets and cakes. It was fun for kids.' And he seemed to be talking about life in general, not just the weddings.

On all this colour mining imposed a certain uniformity: blackened faces ('I never saw my grandfather's face without coal dust,' José told me), terraces ('When my grandfather, Louis Legrand, came home drunk they shouted, "No Louis, further along, further along!"'), graft ('They were poor people. Poor people who worked hard. Courageous people who didn't watch the clock when they were working.'), men distanced from their families by the shared experience of their life in the mineshafts, adored and idealised by young children. José told me, 'I remember all this. And I see him coming in – I used to ambush him when he came in, I loved my grandfather – and picking me up, tiny, and putting me inside his shirt.'

José's beloved grandfather was two metres tall. 'He was called Legrand and he wore his name well. My mother was tiny.'

So was José's remarkable father, who stood four foot eleven in his clogs. 'When he went for his national service, he stood on tiptoe and said he was taller.

'The officer said, "You're on the limit. Don't move."

'"OK!"

'He said it was the biggest mistake of his life. If he'd known, he said, he'd have done things differently.'

José's father was a patient and talented man. José called him 'uneducated but intelligent'. Underground he became a wagon coupler. 'He worked briefly in the coal mines but he was afraid,' Georges told me. So José Senior took up his father's trade and started repairing shoes, learning from a worker he employed to help him.

'He worked all his life without complaining, starting early and working late,' José told me. 'And when he did something, he did it well. He didn't do things he didn't know how to. He learnt how to do them first. It was this way with everything: he measured things carefully, finished them carefully. He took the time things take.'

As well as mending shoes, he found work as a tiler. Later, José told me, 'He was considered one of the best tilers in Paris. He worked with great precision.' He might have served an apprenticeship as a tiler before leaving Belgium for France, for despite his nationality he was employed on the SS *Normandie*, built in a French shipyard using French-built parts to represent France in the nation-state contest of the great liners.

Like many other Flandrians José Senior's passion was cycling. In the north he had ridden as an amateur for ten years. He once told the newspaper *Paris-Presse*, 'I was a very good regional. I won plenty of kermesses, a Grand Prix of Lens, and finished second in the Special Six Days of Busigny . . . I was very fast in the sprint . . . Cycling is so much in my blood that I've always prepared José's bikes and tubulars.'

José's father was an avid reader of *L'Auto*, the sports paper that had founded the Tour de France: 'It was all he read!' He was friendly with a number of former professional cyclists: Jules Lengagne, a professional in the 1930s with the France-Sport and Lapébie teams; Charles Deruyter, an old Peugeot rider who had finished in the top seven of the Paris–Roubaix three times between 1912 and 1923;

Georges Peyrode, who had won the Saint-Étienne Six Days in 1929; a track specialist named André Mouton, who had ridden well in six-day events and twenty-four-hour races; and Robert Jacquinot, a Tour de France stage winner in the 1920s.

José told me, 'He had an amateur licence. He rode a lot on the track because he didn't have time to ride on the road. He was a good little rider but a local rider. There are local riders who are champions but who never have the chance to ride elsewhere. When I was a professional I rode against local riders in Brittany and I couldn't beat them. They were champions but they stayed in their village because they didn't have any sponsorship. In those days only bicycle manufacturers sponsored cycling . . .'

José could remember watching his father race in the velodrome and taking trips to the cobbled roads outside the town to see the riders thunder past on their way from Paris to Roubaix. Cycling became the family sport and what José Senior had been unable to achieve himself he decided his sons would achieve for him.

Organised as well as industrious, he worked all hours and scrimped and saved and finally had enough to move his family away from the hell of the mines and start a new life in the capital. Georges told me, laconically, 'He couldn't read very well, but he could count. He took us to a little hotel in the 5th arrondissement and then, since my father was in the building trade, he bought a tiny house in Bagnolet and built rooms.'

In Paris, as in Lens, many different ways of life were scrambled together and locked in encounters none of their adherents necessarily understood. The French capital had been a haven for refugees from all over Europe since long before the First World War: Armenians escaping Turkish massacres, White Russians escaping the Revolution and civil war, mainly Jewish Poles fleeing Piłsudski's regime, and political fugitives from Mussolini's Italy and the Balkan dictatorships. And that was before the fugitives from Hitler's Germany and the lands he occupied and the flood of Spanish Republicans fleeing execution in Franco's Spain. As we sat talking in a Pantin café Georges told me, 'There were Italians at Bagnolet. Masses of Italians. And here there were lots of people from the north. They arrived through the Gare du Nord and stayed in the vicinity. The Bretons arrived at the Gare Montparnasse and stayed nearby. And at the Gare de l'Est there were huge numbers of immigrants from Alsace. Those were the quarters, more or less, in those days. Afterwards it got far more mixed up.'

Very little of this was picturesque. On the eve of the Second World War almost a third of France's 9.75 million dwellings had been declared unfit for human habitation. In 1920 twelve francs bought a US dollar. In 1925 it took twice that. Inflation made it politically impossible to lift rent controls, which had been imposed in 1914 as a war measure, so landlords were refusing to modernise properties and investors were reluctant to put money into housing.

Bagnolet, crowded with small, cramped dwellings, was something of a black spot. Its population of cobblers, upholsterers, locksmiths and tapestry makers was hit hard by the Great Depression. By 1935 unemployment was among the highest in the region.

It was then that a chance meeting in the street gave the Beyaerts a way out.

José's other grandfather, Evarist Beyaert, five foot six, black hair, brown eyes, born in Nazareth beside the Belgian town of Ghent, perhaps never intended to stay away. He had entered the United States of America on 29 April 1912 after nine days travelling steerage aboard the *Nieuw Amsterdam*. At Ellis Island he was designated a 'non-immigrant alien', meaning he had a return ticket he was required to use. Two other Nazareth men were with him: Theophile Mehuys, thirty-five, Evarist's age; and twenty-six-year-old Auguste Defauw. They told immigration they were farmhands headed for St Louis, Missouri, and a friend named Verhaeghen, whose address in the records is illegible. Evarist claimed he'd been to St Louis in November 1909 although there is no record of an earlier entry into the United States.

Mehuys' trail disappears at the water's edge. Defauw made it to Detroit and beyond: in October 1915 he crossed Lake Huron from Canada with dozens of other Flemish labourers and headed back to lodgings at 1028 Lafayette. He had a hundred and fifty dollars in his pocket. The 1920 census records neither name. Perhaps their stories are hidden behind new ones: Defoe, Mays, Muse? They, in any case, were single men chasing their fortunes. Not Evarist. Chasing a future or fleeing the past, he had left a wife, Leoncine, and children in Nazareth, and had a hundred dollars in his pocket as the Manhattan dreamscape rose over the Hudson: the astonishing Singer Building, the world's tallest, and the Woolworth Building emerging to challenge it. No way of knowing whether any of them reached St Louis, if that was their destination.

Georges told me his grandfather decided not to return to his family. 'In America there were lots of migrants but all of them were men. Evarist couldn't find a woman, so he went back to Belgium to look for one, intending to take her out there. But when he got to Europe the war meant he couldn't go back. He fled to France because he didn't want to fight and in Paris he found a woman and stayed.'

Evarist, a shoemaker, had a small business at Pantin, north of Paris. One day, and according to the family story it was by pure coincidence, Evarist met his son in the street and sold him his shoemaker's workshop. José, Georges and their parents moved away from dank Bagnolet.

José was severe with his grandfather: 'He abandoned his wife with three children. You can't respect people who do that.'

'Did he flee to the US to earn money for the family?' I asked.

'No, it was to earn money for himself. And he was an alcoholic too.'

But if Evarist Beyaert's story met with his grandson's disapproval the memory of it would resurface when José was in his twenties, reinforcing his resolve to strike out on his own and see the world.

José and Georges moved to the school at Rue de Montreuil. Georges told me, 'We didn't go out in the evenings. We worked in the shop with my father because in a shoemaker's there are lots of little jobs children can do. We gave the shoes to the clients, we mounted the glissoires on the shoes. We had to sweep up, clean up. If there was a bit of painting to be done, the boys did it.'

The two boys finished their Certificat d'Études and started work straight away. The workshop was called 'La Cordonnerie Moderne'.

José's father was also a good teacher. José told me, 'We made shoes to measure and I started working on them aged twelve and aged fourteen or fifteen I was already making shoes. I took measurements and cut the leather. I enjoyed making shoes.'

The business gained an excellent reputation. Clients included at least one celebrity. José recalled, 'One day I made a pair of shoes – I was fifteen or sixteen, I don't know which – for a man named André Dassary. He was a great singer.'

André Dassary sang with the Ray Ventura band but he was also a regional athletics champion and played rugby. As well as taking singing classes he became a physiotherapist and accompanied the French team to the World University Games in 1937.

José remembered, 'We'd been recommended to him and I made his shoes personally. When I finished them I showed them to my father, all stitched by hand. My father looked at them: he waited a moment, then said, "Not bad." *Merde!* I got angry. "You don't know how to say, 'They're good.'"

'He looked at me and said, "Listen son, to someone who's learning, you never say, 'It's good.' That way, he always tries to improve."

'He was right.'

Like his father, José would develop an infuriating didactic streak. He would also acquire a beautiful singing voice. Whether he sang for Dassary we do not know.

2

It is easy to imagine José enjoying popularity among his peers at school. No one could have spoken more excitedly about boxing or cycling or have had a better sense of humour or a keener wit or been more fun to be with in the playground or on the walk home, denying the existence of God, boasting of his free-thinking, perhaps even singing with his magical voice. He charmed a schoolgirl named Louise Poulalion, known as Louisette, whom he had known since he was six. Many years later they would marry.

But there was always another side to José. He had the reputation of being a hard case. He was always in trouble. His brother Georges told me, 'From when we were at school absolutely no one bothered me because they knew that if anything happened my brother would get involved. I could relax!'

When José saw his first professional prizefight we do not know: perhaps at the Vélodrome d'Hiver – the Vel d'Hiv or 'Winter Velodrome' – on Rue Nélaton near the Boulevard de Grenelle Métro (now Bir-Hakeim), where the American literary set – Hemingway, Dos Passos and so on – lost entire nights at the legendary six-day series in the 1920s. Fight nights continued there through the war. Or perhaps it was elsewhere: Paris after all was a boxing city. In *A Moveable Feast*, his memoir of life there, Hemingway excuses himself for making 'no mention of the Stade Anastasie where the boxers served as waiters at the tables set out under the trees and the ring was in the garden. Nor of training with Larry Gainst, nor the great twenty-round fights at the Cirque d'Hiver.'

Either way José at once fell in love with the sport. His father seized the opportunity to encourage his enthusiasm and the boys gained access to a gym where boxers trained. The Pantin Ring was home to a couple of celebrated Parisian prizefighters, Théo Medina and Emmanuel 'Titi' Clavel. Medina, born in 1918, was a bantamweight who fought his first professional bout aged twenty and was French champion by the outbreak of war. Middleweight Titi Clavel was José's age. Titi's first professional bout was in 1947. Within two years he would be French welterweight champion. Given their age and size, there is every possibility José and Titi entered the ring together. It would have been an explosive confrontation because, as Georges told me, 'José was the same height as me but his punch was very hard. One blow and it was over. In the beginning he wanted to box. He had four bouts and he won all four with a knockout.' *L'Équipe* made it three: in spring 1948, during the qualifying races for the Olympics, it described José as 'a former boxer (his record shows three bouts in the colours of coach Guérault, of the Pantin Ring. He won all three by knockout)'.

For a couple of years José and Georges Beyaert trained there most evenings. There could hardly have been a greater contrast between the two brothers. Georges was younger, of course, and more slightly built. He would one day be a professional cyclist like his brother, but a climber not a sprinter. José was so robust he developed the habit of speaking with detached curiosity about his own physique. As an old man he told me, 'I was very, very, very, very strong, and I'm not talking about cycling . . .'

He was a natural gymnast too, always walking on his hands. Looking back on those years José told me, 'I did physical culture: parallel bars, the rings, the floor. My father made me do sport. He said, "Do this, do that," but without putting too much pressure on me to achieve results. He was preparing me for cycling. He didn't have money to buy weights so he made them. I built up my chest. I had big lungs so I'd recover more rapidly. My father hadn't had the opportunity to study but he understood things. He knew what would be good for me. Little by little, he prepared me like that. And I enjoyed it.'

A photo among his papers shows the effects. It is a studio shot dated 1941 on the reverse, a portrait from the midriff up, naked but for the tortoiseshell glasses and greased-back hair, with clenched fists, big forearms, a muscular torso. Light, robust, powerful: a boxer's physique but for the glasses. They, and the sweet smile, masked a savagery. José wanted to win every battle he fought and he wanted to do so decisively. He didn't restrict his punches to the ring either: 'He always threw the first punch. At times, an argument started and – wham! We'd say, "José, don't hit people straight away. Try reasoning with them first." And he said, "I do, it's just that I prefer to reason with them while I'm on my feet and they're on the ground!"'

Gymnastics gave José a profound understanding of anatomy. This, the boxing skills he quickly acquired and his innate strength allowed him to bring down much bigger men in seconds. Many years later in Colombia, one of my interviewees gave me an example of José's blend of speed, strength and technique.

'José had a problem in the street. A policeman threatened him with a gun. In a second, José immobilised him and disarmed him and then frog-marched him to the police station.

'"Take me to the General."

'"This officer's a danger to society. You can take him from here. And here's his gun."'

Boxing no doubt imposed restrictions on José's strength of character. It gave him control and inner hardness and some standing away from the street. It may have helped save him from the nightmare of a life of uncontrolled violence. By going to the gym and learning to accept the subtle humiliations of boxers who were better than him – a role Titi Clavel may very well have performed – he might have begun to learn to make a kind of peace with so much that was unsettled in him, although if the Beyaert–Clavel bout took place it left no trace, and José's career in the ring was destined not to last. His brother again: 'He couldn't carry on because he wore glasses. He was told, "You can't box because of your eyes," although he was long-sighted and in a boxing ring he could see perfectly well. That's why, in the end, he wasn't a boxer, despite the fact that he preferred boxing to cycling.'

Years later, in June 1949, after winning his Olympic gold medal, he made *L'Équipe*'s front page by performing a sideways handstand on a chair for a picture. The accompanying article, 'Athlete, Gymnast and Boxer, Too', reads:

> Beyaert, who can ride on the flat, climbs well and sprints, appears to be an especially complete rider. More than that, he's an eclectic athlete who practised gymnastics, athletics and boxing before choosing the bicycle. José gave us proof of his gymnastic talents by performing, in the middle of the editorial offices and before our photographer, a perfect balance, and he had to repeat it a good ten times!

He is described as being as 'at ease with a skipping rope or on the parallel bars as he is on a bike. As you can see, he performed this handstand with a smile. And it's true: the Olympic champion, with his excellent morale, is always smiling.'

But cycling was his calling, and its asceticism, the bruising falls and injuries and pushing on in pain, the dietary self-control, the exertions that left the taste of blood, took over the task of tempering his tremendous strength and energy where boxing left off.

Cycling was immensely popular in France. There was that run of Tour wins, 1929 to 1934. And more than wins, personalities: André 'Dedé' Leducq – '*Gueule d'Amour et Muscles d'Acier*' (how shall we put that? 'The steely-armed love mug'?) – who won two himself and played a supporting role in three more; and René Vietto, who as a twenty year old won four mountain stages and yet sacrificed himself by surrendering one of his wheels, then his entire bike, to his team leader, handing him overall victory too. And there was that 1933 team, a Harlem Globetrotters of cyclists, all French: Georges Speicher, France's first world road-racing champion; André Leducq, winner in 1930 and 1932; Antonin Magne, winner in 1931 and 1934; Charles Pélissier, the winner of eight stages in the 1930 Tour de France; and Roger Lapébie, who would win the Tour in 1937. These were heroes whose images drifted before the dreamy eyes of young French children as they fell asleep. At the 1936 Olympics Frenchmen had won in the pursuit and taken gold and silver on the road. In 1939 the national cycling body issued 950 professional racing licences. Compare that with 157 in 2007.

At the start of the war Paris had seven velodromes: the Buffalo at Montrouge; the Cipale – better, 'La Cipale' – at Vincennes; the Saint-Denis, Vaugirard and La Croix-de-Berny tracks; the Parc des Princes; and the great Vélodrome d'Hiver. The Parc and the Vel d'Hiv were owned and managed by Henri Desgrange and Victor Goddet, whose portfolio included majority shares in the newspaper *L'Auto* and its showpiece race, the Tour de France.

José and Georges made their father's enthusiasm their own, even if it meant an adolescence of rigorous discipline. José told me, with comedic emphasis, 'In my youth, I never went to dance in a nightclub. Never. I never danced. Never. Not once. Never. Because my father had ideas about things. Walking wasn't good. Playing football wasn't good. Beer wasn't good. I did everything for the bike. At times it was good; at times it wasn't good. But it served as experience. There's no secret, you know. There are details, but the accumulation of details allows you to have a small advantage.'

'[My father] was passionate. He loved cycling. He always came to my races. He came by bike. And when I was engaged, he had a tandem and he brought my fiancée to the races and home.'

The roll call of his father's cycling friends is suggestive of the vast reservoir of race-craft and expertise that surrounded José. He rode for the Pantin club JPS (Jeunesses Populaires et Sportives), a small but well-connected organisation whose president, Achille Joinard, was the head of the French Cycling Federation and the future chairman of the Union Cycliste Internationale (UCI), cycling's world-governing body. Joinard was a straight-backed figure who wore a suit indoors and a greatcoat and trilby out. José liked and admired him: 'Achille Joinard was a great monsieur. Religious and all that, but . . . They spoke ill of him in certain contexts, but I would have nothing to do with that.' He was also a Pantin resident.

Pantin was also home to two Tour de France cyclists celebrated for very different reasons. One was Georges Speicher, the national hero. The Beyaert boys used to see him in the street. Georges Beyaert recalled, 'There were only two bike shops in Pantin, and they were next door to each other. One was called Valente. It was run by a woman and Speicher courted her before he won the Tour de France. She didn't want to marry him because he was no more than an apprentice there. When he became champion he decided he didn't want to marry her any more!'

Pantin's other Tour de France cyclist was Ernest Neuhard, who owned the other bike shop in the district. The year Speicher won the Tour de France, Neuhard came last. 'Two Pantinois in the Tour,' Georges reflected, 'and they finished first and last!'

The Parisian cycling stadiums were all full, even after France declared war on Germany, even after the seven months it took before the German army addressed Belgium, Holland and Luxembourg, slicing through them like a razor-sharp knife and emerging in the shadow of Paris. Refugees, eight or ten million, spilled into the streets, but still the bicycle races continued until the German army was within sixty miles of the city. *L'Auto* changed its name to *L'Auto-Soldat* and the journal of the national cycling body talked hard talk:

> There are more than five thousand young men in France capable of covering two hundred kilometres in a day by bicycle . . . If it were only a matter of defending our territory, is that not an interesting mass of rapid manoeuvres [when] the German motorised divisions advance at a mere fifty to eighty-five kilometres a day?

But the bike-bound hordes did nothing to hinder the German troops entering Paris in June 1940, when José was working part-time at the Motobécane bicycle factory a street or two away from the family shoemaker's shop in Pantin. After José had fitted the pedals, the Motobécanes went to the French army, who used them to speed French soldiers to the front.

'I came out of the factory to go and eat something at midday and I found myself in front of a group of German soldiers. I mounted the pavement with my bicycle and they walked past as if nothing had happened. I said to myself, "They've arrived. No more fitting pedals!'"

Alsace-Lorraine was annexed and the north-eastern border of France incorporated into a military administration. The rest of the land conquered by the Germans was divided into the thirty-million-strong Occupied Zone under the German army, consisting of the northern half of France plus the Atlantic coast as far as Spain, and the Free Zone in the south, containing thirteen million Frenchmen under a puppet regime based in Vichy.

In Spain and Italy professional racing carried on. Mussolini waited for the twenty-year-old Fausto Coppi to win the Tour of Italy on 9 June before declaring war on France and the United Kingdom the following day.

In France, racing returned when the occupation was in place. As refugees slowly returned to Paris the streets filled with bicycles and the velodromes reopened. At the top professional level, far from reducing the number of races, the war doubled it. The divided country began to host twin editions of the major races: in 1941, 1942 and 1943 there were two versions of the Critérium National: a Free Zone (or, from November 1942, 'Southern Zone') edition organised by the Lyon offices of *Paris-Soir* and an Occupied Zone (later 'Northern Zone') race arranged in Paris. In 1941 there were two French national titles awarded, and the Grand Prix des Nations – the most prestigious individual time trial in the sport – was held twice: between Condom and Toulouse in the Free Zone on 7 September and around Paris in the Occupied Zone on 14 September.

In 1941 the Flèche du Rhône or 'Rhône Arrow' pitted the best riders of the Occupied Zone against those from the centre and the south. Riders with the prestigious Mercier team like Georges Speicher, Raymond Louviot and Guy Lapébie, plus Émile Idée of Alcyon, took on the brilliant southern climber René Vietto and the hardy Pierre Cogan.

At the race start in Avignon on 20 April the gendarmerie intervened. Nine riders who had crossed the demarcation line without authorisation were prevented from starting. The race took place: Joseph Soffietti first, René Vietto second, Fermo Camellini third. The newspaper *Paris-Soir* put up the trespassing riders in a Lyons hotel. Their permits to return to the Occupied Zone arrived the following day. In Paris, however, they were arrested and held in La Santé Prison for three weeks. The incident could have ended in disaster: soon after their release the Germans began to take prisoners from La Santé and execute them in retaliation for attacks on their soldiers.

During the war years José and Georges worked with their father in the shoemaker's and rode their bikes together. With each pair of shoes and each tip José bought the parts that would become his first bike. 'One day I bought a frame, one day a wheel, another day the handlebars. We put a bike together and with that I went out riding with my father.'

Their father competed in the madison, that hybrid event in which two riders compete as a team, taking it in turns to race and rest. José Senior's partner had come with the Beyaerts from Lens to Bagnolet then from Bagnolet to Pantin. José told me, 'He was a Pole, Meyer or Majère. Léon Majère, something like that. He was like a brother to my father and he had a son called Jean. My father said, "Come and live with us." Jean was a little older than me. He was like an adopted brother. He was a cyclist too.'

José's father had opened a second shoe-repair shop on Avenue de la République in Aubervilliers. José told me, 'It wasn't far, two or three kilometres, but on the way back there was a bit of a climb near the railway and the town hall and it became a sprint between Léon, my father and me. In the beginning my father came first, Léon second and me third. Later I started to come second. And then when I beat my father for the first time we started to think seriously because he thought he was pretty good and I'd beaten him. I was fifteen. That was on my first bike. So he said, "I think from now on we should take this seriously." On Sundays we went on longer rides in the Chevreuse Valley to the east. There were lots of little climbs so we chose our route accordingly. We did sprints from time to time and I always won. I was always the strongest.'

José's first race came soon after his sixteenth birthday, towards the end of 1941. 'It was the last race of the year. Paris–Coulommiers. Ninety kilometres. I remember it as if it were yesterday. I finished in the peloton. I was riding for my brother. My adopted brother, not Georges. All race I'd been ahead of him, helping him by protecting him from the wind. He was dropped on the final climb, three or four kilometres from the finish line. We caught him at the back end of the peloton. I could have done much better and that's when I realised I was a good rider.'

In Paris there were amateur circuits each Sunday. 'There were lots of riders,' José told me. 'I remember at the start there were three to four hundred entrants. You never saw the front of the peloton.'

Some of these events are depicted in photographs I found among José's papers. The earliest is dated 6 September 1942. It shows a country road, slightly uphill, on which a white finish line has been traced, perhaps in chalk. José's bespectacled eyes look down and to the left, where he can see the front wheel of the bicycle that has beaten him by twelve inches and the front wheel of the bicycle he has beaten by the same distance to finish second. José may still have been boxing but he already had an explosive finish as a cyclist.

The next two photographs are stamped 11 April 1943 and marked in pencil, '1st race at Montrouge'. We see the racers, twenty-nine of them, bunched just before the start. One gawps. Several pull nonchalant poses. José's eyes are rimmed by round spectacle frames. He has the switched-on look of the serious racer. He has the same look in the next photograph: a rider bursts past a roundabout with two more side by side, thirty feet behind, and then José, fourth, sitting up, taking a long look, monitoring the break from the slipstream of the man in front, riding with his head as well as his legs.

The next picture shows José holding a bouquet, with his father at his side. It would complete the sequence except that it is dated two weeks later. He is skinny-armed but with huge, heavy hands. His father looks directly at the camera, expressionless. Emotionally choked. Too proud of his boy even to smile. It says a great deal about their relationship.

On 29 May 1944 we see José and a Swiss track rider, Jacques Lohmuller, in cycling uniforms in the stands of an open-air velodrome. Lohmuller is holding the bouquet. He is twenty-three; José is eighteen. They are standing beside men in suits, one of whom is the future UCI president, Achille Joinard.

There was no photograph of José with Roger Rioland. Rioland was a year older and a pursuit specialist: they rode the madison together. A powerful *rouleur* like Rioland who could keep the tempo high paired with a fighting-cock like Beyaert who could win the sprints made a formidable team. In the war years they were Vel d'Hiv regulars. Rioland recalls winning ten or twelve madisons there as José's partner: 'When we were amateurs we were always together. He was full of class. That was as amateurs. As professionals we never had the chance to ride together. He was Olympic champion; I was world champion and French champion. The contract would have been too expensive. It's the regret of my life as a track rider. I'd have liked to have ridden with him again. He had talent, heart: he was out of the ordinary, José.'

And there was more to his memories: 'With any woman he liked he tried his hand.' I heard similar and more explicit stories from many interviewees and formed the impression that, despite his stable relationship with Louisette, José was a Lothario who felt from an early age a raging need to fornicate at no matter what cost to the feelings of others.

Wartime shortages were acutely felt by young sportsmen like José and Rioland. 'The thing we most lacked was food,' José told me. 'When you're fifteen or sixteen you burn a lot of calories. We rode out looking for it! In normal life you carried a rain cape, a spare tyre and things in your food bag. Not a backpack, a *musette*, that's all. During the war you'd carry a kilo of beans in it. Life was hard. It was a special life, and dangerous. Dangerous because certain people took advantage of us youngsters. They made us carry arms in our food bags at bike races. It happened many times. It was abusive because if we'd been caught we would have been shot.'

'You carried arms from one part of Paris to another?'

'Yes: and outside Paris, during training rides. There were times I didn't know what was in my food bag.'

There are plenty of stories of cyclists who put their skills in the service of the Resistance. Jean Bobet has written of Charles Berty, a fine rider and cycle-shop owner who spread clandestine newspapers and provided bicycles for the Resistance, reconnoitred parachute drop zones by bike and passed on information from the Gestapo that he in turn had received from an employee of the Savoy Hotel, where the German police were in residence.

Others lost their lives for their efforts.

'I knew some. They were stopped in an old house they used the other side of Languiche-sur-Marne. The Germans went through their papers: "You're not from here." They shot nineteen of them.'

José was ambivalent on the subject of the Resistance. He helped them but he opposed what the Resistance called 'D measures', where 'D' meant 'Definitive': in other words, physical liquidations. 'We weren't involved in actual attacks. I didn't agree with them because if you killed a German they shot fifty people.' These must have been widely shared sentiments: the Institut d'histoire du temps présent lists only 208 killings by members of the Resistance in the *département* of the Seine. Fifty-seven of those took place after the Liberation.

José was as ambivalent towards the invaders as he was to the Resistance. He had no problem with strictness. He could see through it to their humanity: 'One day I was stopped by a German soldier. I'd been hanging onto a truck and they stopped me. I stopped, the truck left and the soldier gave me a slap in the face.'

'Did he speak French?' I asked.

'Just about. He told me, "Little imbecile, you could have fallen underneath it. You could have died there." Like a father to his son.

'I said, "Yes, sir."

'"Go on, get on your way."

'"Ah, *bon*."

'But that was after two or three years of occupation. He'd slapped me because I'd hung onto a truck and it was dangerous.

'Another example. A train had been attacked. I went in and found a box. I carried it away and looked inside: cognac – *merde!* I took it back to the train. Someone else was coming out. "No, no, no, José, it's too late. Don't go in!" But I went back to the train and found a sack full of nuts. I thought they were beans. Fifty kilos! I put it on my back: the door of the wagon, first, then a gap in the fence. As I come out I see a rifle, boots. I put the sack down where it falls.

'"What are you doing there?"

'A German soldier. He spoke French: in three or four years he'd learnt it.

'"Monsieur, there were other people stealing and they got away. I wanted to steal too. I'm sorry but it's to eat."

'He put down his rifle and helped me because carrying fifty kilos is hard. He helped me! There was a nursery school, leaving Pantin. I told him I was taking it there. He said: "I have young children who are hungry." I couldn't feel the fifty kilos. He was carrying it. I thought he was going to make off with it. I turned the corner. Pum! He gave it to me. I covered perhaps two hundred metres, perhaps more, perhaps less, and then I sat down on the sack for a while. When I'd recovered, I took the sack to the nursery school. When I got there, Pum!

'The woman: "What's in it?"

'"It's full of nuts. You can share them, do something for the kids."

'"Oh! *Formidable.*"

'I met the woman a month or two later. She said: "Monsieur, thank you for the sack." I explained about the soldier. I'd only taken them to the nursery school because he'd been behind me with a gun!

'I can't hate the Germans. It wouldn't be logical because it was an occupation. The German soldiers were afraid of being killed by people who weren't in uniforms, who hid themselves to take potshots at them. That wasn't right either, when you think hard about it. I couldn't, and I can't, hate them.'

The Vélodrome d'Hiver stayed open throughout the war. Every Sunday thousands of Parisians attended the Vél d'Hiv despite the low quality of the riders. There were cash prizes. Such was the demand that the Vel d'Hiv was open on All Saints' Day, Armistice Day, Christmas Day and New Year's Day.

But the Vél d'Hiv fulfilled another function during the war. In the summer of 1941 it was briefly used as a transit camp for Jewish prisoners detained in Paris. A year later, early in the morning of 16 July 1942, 12,884 Jewish men, women and children were seized in a notorious mass arrest. Some were sent directly to the internment camp at Drancy, north of Paris. The remaining seven thousand prisoners were taken to the Vél d'Hiv where for five days they were deprived of food and given access to a single water fountain.

The citywide sweep was planned by the Nazi authorities, but four and a half thousand French officials worked with the SS to ensure its success and the Parisian public transport system transferred the prisoners, following orders from the collaborationist government at Vichy. Not until 1995 did a French president – in the event, Jacques Chirac – recognise the part played by the French state in the operation.

At the time France was partially shielded from the truth about the camps. When the first survivors began to return after the war their rotting teeth and sallow skin and appalling emaciation shocked Paris. I talked about the Holocaust with José. It seemed to exist for him like something filmed – like the footage of Belsen and Dachau that reached the cinemas in 1945, although José never saw it. 'My father didn't want me to go to the cinema because you could smoke in the cinemas. Everything for the bike.' The discipline imposed by cycling shaped every aspect of José's experience.

I was curious to know if he had even been aware that the Vel d'Hiv had been used as a transit camp. There was no heroism in his words or actions. He was a teenaged sportsman totally wrapped up in his life, the way sportsmen often are. 'I knew about it,' he told me, 'but I'm a sentimental man. I don't like sad things. For example, documentaries that show a lion catching its prey; I don't like seeing it. I'm sentimental, even if there are things in my life that run against what I've said . . . I've done things that have nothing to do with what I've just said, but it's true. The circumstances are different.'

Seventy-six days after the arrest of the Jews the Vel d'Hiv reopened its doors for the European middleweight title fight between the Algerian-born Marcel Cerdan, a national hero in France, and the Catalan José Ferrer. Sixteen thousand attended, generating record receipts of 1,420,000 francs. Cerdan knocked Ferrer down four times in eighty-five seconds to win the European title.

Bicycles were important to the Resistance as a more or less silent, inconspicuous, rapid means of transport. On 4 June 1944, two days before the Normandy landings, Resistance fighters intercepted the Tour de la Haute-Vienne. The race had been rerouted the night before: still the partisans knew it would pass through La Croisille-sur-Briance, where they seized eight cars and twenty-two racing bikes, taking the riders' spare tyres and goggles and leaving them on foot. Two days later, at 6.30 a.m. on Tuesday 6 June, the Allied troops landed on the Normandy coast. The freedom fighters perhaps put the racing machines to use in the cause of liberty. Or they might simply have been bicycle thieves.

3

Que ce soient des boxeurs, des cyclistes
Sur le parking ou sur la piste,
Que ça se passe l'après-midi
Ou le soir ou réunion de nuit,
Il y a toujours un monde inouï.
Le Vel d'Hiv, c'est un peu Paris:
Paris qui vit, Paris qui crie,
Paris bon cœur, Paris blagueur.
Si tu n'avais pas existé
Mais Paris t'aurait inventé.

(Whether it's boxing or it's bikes
In the car park, on the track,
It doesn't matter: afternoon, later on
Or through the night,
There's always a tremendous crowd.
The Vél d'Hiv makes Paris proud:
Living Paris, shouting Paris,
Hearty Paris, joking Paris.
If you weren't already there,
Paris would have invented you.)

'Vél d'Hiv'
Yves Montand (1948)

Someone had phoned Édith Piaf. It was 22 August 1944 and in the chaos of the Liberation they needed more volunteers to guard the Comédie-Française. She dispatched her lover and protégé Yves Montand for sentry duty. Montand was twenty-three and not yet the major French singer and movie star he would become, although he was in fact Italian-born, birth name Ivo Livi.

Within weeks the Vél d'Hiv became a prison camp for the third time. Parisians accused of collaboration were arrested early in the day. From the Prefecture of Police on the Île de la Cité they were taken across to the old Conciergerie on the Quai de l'Horloge and thence to the Vél d'Hiv for dispatch to Fresnes Prison or the camp at Drancy. The Vél d'Hiv was a venue for mass political meetings too. None of this was chronicled in Montand's post-war song 'Vél d'Hiv', recorded in the Studio Washington in March 1948. He sings only of the great sporting events that brought all Paris in. The amateur nights when José and Roger Rioland ruled supreme, of course, didn't get a mention.

There was much to forget. Wartime collaboration with the Nazis and the *épuration sauvage* or 'unofficial purge' that followed the Liberation, when mob rule and lynch law provided much of the logic behind the accusations made and the accounts settled, made unhappy memories. Much better to sing of '*les mécanos, des employés, des aristos*' – mechanics, clerks and aristocrats – having a swell time together at the races:

> *Vél d'Hiv, même si on ne connais pas son voisin,*
> *Ça ne fait rien, c'est un copain . . .*

> (Vel d'Hiv, even if you don't know your neighbour,
> It doesn't matter, he's a friend . . .)

The black market was flourishing. Local drug gangs moved in on the petrol racket, stealing and selling such quantities that the continuing attack on Germany was said to have been endangered. Yet in Paris there was every cause for elation. By a miracle the city had been liberated with its artistic treasures, monuments and historic buildings largely intact. Hitler had ordered General von Choltitz, the Nazi commander of Groß-Paris, to defend Paris to the last man and reduce the city to rubble, but von Choltitz had quietly refused to do so. When the church bells rang out across Paris on 24 August 1944 there was celebration among Montand's '*mécanos*' and their neighbours, although not everyone rejoiced. At the extreme there were active ideological Nazis who had joined organisations like the Gestapo, many of whom fled Europe for South America to escape prosecution. Among the '*aristos*' there were committed Pétainists who awaited an uncertain future. And those '*employés*' whose daily work had involved some degree of cooperation with the occupiers could only hope they weren't accused of anything more serious. But there were also hundreds of thousands of citizens who had continued to live their lives much as before, caring little for politics and simply pretending not to see the German soldiers. These citizens included the Beyaerts. To José the miraculous preservation of Paris meant not museum trips but bike races: with the bridges in place and the roads free of mines and snipers, cycle racing, too, could continue.

During the war José had been too young for Compulsory Work Service (Service du travail obligatoire, or STO), which had sent young men due for military conscription to perform forced labour in German factories, often in dreadful conditions.

In 1945, having avoided STO, José was due for military service. He was called up by the regional recruitment bureau at Valenciennes, was asked to be available for military service if required – he never was – and then sent home. Later he told it as if it was just reward for the hardship of war: 'Men born in 1925 didn't do military service because they were the people who'd suffered most during the war at that age. So they passed over that year.'

But his brother Georges, born two years later, performed his national service. He was sent with the French army to Morocco. It was hard to see how José's suffering had exceeded that of Georges. On another occasion José explained that he had worked briefly in the mines at Lens during the war, which had earned him his exemption. I wasn't sure I believed him. Either way it wasn't the end of José's contact with the military.

His military situation was only resolved in 1956, when a stamp went into his call-up booklet: 'Considered as having complied with his legal obligations.' But it still struck me as odd that José should feel impelled to justify his failure to serve in the army. I wondered if it explained some of his macho posing later on.

For most young Parisians, or 'J3s' as they were called, after the ration category for fifteen to twenty-one year olds, the Liberation changed everything. The iron discipline of José's life as an athlete meant that the end of the wartime curfew changed little for him. Not for José the freedom of the streets at night, of the jazz clubs of Saint-Germain-des-Prés.

All the same they were heady times. José began to travel widely with the French amateur team.

The last edition of *L'Auto* was published on 17 August 1944. The following year de Gaulle's provisional government passed ordinances to outlaw periodicals that had continued publication during the war. With the press baron Émilien Amaury, who had founded *Le Parisien Libéré* in 1944, *L'Auto*'s director Jacques Goddet created a new sports title, *L'Équipe*. The first edition came out on 28 February 1946. José made his first appearance nine weeks later:

> The Italians Artioli and Usotti, the French riders Rioland and Beyaert and the Belgians Gauthier and Leroye have been eliminated and reported to the UVI for sanctioning after being surprised clinging to vehicles.

Roger Rioland was also exempted from military service. He's eighty-five now and still rides sixty or so miles during the week, 'for my balance', and sometimes a longer ride on Sundays. I produced the tiny newspaper cutting.

'I remember it! I'll tell you what happened.'

It was the amateur Tour of Emilia in Italy. Rioland and José were members of the French national amateur team. Rioland had won an early stage but the race was too hilly for the French riders and in any case they weren't staying in hotels but with local families.

'Since we were French they brought out their best red, which was excellent, and we drank a bit too much so when we started the stage we weren't exactly drunk but we weren't exactly sober. We were a little euphoric and of course we couldn't follow the peloton.'

They rode up to a car to which a number of Italians were clinging, fought their way through and grabbed it too. 'We rode half the stage that way and at the finish we were eliminated, which was normal and reasonable. We said, "We weren't the only ones hanging on. There were Italians there too." But since they were the organisers, they closed their eyes.'

It was schoolboyish but it made the national press, partly thanks to an Italian rider named Bruno Pontisso, who had forced the organisers' hand by insisting the Frenchmen were disqualified. Pontisso had influence: as well as being the Italian amateur road and pursuit champion he was the nephew of Cardinal Pacelli, who became Pope Pius XII, the cycling pope who urged Catholics to follow the example of Italy's great Tour de France champion Gino Bartali by winning the yellow jersey in the race for salvation.

Rioland had his revenge a month later at the world track championships in Zurich: 'I madly wanted to beat Pontisso. I had the good fortune to be a little stronger than him in Zurich and I beat him in the semi-final on the way to becoming world champion.'

Recognising that his star rider needed the backing of a bigger club than JPS, Achille Joinard encouraged him to move on. José told me, 'Monsieur Joinard said, "We can't give you a training bike – we can't give you anything . . ."

'I said, "M. Joinard, I'll go where you tell me" – and he chose the ACBB [the Athlétic Club de Boulogne-Billancourt] – "but when you have the means to build a stronger team, I'll come back." So I left for a year.'

The ACBB had only one rival among French amateur clubs: the Vélo Club de Levallois, or VCL. And there was no question of José going there: at the end of 1943 the VCL president, Paul Ruinart, had refused to take José on the grounds that he wore glasses.

Even as José began to travel internationally and cycling became something like a profession to him, it remained a family pastime, and a successful one. José had a story about himself, Georges and their adoptive brother Jean: 'One day in 1947, all three of us won different races. [Jean] won in the morning, my brother won in the afternoon and I won Paris–Briare.'

A fourth young friend joined José, Georges and Jean at home, in the shop and on their training rides. Jacques Marinelli too was a second-generation immigrant. Like José he was also destined to become a French national hero. José told me, 'Jacquot was my close friend. He worked in the shoe shop with me. His father was Italian. He went with me to ride in Italy before he was famous.'

Georges remembered, 'We met him during the war. He ate and slept at ours from time to time. He'd lost his mother. He lived with his father, who worked in construction, I think. He had to go to work so he brought his sons to eat at ours. There were two sons; the other was a bit older than Jacquot. He worked in a pharmacy. But we always saw Jacquot. We trained together, raced together, everything.'

Roger Rioland told me, 'He was a good little rider. He lived in Pantin with José. Marinelli built frames for a factory at Drancy. He was young and very intelligent. Very intelligent.'

As the war receded José was a fixture in the national amateur team. One rider who rode frequently against him at international meetings, world championships and the London Olympics was the Englishman Bob Maitland. Sutton Coldfield in the English Midlands seemed the last place on earth to be looking for traces of José Beyaert but Bob's excellent memory and the scrapbooks he filled with cuttings, race programmes and photographs were an excellent resource. He gave me the outside view on José and made one thing clear: even amid the post-war desolation and shortages French cycling remained the envy of the world. Bob Maitland's experiences competing against Continental riders left him with no illusions.

'In Britain in the 1930s, no one had a clue about cycling, which meant there were no coaches for our generation. Our knowledge was limited and we realised what a tremendous gap lay between British and Continental racing.

'Every year there was an international race around the Isle of Man. The French came, ripped the field to pieces and made everyone also look stupid. The VCL sent riders with colour-coded sleeves! [Jean] Baldassari won it two years running. They were streets ahead of the rest of the world.'

The British on the other hand were streets behind, which would barely have been worth a mention had the International Olympic Committee not decided in February 1946 that the 1948 Games, the first of the post-war period, would be held in London. Months, years before it began, the Olympic road race had become a clash of cultures. When the Games were awarded to the British capital a shudder of concern rippled through the international cycling community. In Continental Europe and elsewhere cycling belonged firmly in the cultural mainstream. In Britain it belonged to the margins, at best. Bitter institutional feuds conspired to keep it there. The National Cyclists' Union (NCU), created in 1893 from the earlier Bicycle Union that went back to 1878, promoted track. Its partner, the British Time Trials Council (BTTC), governed road racing, which meant time trials were held at secret locations and at first light. Before the war mass-start races had been strictly prohibited. Riders opposed to the ban had founded the British League of Racing Cyclists in 1942. Since cycling's world-governing body, the UCI, recognised the Union but not the League, British road racers could only compete abroad through private arrangements with breakaway organisations.

In 1947 the cycling editor of the *News Chronicle*, Bill Mills, teamed up with Jean Leulliot, who was both the editor of the French weekly *Route et Piste* and the director of the Paris–Nice race. Together they organised a three-day race from Paris to London. The race was held over the long Whitsun weekend in three legs: two mass-start stages from Paris to Lens and then Lens to Calais, followed by that most British of events, a time trial held over an astonishingly long distance: the fifty-seven miles separating Folkestone and London.

The *News Chronicle*'s race description of the final time-trial stage gives some idea of the quaintness of British cycling rules:

> After being received by the Mayor of Folkestone on the sea-front, the riders set off for the 'secret' starting point of the last

stage to London. For, to avoid congestion on the roads, and to conform with British rules, exact details of start, etc., are restricted to the riders, officials, etc.

From the starting point the riders will be dispatched one by one, first a British cyclist, then a French, and so on in alternate order, at one-minute intervals. Reaching the outskirts of London, the riders cross another 'secret' check point, where their racing time is recorded. From then on the race is neutralised, until the riders enter Herne Hill track, Burbage Road, London, S.E. Here another timekeeper picks them up, and records their time for the final leg of the journey, one lap (503 yards) of the track.

The route of the final stage, we read, avoided traffic lights: 'all the better as French riders are not used to being stopped in full effort'.

The event attracted great interest in Britain and the weekly magazine *The Bicycle* published detailed stage descriptions as if the Paris–London had been the Tour de France.

The race favourite was a twenty-three-year-old Frenchman from Rouen called Roger Queugnet, shortly to turn professional with La Perle. Bob Maitland told me, 'Only about ten of the Brits were any good. I could only name a dozen riders in the whole country at that level.'

Stage one, Paris to Lens, 112.5 miles, started alongside Le Bourget airfield under a clear blue sky and in blazing heat. According to *The Bicycle*, the French were 'neat and well-equipped . . . with carbon dioxide tyre pumps, multi-speed gears, and alloy gadgets'. The British were inferior in every way: 'not so neat and by no means so well equipped'. On the first hill, one of the British bikes fell apart: 'Kempshall (G.B.) pulls up, his gear lever and cable hanging loose. He winds the cable round the frame and resumes.'

It was only the first of an eventually comic sequence of incidents:

Front tyre bursts and Kitching crashes. Gear wrecked, no spare tyres left, Kitching finishes up in a lorry . . . Stanway, saddle broke in half, rode fifty miles on the wreck (over the cobbles!)

and then had to quit, suffering acutely . . . Woolley, gear cable snapped . . . Robbins, gear jammed in wheel . . .

At the front, 'Edwards is strong – too strong. He even splits up his own countrymen. The British have no idea of team work.' But the pace was high and after three hours the leading group of riders had covered seventy-one miles.

> The Scotsman Edwards, riding strongly, breaks away in company with a Frenchman, Beyeart [*sic*]. They go through Peronne, crossing the historic river Somme. Beyeart drops Edwards, who is caught by Clements, Dominique Forlini, and his brother Louis . . . Half an hour later – Beyeart is caught by the Edwards–Clements group.

Twenty-five miles from Lens the five led the next group by a minute. Then they reached the cobbles. Clattering over the *pavé* the pace plummeted. Another Frenchman joined the leaders, and after four hours they completed ninety-four miles. In Arras the cobbled road surface worsened. The steep hill leading out of town weakened Edwards, and nearing Lens the six were reduced to five, with Ernie Clements alone against four Frenchmen, three of them, Louis Forlini, Georges Delescluses and José, members of the ACBB and working together. Louis Forlini's brother Dominique, a VCL rider, was as isolated as the Englishman. Yet . . .

> Clements leads the other four into Lens – is the first man to enter the Lens track! He and Dominique Forlini pull ahead – the last banking . . . Clements leads!
> Then he eases (his front wheel skidded in a loose patch at the foot of the shallow concrete track). Forlini whips by the line – Forlini wins. Clements second!

To the British press it was a victory for France. The French riders saw things rather differently. To them it was a win by a lone VCL rider over no less than three ACBB rivals. The rivalry between the two foremost amateur cycling clubs in France shaped the rest of the race. The following day between Lens and Calais, at sixty-three miles a short stage made formidable by coastal crosswinds and more cobblestones, the ACBB's Louis Forlini made a nine-man breakaway containing six Britons. Forlini's eight team-mates refused to cooperate with the eight VCL participants in the chase. This allowed the early escapees to open a substantial lead. Twenty miles from Calais four of the morning breakaway riders still held their lead. Behind them the former favourite Queugnet gave up and left the race.

With seventeen miles to go Britain's George Fleming attacked out of the leading group. *The Bicycle* described the anxious minutes:

> Thousands upon thousands of people line the streets – the finish is on the main road in front of the town hall.
>
> We disembark, stand and wait. A figure hoves in sight in the distance. Is it Fleming? Of course it is!

The squabble among the French had handed the stage, and a high probability of overall victory, to the Briton.

After the evening ferry from Boulogne the race ended with the time trial. It took even the fastest of the riders more than two hours twenty minutes. The fastest of them again turned out to be George Fleming. *The Bicycle* raved:

PARIS TO LONDON –
TURNING POINT IN BRITISH CYCLING

In a letter to *The Bicycle* George Fleming wrote: 'I feel sure that I voice the opinion of all the lads . . . in saying that we learned more about real mass-start racing than any other race at home has ever taught us.'

The *News Chronicle* noted, quietly: 'Beyaert too was fast in the time trial, and his 2 hr. 27 min. 20 sec. . . . enabled him to take third place [overall], pushing Delesclueses [*sic*] back to fourth.'

Largely unnoticed, José had ridden onto the podium. It was a competent performance from a young man who was already thinking of the Olympic Games. Bob Maitland, fifth overall, had José sign his race programme. The autograph suggests José had been having fun: 'I am very happy!' he wrote, using the only English expression he knew, 'José Beyaert'.

'That was probably the first time I saw him,' Bob told me. Over the next fifteen months he rode a number of international amateur events with José. But he said something else about the Frenchman that seemed remarkable: 'Looking up the figures I noticed he was often in the breaks I was in. But I didn't see him.'

In the life José would later live, this phantom quality would serve him well.

When José easily outsprinted his breakaway companion and French national team-mate Fernand Decanali to win the Prix du Docteur Garnier race on 20 July, *L'Équipe* named him a 'contender for the world amateur championship' to be held on 3 August in Rheims, the capital of the Champagne region. The final French selection was made in an impromptu race from Meaux to Fontainebleau, in terrible heat, the Sunday before Rheims.

José bided his time, attacked on the final climb and took Jean Baldassari with him. Recognising José's finishing speed Baldassari attacked early. José let him go and settled for second place, intelligently saving energy for the following week.

The day before the world championships, *L'Équipe* commented: '[Beyaert's] great enthusiasm could be his only weakness . . . however, if he's on song . . . he could allow himself any fantasy to arrive at a positive conclusion.'

José's fantasy took place on the tenth of twenty-one 4.86-mile circuits. It did not go well. By that stage one of José's team-mates, René Rouffeteau, had been taken to hospital with a head injury after a fall on lap one and another, Fernand Decanali, was having an off-day. On lap six, after thirty miles of high-speed riding, the first serious attack had formed. Six riders had gained nearly a minute over the main group and had been joined by two more. These eight held off the peloton for three full laps.

The race was not yet half over when José made his move. Halfway into lap ten, on the one short, steep hill, the chasers caught the fugitives. Britain's George Fleming attacked. José went with him.

A group of fourteen formed behind them. It was the definitive breakaway. Fleming and José had created it but José's place within it was temporary. A mechanical problem, perhaps a slipped chain, sent him careering backwards through the field. By lap fifteen the leading group of fifteen riders, still containing Fleming and with Baldassari, the sole Frenchman, was followed by a second group of ten, twenty-three seconds back, led by José.

With four laps to go Italy's Aldo Ferrari attacked. A Swede, Harry Snell, gave chase. The three other Swedes and the one Italian in the group refused to pursue their team-mates. Baldassari had nothing left. The gap grew. With two laps remaining Snell began to suffer from cramp and dropped back. Eventually, paralysed by fatigue, he fell. Ferrari, slowing all the time, carried on alone. Behind him the group containing Fleming and Baldassari began to fragment. Ferrari crossed the finish line alone, so exhausted he was unable to turn the pedals. Baldassari, sixth, had ridden anonymously. José had at least shown some flair. Indeed, in the final kilometres he had scythed through the remains of the leading group. 'I was ahead, but I broke my handlebar and coasted to the line.' He finished eleventh, convinced he could have won the 1947 world amateur championships. The following morning *L'Équipe* expressed its disappointment with the French team:

> The victim of an accident, Rouffeteau was out of the race. Decanali never behaved like a world championship rider. Baldassari was stronger and stronger but stayed on other riders' wheels. As for Beyaert, the most engaging and deserving of our riders, he rode such a disorderly race that it is scarcely possible to believe in him.

It must have been frustrating to read. Yet José told me, 'In my bad luck was my good fortune because if I'd won the world championships in 1947 I'd have turned professional and I'd have been in the peloton. So that bad luck was good luck for me.'

Something in his extraordinary make-up always transformed frustration into something positive. It had been a successful year but in 1948 José returned to JPS. The bicycle manufacturer Helyett had agreed to equip his local team, so José told Albert Gal, the ACBB chairman, 'I have nothing against you, but I love my little club.'

In mid-June 1948 *L'Équipe* sent a reporter to take a look at the Olympic road-race course around Windsor Great Park. He wrote back:

> The finish line, which is perfectly clear but scarcely any wider than the rest of the route, follows Breakheart Hill, which isn't six hundred metres long and has an average gradient of 4 per cent, although the final hundred metres touch 11 per cent.
>
> The setting is pastoral. You cross meadows and woods bathed in sunlight, their greens singing a chromatic symphony. Shafts of sunlight filter through the foliage and pose sweetly in the road like paintbrushes!
>
> Put briefly, this little frequented road, passing no villages and comprising only a few B-roads, is an excellent promenade for lovers or for ladies and young women whose physicians have prescribed a little gentle bicycling.
>
> It's also wonderful propaganda for the countryside around London. But it isn't worthy of an Olympic road race.

In one respect *L'Équipe*'s correspondent Marc Hauguet was right: it wasn't a course for climbers. But Hauguet's analysis was based on two errors of judgement and one omission. The errors first: he somehow forgot the truism that it is the race that makes a course easy or difficult. Worse, he failed to take the British summer into account: when race day came the wind gusted and the rain poured, no weather for young ladies to take their restful constitutionals. The omission was more chauvinistic; he forgot to mention that France's Olympic preparation had been just as disorganised.

In January 1948 the French Cycling Federation's Olympic Committee decided that preselection for the Games would depend on the results of seven races held in quick succession over the seven weeks separating 29 March and 16 May. The five riders with the best results would qualify automatically. The final place would be a wild card awarded at the selector's discretion, taking accidents and injuries into account. The six preselected riders would travel to London. Four would be selected to race.

Five weeks after publishing the selection procedure the Federation appointed the selector. Their choice was Georges Speicher. He accepted the post but distanced himself from the Federation's criteria by making it plain to *L'Équipe* that he hadn't been consulted on it. For the next three months he bit his tongue. Then, after the sixth qualification race, he spoke out:

> To tell the truth, I only saw four of the 133 participants today . . . Our amateurs don't know how to impose their will on the race. Most of the time the breakaway hero doesn't get away on his own merits, he gets away because the peloton hesitates before chasing. They're trying to qualify, it goes without saying, and only the result counts. Which is why, to my mind, we should never have based pre-selection on qualifying races. We should have given these young men the chance to distinguish themselves without obliging them to finish in the top five. Then they would have fought properly. They'd have shown what they were capable of and I'd have a better idea of their real abilities.

The manner in which José began to ride over the coming weeks is highly suggestive. It is as if he had been told – and this can only have been by Speicher, who resisted any bureaucratic interference with his work – to work his body hard over the coming weeks and not to worry about his results. José was among the front-runners for Olympic selection.

In March the bicycle manufacturer Helyett, based in Sully-sur-Loire, due south of Paris, had provided the JPS riders with brand-new machines. Armed with his beautiful new Helyett bike José was among the few French amateurs invited to compete in Italy on a regular basis. On 2 May, in the middle of the Olympic pre-qualifiers, José made the trip to take part in the Matteotti Trophy around Pescara. After working hard in a long chase-down he attacked alone. With twenty kilometres left to ride he led a group of six by a minute. But he had worked too hard, too soon. At the city gates he was caught and the race came down to a sprint. José took third place despite his exertions. He wasn't in top form yet but it was just a matter of time.

L'Équipe had decided to comment no further on the disagreement between the Federation and its selector, and this allowed Speicher to jettison the Federation's plans in silence. Georges Beyaert remembered a detail that never made the press and ran against the Federation's selection criteria and might have caused a rumpus if it had got out: by the time of the Paris–Caen qualifier on 16 May José knew he was on Speicher's list.

José liked working with Speicher. He told me, 'He was intelligent: not super-intelligent but he knew how to handle me. You have to realise that an athlete isn't a normal person. You don't talk to him the way you talk to normal people. It depends who, of course. You have to know who you're taking to. With one, a smile is enough. With another, you have to talk about sentiments . . . All that is the intelligence of the trainer, the preparer who has to know his athletes. With me, he hardly spoke.'

If Speicher had quietly given him the nod it was an inspired choice. At the end of May *L'Équipe* organised a three-day stage race called the Peugeot Trophies, from Paris to Le Mans, Le Mans to Saint-Brieuc and Saint-Brieuc to Nantes. *L'Équipe*'s account suggests that José rode them as he had ridden the Matteotti Trophy.

On the two hundred and five-kilometre stage to Le Mans he sprinted out of the peloton at Chartres, eighty-four kilometres into the race. Only one rider had the reflexes to get on his wheel. Two more set off in their slipstream, shared the workload for fifteen kilometres and joined the leaders. Working together, the four-man group extended their lead to two minutes fifteen seconds. Behind them six riders attacked out of the peloton. This brought a reaction and after one hundred and seventy-two kilometres, under a storm of rain and hailstones, the field regrouped.

Seven kilometres from the race finish José was one of six riders in another breakaway. They were caught within sight of the finish line. But José still managed eighth place despite his workout and

Jacques Augendre, who would one day be *L'Équipe*'s most prestigious cycling writer, wrote, 'Émile Dangière, José Beyaert and Roland Danguillaume seemed most at ease over the distance.'

Across the Channel, Olympic preparations were coming on apace. The second Paris–London race had been planned as a pre-Games test for teams of Olympic 'possibles' from Britain, France, Belgium and Luxembourg. It would also reassure the international cycling community that the British could be trusted to organise a competent road race in view of the coming Olympic Games. Lens had been replaced by Arras as the destination of stage one and the start of stage two. The only other change was a minor scheduling issue that quickly developed into a major spat between the BTTC, affiliated to the NCU, and their sworn enemy, the British League of Racing Cyclists.

The BTTC met with the NCU to discuss the final time trial. The NCU then notified the race sponsor, the *News Chronicle*, that a permit for the event would only be issued if the last rider in the time trial set off from Folkestone at 7 a.m.

The early start would have meant a 3 a.m. rise for the riders. The French and Belgian authorities opposed the change. Kent police, the promoters and even the NCU preferred 11 a.m. But the BTTC was adamant. It ended in fiasco. Refusing to associate itself with the feud, the *News Chronicle* pulled its sponsorship in early April.

Four months before the Olympic Games serious doubts surrounded London's ability to organise the Olympic road race. Holding the event on the public roads – the Continental solution – was never even considered. Richmond Park was mooted until it was realised that the parliamentary Act that governed the area ruled out the park's use for this sort of event. To avoid more red tape the organisers went beyond bureaucracy to the monarch himself, although the tension between the starched British amateurs and the frustrated cycling officials accustomed to the professional racing scene in Continental Europe simmers beneath the hidebound tone of the Organising Committee's Official Report on the Games:

By permission of His Majesty The King . . . the Organising Committee were allowed to hold it in Windsor Great Park, and initially a track of four-mile laps was mapped out, lying entirely within the Park itself. Due to representations made to increase the length of lap, the course was re-planned to pass over a short stretch of public road between two of the Park gates, giving a lap of seven miles.

The average width of the road was sixteen feet: dangerously narrow, especially for the finish line. The riders would ride seventeen circuits. It was a compromise and of course pleased no one. Accusations of incompetence flooded in from cycling's heartlands.

On 6 June many of the Olympic hopefuls assembled at the Autodrome de Linas-Montlhéry south of Paris for an event billed as the Olympic road-race rehearsal. The Montlhéry track was one mile shorter than at Windsor and the main climb much steeper. The road was also considerably wider than at Windsor. Still, it was probably as close as any Continental circuit could be to the Olympic course.

The Italians were there albeit without the world champion Ferrari. So too were the British although with no Fleming. Australia, Belgium, Holland, Denmark, Luxembourg and Sweden completed a field full of quality. For the French riders a good performance was doubly important: Speicher had won three French national championships at the Autodrome de Linas-Montlhéry (in 1935, 1937 and 1939) and had been known as 'the prince of Montlhéry'. José, acutely aware of this, rode brilliantly.

It was a cool day with plenty of wind and small breakaways by riders from the fancied teams kept the pace high. After sixty miles the peloton split. Ten riders were ahead, three of them Frenchmen, including José. An eleventh man, Denmark's Christian Pedersen, raced frantically across the gap and made the break in the nick of time.

The miles reduced the leading group to nine, then to seven: two Danes, two Belgians, two Frenchmen and a Swede. The Danes worked the endgame perfectly, Børge Saxil Nielsen piloting his team-mate Pedersen to a convincing win by half a length over the Belgian Henri Evens. Nielsen was third, Evens's team-mate

Jean Storms fourth and José was the first French finisher in fifth place, after playing the part of the 'slice of ham in the sandwich', as *L'Équipe* put it. But José, it said, had been 'excellent' although the two Danes had to be considered Olympic favourites. However, the Olympic dress rehearsal at Montlhéry was twenty-five miles shorter than the real thing and the extra distance would make all the difference.

José continued punishing himself. In late June a second series of qualification races started around an eleven-kilometre circuit in the forest of Saint-Germain. During the first of these José was the author of a fifty-five-kilometre breakaway with four others. The peloton caught the breakaway within sight of the finish line. The winner, Pierre Rouchet, had booked his Olympic place. José, perhaps knowing he had been preselected, finished tenth.

Four days later José missed the winning break but led a three-man chasing group and eventually finished eighth. The day's victor, Jacques Dupont, had reserved his trip to London.

Three days later José attempted to tear the field of Olympic hopefuls apart:

> The day was gruelling for riders, who had to climb continuously and the agony of J. Beyaert, Huraux, Bourgeteau, Huguet and Trubert, the authors of a breakaway driven by the implacable Beyaert until the 140th kilometre, was real.

José had enough strength left to finish third in the final sprint. The two riders ahead of him, René Rouffeteau and Joannès Socquet, entered the Olympic shortlist.

By 13 July rumours of the Olympic selection seeped out. José was one of the riders mentioned:

> Monsieur Abadie, the vice-president of the French Cycling Federation, told us ... 'From the conversation I had with Georges Speicher when the Tour de France stopped at Bordeaux, it sounds as though our road-race delegation for London will certainly include Rouchet, Dupont, Rouffeteau and [Alain] Moineau [another regular with the French amateur team], probably with

59

José Beyaert and [Robert] Varnajo [the winner of the 1948 Paris–Briare]. But nothing is definitive yet.'

By Monday 19 July, something definitive had emerged:

PARIS–SAINT-VALERY-EN-CAUX

JOSÉ BEYAERT PROVES HE IS READY FOR LONDON

Riding into a violent headwind and intermittent rain, José and Georges made a series of attempts to start a breakaway before the leading group of twelve took shape. In the sprint Luigi Malabrocca, five years older than José and the winner of the 1947 Paris–Nantes, beat José by a whisker. Yet *L'Équipe* praised his performance: 'Beyaert rode an excellent race. He suffered a puncture after Gaillon and rode back very easily. Selected for London, he wanted to prove that the choice was a good one.'

Georges Beyaert finished fourth.

On Sunday 25 July the official list of the three hundred athletes France was sending to the Games was published. The cyclists for the road race were José Beyaert, Jacques Dupont, Alain Moineau, Pierre Rouchet, René Rouffeteau and Joannès Socquet.

To celebrate, José rode an excellent Paris–Cayeux on 1 August, riding hard in a breakaway and then, when the field came together, a punchy, Moroccan-born rider (and future Tour de France stage winner) named Custodio Dos Reis took the win, with José second, only inches behind.

4

The Olympic road race was to take place on Friday 13 August 1948, the final day of the Games. Speicher prepared his riders meticulously. Jacques Dupont, who was also competing on the track at the Olympic Games, would travel on Monday 9 August. The rest of the road-race team would travel a day later.

Speicher had his riders out on the road towards Chartres at 6 a.m. each morning, starting on Wednesday 4 August. He drove behind them, keeping a close eye. José told me, 'On the training rides Speicher made us rotate by sounding his horn. I noticed he made me ride three hundred metres and the others ride one hundred and fifty metres. He was thinking something there to make me ride more than the others.'

The riders went for a medical on the Friday before the race. Over the weekend the morning rides covered just one hundred and fifty kilometres. Then the distances shortened to leave the riders fresh and strong on the big day. *L'Équipe* covered every move. On the Sunday, it observed, Speicher accompanied his six over one hundred and fifty kilometres through Magny-en-Vexin and Pontoise: 'Rouchet had to join the car halfway after a mechanical problem. J. Beyaert, Rouffeteau and Moineau rode a good session.'

The following day the French pursuit team pulverised the Herne Hill track record in the Olympic semi-final, then left the Italians for dead in the final. It was a major morale boost as José and his companions prepared to leave for London. But José faced an unexpected hitch.

'To go to the Olympic Games, I needed a certificate of good conduct issued by the town hall. When I went to ask for it to go to London, the mayor said no. He didn't want to give it to me because I was often there at the police station for fighting. I was the strongest in the *quartier*!

'"But I'm going to represent France."

'"If types like you are going to represent France, France has got problems."

'So I spoke to Monsieur Joinard. He went to see Borotra, the Minister for Sport. He had been a tennis player.'

Pantin had always been a stronghold of the political Left. In 1948 the mayor, André Jean Faizas, was a member of the French Section of the Workers' International. The incident may underlie a lifelong antipathy towards Communists that would emerge when, as a professional cyclist, he found himself riding under the direction of the left-winger René Vietto. But that was later: to get José to London, 'Borotra signed a special document. That's why I arrived after the others.'

'Borotra was a team-mate of René Lacoste in the French Davis Cup team that dominated in the 1920s and '30s,' I commented.

'I don't know,' José said. 'I didn't know about tennis. To me it was a game for the rich.'

José's story conflicted with *L'Équipe*'s report on Thursday 12 August:

> All the French riders selected for the road race, which will take place in Windsor Park on Friday, arrived in London this morning [that is, Wednesday 11 August].

But Georges Beyaert confirmed that the problems surrounding the certificate of good conduct were real.

The riders went to their accommodation at the RAF camp in Uxbridge, seven miles west of Wembley. With the exception of Jacques Dupont, who rode and won the kilometre time trial at Herne Hill that afternoon, another spur for his road-race team-mates, José and his Olympic colleagues observed a day of complete rest.

Speicher went to Herne Hill and scoured the riders' area for news. 'We will go and look at the race route as a group tomorrow,' he told the press. 'I can't give you the composition of the team I'll field. I'll decide tomorrow.'

L'Équipe speculated, 'On the basis of rumours from French officials, Speicher will align Moineau, Dupont, Rouffeteau, and either Beyaert or Rouchet.'

The Windsor circuit measured 7 miles 202 yards, or 11.45 kilometres. The riders faced 17 laps, or 120 miles 914 yards; not 1946.33 kilometres as the official map had it but a tenth of that. The single difficulty on the course, Breakheart Hill, was no more than a pimple, gaining 86 feet from Johnson's Pond to the crest, a distance of 629 yards. The average gradient was 4.5 per cent. Even if it touched 11 per cent towards the top it was, for lean, hardened, soon-to-be-professional cyclists, an easy climb before the final flat, windswept thousand yards to the finish line. Speicher looked at the climb and came to his decision. There was no easy way of informing the riders who would be left out. When the moment came even the blunt, taciturn Speicher baulked. José told me, 'Until the evening before the race, we didn't know who the four would be. Speicher took our bikes to have them stamped. When he came back he left them outside. Four of them were stamped and two had no stamps. He said to me, "I hope I've made the right choice." We went out and I saw my bike had been stamped. I knew I was in.'

Moineau, Dupont, Rouffeteau, Beyaert: that was Speicher's inspired choice.

That evening José received a visit.

'The night before the race, a race organiser came to see me to talk about "The Olympic Revenge", which was a series of ten or so races in Switzerland, ten or so races in France, Italy, Sardinia, Sicily ... everywhere. I signed a contract with him for a three-month tour with races almost every day, moving around by coach and plane and staging reruns of the Olympic Games. It was nonsense, really: a spectacle. I told the promoter who had the contract, "I want another clause in my contract."

'"What clause?"

'Everyone else had agreed to the same conditions.

"'If I'm Olympic champion tomorrow, I want you to pay me double."

'He took his pen and wrote it: "In this case the contract shall be doubled."'

'You were confident of winning?' I asked.

'That was what I was there for.'

José had another visitor that night: the father of a team-mate José believed should never have been sent to London. 'X had the physique, but he didn't know how to suffer. His father was some sort of industrialist and he was a daddy's boy. I remember the evening before the race, his father came to see me.

"'José, I want to talk to you. Tomorrow, would you mind riding for my son? If you ride for him I'll pay you a hundred thousand francs."

'For a shoemaker like me, it was a lot of money. I said, "Monsieur X, I appreciate and I understand your devotion to your son, but, between us, he won't be there at the finish." I'd seen him in training and I couldn't understand what he was doing there. Perhaps money had changed hands there, too. "And Monsieur X, I came here to win. I'm sorry."

"'It's all right. I understand."'

The following morning, *L'Équipe* ran the following front-page headline:

LAST BIG DAY, THIS FRIDAY 13, AT THE LONDON GAMES
REAL CHANCES FOR J. DUPONT AND
A. MOINEAU IN THE WINDSOR ROAD RACE

The circuit was closed from 10.30 a.m. to all traffic other than the riders and the motors under the control of the race controllers.

As the riders gathered on the start line rain was falling and a cold wind was blowing. The start was delayed when it was found that the Pakistan Cycling Federation had not paid its eleven-pounds-subscription to the UCI, which meant that the Pakistani entrant, Wazir Ali, had to be removed from the field of play.

Then at 11.24 a.m. the Duke of Edinburgh started the race.

The treacherous road surface and a number of right-angle entry and exit points into and out of the park made it a day of punctures and mechanical problems.

As the race started, everyone had the same idea: the safest place to be was at the front. This, combined with an early attack, generated an abrupt increase in pace on the approach towards each hazardous feature of the course. The attack came from a formidable Dutchman named Henk Faanhof who would be world amateur road-race champion the following year and a Tour de France stage winner in 1954. He had a hundred-yard lead at Prince Consort Gate, just over three and a half miles from the start. His attack kept the peloton moving fast enough to drop no less than seventeen riders in the first lap.

As Faanhof reached Blacknest Gate, five and a half miles into the race, he was joined by a muscular Swede named Nils Johansson and then by Orhan Suda of Turkey. The trio led the peloton by a hundred yards.

Johansson, committed to the attack, dropped his companions and pressed on alone. Passing Ascot Gate for the second time after eleven miles of racing, he led Faanhof by fifty-eight seconds. The Dutchman slipped back briefly into the peloton. Then on lap three, another attack. Faanhof's compatriot Gerrit Voorting burst past the group and into space. Faanhof gave chase. Soon the two Dutchmen were working flawlessly together, each taking turns to lead, riding through and off into the wind. They were a formidable pair – in later years, Voorting would win a couple of Tour de France stages and wear the race leader's yellow jersey – and on Breakheart Hill they homed in on the heavier Johansson, making contact as the lap finished. By lap seven the trio of Johansson, Faanhof and Voorting had a lead of three minutes forty-five seconds over the peloton.

By then José had made his first attempt to free himself from the peloton and ride across to the leaders. He made his attack on lap six with two other riders but the peloton reacted and by Blacknest Gate he had been absorbed back into the group. The highly feared Italians raised the tempo at the front of the peloton but still the leading trio maintained its advantage.

On lap eight José made a second attempt to break free. With the South African Dirk Jacobus 'Dirkie' Binneman, Luxembourg's Henri Kellen and Gordon Thomas of the host nation, he had a fifty-yard lead as he passed Prince Consort Gate. His quartet was then joined by two Belgians, Léon Delathouwer (the future winner of two Tours of Flanders) and Liévin Lerno (who would finish second in the world amateur championships two weeks later), and by Lorang Christiansen of Norway.

Far ahead of José and the six riders around him, Nils Johansson had punctured at the foot of Breakheart Hill. After a rapid wheel change and the climb he trailed the two Dutchmen by two minutes twenty-nine seconds as he completed lap eight.

José's team-mates were enjoying mixed fortunes. Jacques Dupont had suffered two punctures. He had ridden back into the peloton easily enough after his first wheel change. After the second he made the mistake of wanting to change bicycle. He rode against the flow of traffic to the team paddock, not realising that the Olympics were held according to their own rules and that bicycle changes were strictly prohibited.

Alain Moineau, by contrast, was staying close to the dangerous Italians, who were staying close to him. Caution paralysed both parties.

The rainfall was sporadic. As the race entered its ninth lap, nearly ninety-two kilometres (fifty-seven miles) into the race, the downpour became torrential. Voorting and Faanhof passed Chapel Lodge two minutes twenty seconds before Johansson reached the same point. Delathouwer, Lerno, Thomas and Christiansen followed just twenty-five seconds behind. In the race descriptions José's name momentarily disappears at this point. One of any number of small problems, now forgotten, may have forced him to drop out of the group. Ahead of him these four joined Johansson at Whitefield Gate. By the end of lap nine these five lay two minutes seven seconds behind the leading pair.

Johansson, still powerful, launched a sudden attack. The chase was led by Thomas, who gave the two Belgians and Christiansen an easy ride in his slipstream. With forty seconds separating the

Johansson group from the two Dutch leaders, a second knot of riders containing Bob Maitland joined it. Still José's name is missing from the reports.

It was at Chapel Lodge that the chasers caught the Dutchmen and formed a leading group eleven strong, including an Indian named Havaldar who had been lapped. The group led the peloton, containing the Italians Ferrari and Pedroni, by one minute and fifty seconds. It was at this point that José made contact with the leading group.

He told me, 'I'd ridden across on my own and if I'd caught them immediately they'd have known I was strong. I knew everyone in the breakaway and I didn't want them all against me so I didn't ride straight up to them. I waited a while behind them and grimaced as though suffering, as if I couldn't make it. A bit of theatre to fool them. Then, finally, I rode up to them. They didn't worry too much about me after that.'

On Breakheart Hill, the Dutchmen increased the pace and opened a small gap but the others responded. Eight men crossed the finish line bunched.

There is some confusion over the composition of the leading group at this point. There were certainly two Britons: Bob Maitland and Gordon Thomas. There were two Belgians too: Léon Delathouwer and Lode Wouters. There was an Australian, Jack Hoobin (little known in 1948, but world amateur champion within two years); the big Swede Nils Johansson; the Dutchman Gerrit Voorting; and José, whom *L'Équipe* describes as looking over his shoulder, vainly expecting his team-mate René Rouffeteau to join him. *The Bicycle* says Rouffeteau not only made it across but also joined José in accelerating on the fourteenth ascent of Breakheart Hill to test their opponents' strength. Still the group held.

There were 34.35 kilometres (21.34 miles) left as the riders finished the fourteenth lap. The last opportunity for the riders to collect food and drink at the official station near Cumberland Gate was approaching.

Rouffeteau darted to the front to collect his *musette*. As he collected his feedbag it caught in the spokes of his front wheel and became wedged in the fork. The wheel stopped dead. The front of his bike slid away beneath him and he fell heavily to the left, striking his head on the road surface. Blood spurted from a deep head wound. Speicher helped him to his feet and put him back on his bike: winning the team prize depended on him. But Rouffeteau fainted. When he came to he was led away to the first-aid tent, where the wound was closed with four stitches.

Bereft of a team-mate in the leading group, José may well have felt a sense of liberation. It was him against the world: his favourite odds.

Two minutes behind the leading seven, the Italians had assumed control of the chase, sacrificing themselves for their leader, Aldo Ferrari. But nothing they could do had any effect on the gap. Even when Faanhof punctured at Blacknest Gate, a mile and a half before the start of the penultimate lap, and lost all hope of disputing the finale, the pace remained electric and as the leaders crossed the finish line at the end of the fifteenth, and then the sixteenth, lap, it was José who led the line, perhaps already visualising the denouement as the urgent jangling of the bell penetrated his consciousness and the crowd roared from the tribune.

There are many photographs of those closing laps. In all of them José's head is up and his gaze focused on the riders around him. He is awake, alert, ready for anything.

On the narrow lanes at the north end of the circuit, where the land drops away and vista opens out towards the castle, Delathouwer jumped. Thomas went with him. On the sharp descent to Long Walk the pair had a small lead, with Voorting leading the pack.

They made it at speed through the dangerous turn into Blacknest Gate and sped across the lakes before the climb. By the foot of Breakheart Hill the group was together again. Then, the final climb. Gordon Thomas attacked again. Voorting was even stronger and approaching the crest of the hill he had the lead.

José was some way back, 'a good five lengths down on Voorting' said *The Bicycle*: 'Still climbing, in fact, when the Dutchman reached the top.'

But as the road began to run out José was watching, biding his time.

Then came Beyaert's gamble. A sprint from the rear and he passed them all and made eight lengths on Voorting in as many seconds. Back wheels switched as the remaining seven took up the chase.

Fifty-six years later José gave me his version of the race conclusion. It was a tale he had told so frequently it had become canonical: 'I saw it this way: if I wait for the sprint everyone will be on my wheel because I'm a sprinter, and I'll have no one's wheel. So I made a little acceleration from the front with two kilometres to go, just to start things off. That put me at the front of the line. I reached for my *bidon*. You know how it is: one drinks, everyone wants to drink. So I reached for my water bottle and when I saw that two or three of them had reached for theirs I threw it away and attacked. They were off guard. By the time they reacted I led by fifty metres.'

Kidding the other contenders into reaching for their water bottles in the final mile or so of a race, and such an important race? It seemed unlikely, although there was no way of being sure. As the seven contended for the victory that would change their lives there must have been so much going on, mentally and physically, and seen from so many different points of view, that I had no hope of coming to a consistent story, free from contradiction. There were only fragments of broken narrative that refused to sit together. Bob Maitland had no recollection of the ploy. He might not have been one of the riders fooled. But isn't it the essence of the confidence trick that its victims refuse to accept, even fail to recognise, that they have been taken in?

José's muscles emptied their power into the gusting headwind. His lead began to wither as Voorting gathered speed behind him.

'But it was useless,' said *The Bicycle*. 'The Frenchman could not be caught.'

The winning margin was 3.6 seconds and José had won two Olympic medals: gold for his individual victory and bronze in the team category. It was his day and he could tell it any way he liked.

Speicher met José at the finish line.

'He said I'd done '*un grand truc*' ['a great trick']. That's all he said. I like people like that. That's how you should be – not blathering on all the time.'

Informed that Prince Philip wanted to congratulate him, José, even after 5 hours 18 minutes and 12.6 seconds of effort, still had the quickness of mind to quip, 'Tell him I take visitors from seven to nine.' When the Duke of Edinburgh shook his hand José told him, through his beaming smile, 'I am very happy!' They were the words he had written above his autograph on Bob Maitland's Paris–London programme the previous year. He had no doubt learnt from his British rivals during the event.

'Prince Philip said, "You speak English?" I said, "No!" I'd said everything I knew. So he started speaking in perfect French.'

That evening, the promoter of the 'Olympic Revenge' tour saw José and commented, 'You've earned a nice little packet today!'

'WEE JOSE – TOUGHEST CYCLIST THERE' was the *Daily Mirror*'s headline. Oblivious to José's penchant for fist fighting – oblivious of any detail about his existence apart from his trade – the *Mirror*'s Armour Milne wrote:

> But for his cheeky smile, José Beyaert, bespectacled French shoemaker from a small town on the outskirts of Paris, might have been mistaken for a scholar, possible winner of a literary prize in the Olympic arts competition.
>
> Instead, he won the Olympics championship [*sic*] in one of the toughest of all sports – the 120 miles road cycling race – in 5h. 18m. 12.6s. in Windsor Great Park yesterday.
>
> A little man, almost wispy in shape, standing just over 5ft. in height, José, 22, let a field of ninety-nine tough he-men play cat and mouse games with each other over seventeen laps of undulating roads.
>
> Then, about a mile from the finish, he shot out from the back of the leading bunch to rip into a lead that the others were unable to wipe out.

Appropriately, Breakheart Hill was where José made his effort, one of those tough climbs at which one expects the giants to excel. And it was here that little José became the giant-killer.

It was condescending, and quite mistaken in every substantive detail of cycling lore (Breakheart Hill was not a tough climb, and if it had been, the slowest riders up it would have been the giants and so on) but it ensured José his moment of fame in Great Britain.

France, of course, lionised him. *L'Équipe* ran the front-page headline:

BEYAERT, THE ROAD MAN, CONFIRMS THE OVERALL SUPREMACY OF FRENCH AMATEUR CYCLING

And in *Paris-Presse*, the chief sports editor, Gaston Bénac, wrote:

The victory of the little Parisian Beyaert, the rider with glasses, was so clear, so eloquent and had seemed from the start, if not probable, that at the very least possible, so great was his ease and so absolute his dominance on the climb, that it requires no comment. He gave the impression that he could have ridden away from his adversaries earlier and won alone. But the little chap had calculated his attack well. Several times he tested his rivals on the little climb a kilometre from the finish and after the weak response of the Belgians, the British and the Dutch, he realised that it would be easy to win on the final lap by attacking at the foot of the climb. It was a wise solution [and] he carried out his battle plan to the letter, finishing the climb alone and maintaining his lead over the last flat straight six hundred metres.

The report revealed another detail: José had won the race on his mother's birthday. He told me, 'My mother was very superstitious. You couldn't spill the salt or put the bread upside down, all sorts of nonsense. And then I became Olympic champion on Friday the thirteenth! I said, "Yes, but it was Friday the thirteenth for everyone else, too."'

José flew back to Paris the day after the race. The Air France flight touched down at Le Bourget at the end of the morning. Photographers were waiting for him as the aircraft door opened. By 1 p.m. José was with his family: a photograph shows him seated at the head of the table, flanked by Louisette and his father on one side, Georges and Jean on the other, and friends along the table. As always everyone around José is smiling and laughing.

Then an exhausting round of appointments began, starting at 3 p.m. that afternoon, when José paid a visit to *Paris-Presse*. The Monday after his triumphant return José and the other Olympic cyclists visited the offices of *L'Équipe* for wine and photographs.

Olympic victory brought José into contact with high Parisian society for the first time. This led to a series of excruciating moments as the poor cyclist improvised his way through the etiquette of the very rich. He was invited to dine with the President of the Republic Vincent Auriol at the Champs-Elysées. The world-champion boxer Marcel Cerdan was there. So too was the great-niece of the author Victor Hugo, the remarkable and beautiful Micheline Ostermeyer, a concert pianist as well as the winner of Olympic gold medals in the shot-put and discus and silver in the high jump.

José surveyed the table. 'I looked at all the cutlery and Vincent Auriol said, "What is it, *filston*?" He called me "*filston*" [meaning "my boy"].

'"I was just counting the knives and forks. There are six of us at home and we have five forks. When the first one's finished, the last one can eat."

'He called the sommelier and spoke into his ear. He came and took all the cutlery away except for a knife, a fork and a spoon.

'"Is that better?"

'"Thank you."'

Afterwards there were speeches. But José was still hungry.

'Everyone ate a little. They didn't eat like us. The meal was no bigger than that: a dish, two or three dishes. I looked around for Cerdan.

'"*Filston*, what are you looking for?"

'"It's all right, Mr President, I was looking for Cerdan."

"'He left ten minutes ago.'"

José made his excuses but before he could leave, the president called the sommelier, who handed José a small packet.

"'Thank you, Mr President."

'I looked at him. He looked at me. He'd given me those knives, forks and spoons.

"'From now on you can eat together.'"

José left the palace and went into the first restaurant he could find. There was Marcel Cerdan tucking into a huge meal. José sat down beside him and ordered.

The sponsors of JPS presented him with a small cheque at another celebration meal, this time in a Russian restaurant.

"'Do you want caviar?"

'I'd heard people talk about caviar, but I'd never eaten it.

"'Yes, yes."

'So they brought me caviar on a plate, like that, with a big spoon. There were twenty of us.

"'Serve yourself, José."

'I took a great pile of the stuff and immediately realised I'd committed a gaffe.'

At least it made his mind up about caviar: 'I wouldn't cross the street to eat it.'

There was another personal detail that did not make the press. José and Louisette wanted to marry. José's father was opposed to the union on cycling grounds.

'He was afraid that marriage would weaken me. Later it was proven that married champions are more serious than those who aren't married. But he had said, "If you're Olympic champion, you can get married." He made a mistake there!'

On the Wednesday after his Olympic victory, as Louisette started the preparations, José left Paris with the French team for the 1948 world road-racing championships at Valkenburg, Holland. The race was to be held over twenty-two laps of a demanding ten-kilometre circuit with the terrible Côte de Cauberg at its heart. José told me, 'Those were the climbs for me: short and hard.'

Given the distance he fancied his chances. However, the distance was reduced to eighteen laps shortly before the start. It must have disappointed José, who showed himself at the front of the field as early as lap seven. *The Bicycle* reported: 'Near the top [of the Côte de Cauberg] Johansson, the Swede, Fanti and Isotti, Italy, and Olympic champion Beyaert, France, forged ahead.'

But a hard chase ended the breakaway a lap later and on the eleventh lap the Swedish rider Harry Snell, who had lost the previous year's event to Aldo Ferrari and a bad attack of cramp, joined a four-man breakaway with his compatriot Olle Vanlund, the Belgian Liévin Lerno and Wim Van Est of Holland.

José told me, 'Speicher made a mistake that day. And he said, "Wait, wait, wait." We were watching the Italians but there are days when they ride badly. And after Dupont had fallen and recovered I was all alone. He said, "Do what you want." I attacked but I could no longer catch the leaders.'

The Bicycle corroborates his memories: 'Beyaert, of France, was organising the chase by the main group, and he led the bunch over the line' at the end of lap twelve.

But there was no way back. Snell deservedly won the race with Lerno second and Vanlund third. Van Est, an outstanding one-day racer as a professional in the 1950s, finished fourth. José could do no better than eighth. *L'Équipe* published a table showing that José had been the most consistent finisher at Montlhéry (fifth), London (first) and Valkenburg (eighth) but it was not enough for José: 'I could have been world champion at Valkenburg,' he told me.

As he grew older, José could be a bit of a bore on the subjects of diet and heart rate; he came to resemble the old fighter Hemingway created in his story 'The Battler':

> 'You know how I beat them?'
> 'No,' Nick said.
> 'My heart's slow. It only beats forty a minute. Feel it.'
> Nick hesitated.
> 'Come on,' the man took hold of his hand. 'Take hold of my wrist. Put your fingers there.'

This tendency probably had its roots in his experiences with a group of sports scientists who contacted him after his Olympic win. 'They wanted to do analyses. There were six of us in the same conditions: the American decathlete [Bob Mathias], Emil Zátopek; I can't remember the others. We all had an Olympic title. Afterwards they followed up on those cases – Zátopek in Czechoslovakia, me in Pantin . . .

'I walked in. There was a group of men in white jackets.

'"Bonjour Monsieur."

'"Take a seat."

'Heart rate: forty. Lung capacity: seven litres. Thoracic expansion: *formidable.*

'Questions: "Are you a vegetarian?"

'"No."

'"No?"

'"No, I eat raw meat every day."'

All his life José's favourite meal was steak tartare.

'They were all looking at each other. The other five were all vegetarians. When I got home I said to my father, "Perhaps we've got it wrong: I should be a vegetarian."

'So I became a vegetarian. I was in good health and everything but I didn't have . . . I called them "accesses" of strength, moments when I had the feeling I could take an iron file and twist it. Moments of strength like that. I was unbeatable when that happened. And for several months I couldn't ride at all. I was in the peloton; that was all. Good health, everything – except that I had no more accesses. My father started giving me meat again and I started having accesses again.'

5

After José's Olympic success he readied himself to become a professional cyclist. 'I'm not twenty-three but I don't see why I wouldn't ride the Tour de France next year,' he told *Paris-Presse*.

The Olympic win was a major publicity coup for the bicycle manufacturer Helyett. In the 1930s Helyett had backed a professional cycling team led by the climber René Vietto. The company had let the team lapse but now, with an Olympic champion riding its machines, the Helyett professional cycling team was revived for the 1949 season.

Anticipation surrounded José's transition to professional cycling. *L'Équipe* named him '*L'Espoir* 1949', in other words, the rider to watch. José's debut came in February at a series of events in the French colony of Algeria. After three thousand kilometres of preparation rides he started 1949 much as he had finished 1948: with impressive consistency.

In the Critérium de L'Écho d'Oran on Sunday 27 February José finished fifth and prompted Albert De Wetter to call him 'fizzling, sharp, fired-up ... he showed he likes a fight and rejects the primitive, unworthy practice of delaying tactics'.

Two days later he finished sixth in a town-centre race around Aïn Témouchent. There and in Oran the top French sprinter Louis Caput had beaten into second place *L'Équipe*'s Star of 1948, Louis Bobet, who had finished fourth in the Tour de France.

The following Sunday the same group of riders met again in the Critérium de l'Écho d'Alger, or the Algiers Grand Prix, the biggest of the triptych. In strong winds José rode pugnaciously from the start. At Guyotville he and Bobet were two of six riders to dart ahead of the pack. The attack was short-lived. On the Côte de Douaouda, the first rise in the road, José, alone this time, flashed out of the group. Three gave chase. At Fouka this quartet had a meagre lead of forty seconds. Yet with one hundred and sixty kilometres remaining the race had taken shape. At Zurich José accelerated to win an intermediate sprint and Lauzé dropped back, unable to sustain such high speeds. On the short ramp at La Chiffa, sixty kilometres from the finish, José and Lambrecht left Molinès trailing. The Côte de Douera was thick with crowds who cheered the leading pair, then waited four minutes for the mass of riders. There were thirty kilometres still to ride.

Louis Bobet made his counter-attack on the cobblestones of La Cressonnière. He moved within three minutes of the leaders, but too late. One hundred and seventy kilometres after riding away from the peloton, José led Lambrecht into the velodrome at Algiers. Lambrecht moved ahead but two hundred and fifty metres from the line José made a vicious acceleration and his rival conceded defeat.

The following day *L'Écho d'Alger* displayed a prominent photograph of the winner on the front page. It was not exactly the first race of José's career but *L'Équipe*'s headline writers found a way around this:

IN HIS FIRST MAJOR RACE AMONG THE PROS JOSÉ BEYAERT DICTATES THE RACE AND TRIUMPHS AT ALGIERS

José was naturally full of beans: 'From my first contacts with [professional riders], I understood that you have to ride your own race and not just stay cautiously on others' wheels, marking this or that champion in the hope of stealing victory by a hair. The pros like you to pay for your wins with sweat. That's how I rode and it worked. I'll do everything I can to go on that way.'

The Helyett *directeur sportif* Paul Wuyard told *L'Équipe*:

José has always trained like a pro. He likes long distances. That's surely why he doesn't feel out of place. Last year, José was a candidate for the Tour de France. He waited to ride the Olympic Games in London.

But when José returned to metropolitan France the press talked him up and he let them down. Before the seasonal curtain-raiser in Belgium, sponsored by the newspaper *Het Volk*, there was some excitement in the columns of *L'Équipe* over José's appearance. The front-page headline read:

AT THE 'HET VOLK' MAHÉ, IDÉE, BEYAERT WILL FIGHT IT OUT WITH SCHOTTE, CLAES, KETELEER

Albert De Wetter wrote of the other French riders taking part:

> Only echoes of their training allow us to situate their current form. They can't have the same value as the first performances realised by Mahé, Beyaert, Danguillaume and Idée.
>
> These four names come immediately under the pen when it comes to determining our chances in *Het Volk*. Mahé showed himself at the Cannes Grand Prix, Idée and Danguillaume at Oran, Aïn Témouchent and Algiers, and Beyaert won at Algiers.

A note on page two of the Monday paper commented, 'Beyaert, ill, was non-existent'.

Three weeks later *L'Équipe* reproduced a photograph of José sharing his feedbag with another rider during a training ride before the Critérium National. 'What we won't see tomorrow . . .' is the caption, anticipating a blistering performance from the Olympic champion.

But in strong winds, José, described with Marinelli as 'for a long period excellent', could only finish fifty-eighth, over forty minutes after the winner, Émile Idée.

Days later there was reason to celebrate: at the Malinvaud Grand Prix in the town of Niort, a small race on the same day as the Tour of Flanders, José tried to break away twice, after sixty-five kilometres with Molinès and after one hundred and five kilometres with Marcel Dussault. He finished seventh overall. He was riding back into form. *L'Équipe* rejoiced in the headline:

EIGHT DAYS BEFORE PARIS–ROUBAIX MIGNAT, GAUDIN, BEYAERT, L. ET R. LAUK HONE THEIR FORM AT NIORT

In La Flèche Wallonne on Wednesday 13 April 1949 Beyaert finished an honourable 24th, 12 m 56 s behind the winner, Rik Van Steenbergen, who beat Coppi in the sprint.

Paris–Roubaix, the biggest race of the season so far and for many the biggest race of the year, was the following weekend. The race saw the most notorious finish in Paris–Roubaix history. Approaching the race finish in the Roubaix velodrome the three leaders, André Mahé, Jésus-Jacques Moujica and Frans Leenen, were leading by three hundred metres when they were misdirected. They found themselves behind the velodrome. Mahé managed to get into the stadium, climbed a barrier and crossed the line first. Soon afterwards Serse Coppi, the brother of the already legendary Fausto Coppi, won the sprint at the front of the chasing group. José told me, 'In Paris–Roubaix, ten of us got away and in the final kilometer I punctured. I had been with the guy who won the sprint. I'll say it because this is what I've always thought: in principle, I was the one who was going to win the sprint. I'd beaten all of them before in sprints. So I never won Paris–Roubaix.'

The press reports confirmed the bad news: José, despite a puncture, a fall and a broken brake, finished one minute forty-three seconds after Serse Coppi. But there was good news too: in these very long and gruelling races against the very best professional competition, he was beginning to find his way.

In mid-April José flew back to North Africa to take part in the Tour of Morocco. He told the press, 'Look out for my brother Georges,' who was performing his military service and riding with the French army. It was the first time Georges was noticed by the media: *'Voilà un brillant tandem!'* wrote *L'Équipe*: 'Now there's a brilliant duo!'

By finishing third in stage five, from Agadir to Taroudant, José took the race lead. Georges was eighth that day. *L'Équipe*'s race report read: 'The Olympic champion's performance should surprise no one, but his young brother should be warmly congratulated for having shown himself his equal.'

'I was the yellow jersey for one day,' José told me. 'I punctured in the square at Aïn Témouchent in the snow. I couldn't change my tyre. My hands were frozen. In the snow! In Morocco! The snowplough had passed: the road was blocked, there was no way past. I punctured there, in front of the *commissaires*. My brother offered me a wheel but we weren't on the same team – he was riding for the army and I was riding for Helyett – and in any case we didn't have the right to receive help from a third party: you had to do everything alone. So I lost the yellow jersey. I might have lost it later anyway, but all the same . . .'

He was misremembering the location: Aïn Témouchent is over the border in Algeria. But the snowstorm was real enough. The stage was ridden through 'snow, water and mud', said *L'Équipe*, and 'a terrible storm broke close to the finish at Marrakesh'.

José finished twelfth that day and dropped into second place overall, over two minutes behind the new race leader, the Italian-born naturalised Frenchman Urbain Caffi. The next was the hardest, longest day of the race, a 268-kilometre mountain stage from Tadia to Meknès, over the Foum Téguet and the Col d'Ifrane. It was a day of fascinating warring among the contenders. The overall race lead was taken and taken back six times: José attacked and gained enough time to become the race leader on the road. Caffi countered. José attacked again. The Belgian André Blomme launched his bid for victory. The Frenchman André Brulé made his move. Then it was Caffi, who seized the race lead back and kept it to the end. José lost time and finished the stage sixteenth, one place behind his brother, who no doubt piloted him to the finish line. José dropped into eleventh place overall. That was where he remained, despite taking third place on stage twelve between Ouezzane and Rabat and suffering two punctures in the final stage from Rabat to Casablanca. The last of these took place in the velodrome. José ran the final lap and crossed the finish line on foot.

L'Équipe's race summary praised the Beyaert brothers:

Don't let us forget to sing the praises of Georges Beyaert, admirable from start to finish and potentially a great hope for the Tour de France, where he might do well in two or three years alongside his brother José, one of the best metropolitans, but unfortunately one of the most unlucky. What a magnificent tandem the Beyaerts are going to form!

But José's forced, extended stop in that Moroccan snowstorm, as he fumbled to mend a puncture with frozen fingers, caused damage that even he was unaware of. His performance there earned him selection for the Helyett–Huchinson team that would take part in Paris–Tours in mid-May. José's name was even on the start list. But he did not race. 'After the rigours of the Tour of Morocco, he preferred to rest,' wrote *L'Équipe*.

In mid-June José admitted to *L'Équipe* that he had been suffering a pain in his side since the Tour of Morocco. It affected his strength for the rest of the year.

He had returned to racing on 22 May in the Vergeat Cup over a series of challenging climbs: the Col des Brosses, Mont Pilat, the Col de la République and then the finish at Saint-Étienne. *L'Équipe*'s race preview includes a paragraph about José: 'Beyaert wants to show us more of his repertoire . . . after showing us his potential in a one-day race (the Algiers Trophy) then in a stage race (Tour of Morocco), he wants to convince us of his class as a climber.'

But José doesn't appear to have finished either the Vergeat Cup or the Boucles de la Seine the following week. Then, as if enough damage had not been caused, José made it worse:

> 'Two hundred kilometres! Yes, two hundred!' the dynamic José Beyaert emphasised to us last night as he told us about the ride he'd just completed during the day.
>
> 'And the weather was disgusting all the way,' added the Olympic champion. 'Twenty times I said to myself, "*Mon petit* José, you'd be better off at home reading a good detective novel." Twenty times I wanted to turn around but I stuck to it. I only turned around at Sézanne. I think that if I say two hundred kilometres I'm telling no more than the truth.'

81

The interview was splashed over *L'Équipe*'s front page on Friday 10 June 1949 beneath the charming photograph that shows José in a checked shirt, tweed plus fours and a broad smile performing a sideways handstand on a chair. The interview went on:

> By fine-tuning his condition Beyaert has tempered his will. He knows an ordeal awaits him in Sunday's Paris–Limoges . . . It is with the intention of winning that José – resident at Pantin – will rise at 3 a.m. to reach the start at dawn at Croix-de-Berny . . . the man who wore the yellow jersey in the Tour of Morocco wants a brilliant return. If he has chosen Paris–Limoges, it is because he wants above all to prepare himself for the French national championships at Montlhéry by competing in a long race.

José had extra motivation to ride well in the Paris–Limoges classic. Two days later the French regional teams for the Tour de France would be announced. José was certainly hoping a good performance would reinforce his candidacy.

He achieved more than a good ride. José was in the thick of the race from Paris to Limoges. After a first brief breakaway that was quickly caught, five riders launched a new attack. José was one of three who crossed over to them. These eight gained an advantage of three minutes before taking two successive climbs at forty kilometres per hour: breakneck speed! Five of the eight were dropped, leaving José, Georges Ramoulux and Raymond Haegel at the front. They held off the peloton until kilometre 274 when, exhausted, they disappeared behind the speeding peloton.

Even so, when the line-ups of the French regional teams for the Tour de France were published, José was not among them. *L'Équipe* explained, 'Beyaert, despite his class, is still unhardened for such a rude task. His Tour of Morocco, where he weakened markedly after several stages, showed it. But José has the future ahead of him . . .'

He was 'a little disappointed', said *L'Équipe*, and he was 'trying to console himself by thinking that he'll ride the Tour de Suisse.

"But I'd have preferred to have started the grand Tour. I'm assured I'll have my chance in 1950. But a year is long . . .'"

Two days later, in the French national championships, José was brought down in a crash on the fourth of twenty laps. At the start of lap six, five minutes behind the leaders, he abandoned.

Instead of riding the Tour de France José signed a contract to ride a series of Sunday races in Switzerland from 3 to 24 July. He could only follow the Tour at a distance as his dear friend Jacques Marinelli rode a brilliant race.

After a brave attack to Brussels on stage two Marinelli had finished second to Roger Lambrecht, the man José had defeated in the Algiers Grand Prix in March. The pair had gained three minutes on the race favourites, Fausto Coppi and Gino Bartali. Two days later Marinelli had joined Lucien Teisseire on a similar adventure on the road to Rouen, taking second place again and gaining thirteen more minutes on the favourites. The next day, from Rouen to Saint-Malo in Brittany, he got into yet another breakaway with the great Swiss rider Ferdi Kübler. Kübler won the stage but Marinelli gained still more time: five and a half minutes on Gino Bartali and no less than eighteen on Fausto Coppi, who had fallen. By the end of stage five Marinelli led the race by fourteen minutes and fifty-eight seconds.

Against the onslaught of the brilliant Italians – not just Bartali and Coppi but the younger Fiorenzo Magni too – Marinelli weakened. But he managed his position wisely and finished third overall.

Marinelli spent his August capitalising on his Tour performance by riding city-centre criteriums through August for handsome fees. In September, when he made his first post-Tour appearance at his home track in Le Blanc-Mesnil, he invited José, who duly won the elimination race. In the fifty-lap scratch race José looked the fastest man there before his usual bad luck struck and he suffered two falls.

The next day José signed a new contract with Helyett for 1950. The value of his contract is unknown. Jacques Marinelli was discreet about his earnings but he told me, 'I was the third-best-paid cyclist in the world, but it would be better to say the third-least-badly paid. Even Fausto Coppi spent the winter racing to earn appearance money.'

José did the same. He went to Italy with four other French colleagues. Between the Italian races, he went to Vienna for a Grand Prix around the town hall. There he met the Italian idol Gino Bartali and, more pointedly, Bartali's Sicilian *domestique* Giovanni Corrieri. Corrieri had a common but largely unrecognised role in professional cycling: he was paid, in part, to impose the will of his team leader on other riders, by force if necessary. In other words, he was Gino Bartali's enforcer. In Vienna, if José's ripping yarn of infamy and fisticuffs is to be believed, the immovable enforcer collided with the irrepressible José Beyaert.

'Bartali was there with Corrieri and the Swiss brothers Jaerlemann, who all rode for Bartali. I was riding with no one. The race had sprints. I won the first one. The race continued and at a sharp bend I saw Corrieri coming to launch me into the public. I grabbed hold of him because I knew how to handle a bike. I said, "You've made a mistake here. It'll be my turn on the next corner." I sent him flying. It was war.

'Bartali rode up to me straight away. He said, "Why did you do that?"

'"He pushes me but I can't push him? I won't be taken for a fool."

'I was very, very, very, very strong.

'He said, "Today, I have to win."

'"But we're professionals. Win it racing."

'"What do you want?"

'"First prize in the race, because if I win, I'll get it anyway. If I don't win, I want the money."

'It was only right.

'He said, "I own a factory here. I have to win."

'"So buy it."

'So I was second and he won.

'After the race, I went to the changing room. Corrieri was waiting for me with a knife.

'He told me, "Come on then!"

'Behind me there was a door with an iron bar to lock it. I grabbed the bar. I didn't hesitate: Bang! I struck him once. Bang! Again. He went down.

'Bartali walked in.

'He said, "What's going on?"

'I said, "He was waiting for me with a knife." I turned to Corrieri and said, "Next time, your wife will have to identify you from your shoes."

'He didn't bother me again.'

It was classic Beyaert. There was no way of telling whether he was telling the truth. I spoke to Giovanni Corrieri, but too many years had passed and his memories had dissolved.

That evening, José told me, he sat down with Bartali to iron out their differences. Max Bulla, the old Austrian champion, was there. José had a couple of old photographs documenting the encounter. The body language and facial expressions suggest an animated exchange.

There were at least two factual errors in José's account. The first lay in the race results. These appear buried at the foot of an inside page in *L'Équipe*. Bartali was the winner but José was not second but fourth, with Giovanni Corrieri sixth.

The second surrounded José's final comment. For Giovanni Corrieri manifestly did bother José again, but that was in another country and six months hence.

Shortly before the Tour of Lombardy José summed up his first professional season: 'I felt the effects of the cold I was exposed to at the Tour of Morocco for a long period. It is the sole cause of my loss of form. But I feel much better now and I want to finish the season on a high note in the Tour of Lombardy.'

Instead José rode anonymously and was unmentioned in race reports. Ten days later he was in Algiers for an evening track event and a mountain trophy the next day. Already he was travelling widely in search of races and income.

Over the last weekend of October France was shocked by Marcel Cerdan's death in an air accident in the mountains of Saõ Miguel, the largest island of the Azores. He had been on his way to fight Jake LaMotta. He left a wife, three children and a lover, Édith

Piaf (who had moved on from the singer Yves Montand). Cerdan's death surely had an impact on José, who knew him and enjoyed his company. Talent as a sportsman and international celebrity were no shield against catastrophe. This was demonstrated repeatedly over the coming months as cyclist after cyclist met an untimely end.

José had known the director of the Helyett team, Paul Wuyard, since his JPS days. In late October 1949 talks between the manufacturer and its former star René Vietto leaked into the press:

> René Vietto left the Côte d'Azur for the Loiret [yesterday] and the directors of Helyett to discuss the conditions according to which he might manage the team next season.
>
> Vietto will choose eight professionals, the 'Riviera Musketeers' among them, of course, and some young riders . . .

The Riviera Musketeers were Vietto's protégés from the Mediterranean coast: the Italian-born Nello Lauredi; the Athens-born Lucien Lazaridès and his younger brother Apôtre, known as Apo; and the two Teisseire brothers, Lucien and Émile.

Lauredi had a hard, fleshless face that crumpled into a bitter rictus when he rode. Apo was his opposite. It was said of him: 'Many fans have, for Apo Lazaridès, a sympathy nuanced by the indulgence usually extended to talented children.'

The team that had the year before been built around José now became an extension of someone else's personality. The someone else concerned was the quixotic René Vietto.

Vietto had been born with astonishing athletic gifts. Aged eighteen he had won Nice–Puget-Théniers–Nice, the Nice Grand Prix, the Cannes Grand Prix and the Mont Agel hill climb. Aged nineteen he had finished thirteenth in Milan–San Remo and twenty-second in the Tour of Italy. Aged twenty he had won the Wolber Grand Prix, finished fourth in the Tour of Lombardy and represented his country in the 1934 Tour de France, where he won no fewer than four mountain stages. Yet his misfortune matched his achievements. On the Puymorens between Aix-les-Terms and Luchon, his team-mate Antonin Magne fell. Magne was leading the race and Vietto leapt from his bike to give him one of his wheels. By doing so he lost precious time. The following day between Luchon and Tarbes, Magne was several hundred metres behind Vietto when he fell again, on the descent from the Portet d'Aspet. A motorbike pilot told Vietto, who had darted away from the group of leaders and was perhaps speeding towards his fourth stage win. When he heard of his team leader's difficulties he turned around, rode back to Magne and gave him his bike. Vietto was photographed sitting on a wall beside the road, his head in his hands, weeping.

The leading cycling historian Christophe Pénot is right to insist that Vietto achieved results in the mountains that outstrip anything attained by Charly Gaul, Federico Bahamontes, Marco Pantani, Vietto's model Alfredo Binda, and also Fausto Coppi and Eddy Merckx. 'René Vietto was the greatest climber in the history of cycling!' Pénot insists – and this, despite losing what might have been his finest years to the Second World War. Vietto's prodigious abilities as a rider and the frustration of his lost years did not make him the most understanding of team directors.

The Helyett riders were invited to meet their new boss at the Salon de l'Automobile, du Cycle et du Motocycle in the Grand Palais in Paris. José was flying to Algiers that day for his end-of-season appearances. It might have been just as well. Vietto arrived late and flustered. He had walked out on his previous employers, France-Sport, and intended to take the Lazaridès brothers with him. On his way to the Helyett stand at the Salon he had walked into the commercial director of France-Sport and his former team director, Fred Oliveri. The encounter was frosty.

Vietto began to sack riders hired by his predecessor. The Italian-born Frenchman Pierre Tacca held a signed contract for 1950. No matter: he found himself out of work. José knew he had Helyett's confidence. The team even took his brother Georges on. But Vietto had a habit of forming a clique of Mediterraneans around him. The Beyaert brothers were of a quite different temperament.

A short piece by Albert De Wetter about a late-night rendezvous with Apo Lazaridès let slip his view of Vietto's personality. De

Wetter had met up with Lazaridès at one o'clock in the morning at Ducaseau's, a café on the Faubourg Montmartre. The rider's eyes were red with stress. His loyalties were torn. France-Sport, he said, had always shown him generosity, but he owed René Vietto too much not to join him: 'Without him I'd still be a little mechanic. He fed me when I was hungry. He helped me break through and make a name for myself. The time has come for me to repay my debt to him.'

De Wetter's advice betrayed the low view he held of Vietto: he was convinced Apo would be better off fleeing what he called Vietto's 'tyranny'. For the *L'Équipe* journalist, Vietto had been making superhuman efforts 'not to consider himself the navel of the cycling world to whom everyone owes everything'. But those efforts were probably doomed, he went on, 'unless Vietto the team director really is the man he is making himself out to be . . .'

The more the journalist dwelt on Vietto's struggle to mask his self-involvement, the more caustic his pen. Vietto claimed to have resisted the urge to force his ideas on his riders. They could dictate their frames' dimensions and choose their positions on their bikes. 'To all requests,' says De Wetter, facetiously, 'Vietto responds with agreement.' He has, he says, 'no other goal than that of serving'. Training was the one matter about which Vietto was uncompromising. He arranged a training camp early in January where he would supervise his recruits.

> 'All they'll have to do is eat, sleep and train,' he tells us. 'I'll worry about the rest, the *soigneur*s and the equipment. If need be, I'll pump their tyres up for them!'

It was a tempting picture. 'Rather unexpected, you have to admit,' De Wetter added.

A foretaste of the problems to come was hinted at in a report by another *L'Équipe* writer, Jean Heltey. Vietto resented the commotion surrounding his new role. As ever, his argument started reasonably and ended sounding bombastic: 'Cycling has no more mysteries than any other sport and I'll be no more demanding or tyrannical as a *directeur sportif* than anyone else.'

In December Vietto went to Milan, where he signed agreements to take part in the Milan to San Remo one-day classic and the three-week Tour of Italy. In exchange for entry to the Tour of Italy he agreed to some rather extreme conditions: his riders would not be allowed to withdraw from the race: *'Pas question d'abandons! Avec moi, on n'abandonne pas!'* – 'There'll be no question of abandoning. With me, you don't abandon.' It was unheard of and, anyway, unenforceable: riders fall ill, break bones, die. But Vietto felt able to give his word.

In the pretty Provençal village of Lorgues, the chosen location of Vietto's training camp, Cauvin the hotelier, Vigne the butcher, Luraschi the doctor, Descoustes the pharmacist waited impatiently with the rest of the village for 'their' cyclists to arrive. The training camp was held at Lorgues partly because Apo Lazaridès wanted to be near Bernard Nehr, a former *soigneur* who had left cycling in 1943 when he moved from Rocheville, Cannes, to Lorgues.

Nehr was a qualified masseur. More importantly he had been involved in sport since the age of fourteen as a wrestler, then a boxer. He claimed to have sparred with Jack Johnson. It was possible: Johnson had fought at the Vel d'Hiv in December 1913 and June 1914. Nehr had worked with the middleweight Édouard Tenet early in the career of the future European champion. Then, after moving to the French Riviera in 1923, he got involved in cycling and helped launch a number of young riders, the Lazaridès brothers being the best of them. Nehr and José had much in common, although the *soigneur* belonged to the Riviera Musketeers.

In January 1950 Vietto finally assembled his riders in Lorgues to oversee their preparations for the new season:

> They'll have to train hard without thinking about cold or clouds. Every morning, reveille at six. Outings reaching, by the end of February, 250 km at least one or two times a week. I'll be there on my bike and I'll see that everything goes properly. Each rider will have his weight card kept strictly up to date and the menu will be what it has to be.

A conflict over José's steak tartare seemed to be in store. It was not the only topic that boded ill for relations between José and his new boss. Vietto announced his January training camp with characteristic overstatement:

> The Teisseire brothers, the Beyaert brothers, the Lazaridès brothers, Lauredi, Cogan, Vercelonne, Giocomini, Thiétard and I are meeting in our little village, Lorgues, lost in nature, where my comrades will begin their life as true champions . . .

His use of the French word *camarade* ('comrade') was not incidental. Vietto did not hide his sympathy for the French Communist Party. The Communist newspaper *L'Humanité* called Vietto '*notre camarade*' ('our comrade'). And Vietto was a regular contributor to the newspaper during the Tour de France, offering his views on each stage for publication.

José was apolitical. Dogma and rhetoric left him unstirred. He had no feelings at all towards Communism but very definite thoughts on Communists, starting with the Mayor of Pantin. There was little prospect he would welcome Vietto's politics.

Even so, José was positive about having Vietto as his team leader. With more care off his bike – specifically, if the exposure he suffered in Morocco had been diagnosed and treated – he might have achieved so much more. And there was always more know-how to acquire, which Vietto could provide. For example, during the Mountain Trophy in Algiers, on the climb up the Chrea, the heat was draining. José asked for water to be poured over him. 'At the top I was soaked through. Obviously, with the wind and the speed of the descent, I was frozen. The shivering cost me precious time . . . Vietto had warned me.'

L'Équipe put the interview on the front page:

TO BECOME A TRUE 'TOUR DE FRANCE'
JOSÉ BEYAERT TRUSTS ENTIRELY IN RENÉ VIETTO

'I STILL HAVE EVERYTHING TO LEARN,'
THE EX-OLYMPIC CHAMPION MODESTLY CONFESSES

The 'ex' before 'Olympic champion' was not strictly justified. *L'Équipe* used the prefix systematically; it dramatised the transience of sporting glory. José's prospects of achieving more greatly depended now on Vietto. The first signs were that José was going to get on just fine with him:

> He has never said much to me but he has been right in everything he has told me so far . . . He advised me not to drink coffee any more because I'm already restless. I listened to him and it has served me well. [Our relationship] is simple . . . I trust him implicitly.

José had just two requests. The first was to be allowed to ride the Algiers Grand Prix and the Tour of Morocco ('where I have revenge to take'). The second was to be selected for the Tour de France. This, however, did not depend on Vietto. Trade teams did not compete in the Tour de France. Instead riders represented either their country or their French region. There was little prospect of José riding for France. But he knew he just might qualify for the Paris selection or for Île-de-France, if he could catch the eye of the members of the newspapers *Le Parisien Libéré* and *L'Équipe* who elected the teams.

At Lorgues, José gathered the material for another of his favourite anecdotes.

'I met Picasso,' he told me.

'You met Picasso?'

'I was training in the Vars, and in the village there was a carpenter with a son who was a cyclist. Picasso had a mansion in the Vars and one day he went to see the carpenter because he wanted a piece of furniture. He drew what he wanted and asked the carpenter, "How much will it cost?"'

'The carpenter said, "Just sign the plan."'

Picasso's mansion was actually at Vallauris, close by Cannes, some hundred kilometres from Lorgues. It represented his escape from the social demands of life in the French capital. 'Paris was liberated,' Picasso had said to his friend Georges Brassaï, 'but I was beseiged and I still am.' Everyone wanted to visit him in his studio. But the encounter between the artist and the Olympic champion could have taken place at Lorgues or Vallauris or anywhere in-between. Vallauris was well within range for a long training ride. Either way, Picasso might have been the only Communist alive José would have boasted about meeting.

He might well have pardoned Picasso on the grounds of pragmatism. When the front page of *L'Humanité* declared, on 5 October 1944, the day before the opening of the Salon d'Automne, 'Picasso, the greatest of all living artists, has joined the Party of the French Resistance', many considered his rise to political consciousness a sort of insurance policy to safeguard a fortune reputed to be worth six hundred million francs. Right-wingers were said to have gone round Paris altering '*Pétain au poteau*' ('Pétain for the firing squad') graffiti to '*Picasso au poteau*'.

The riders were accommodated in the Hotel Moderne in Lorgues. The Lazaridès brothers roomed together. José seems to have shared not with his brother but with Émile Teisseire. Pierre Cogan, who celebrated his thirty-sixth birthday on 10 January, shared with Lucien Teisseire.

The mornings were dedicated to training sorties. After a shower and lunch, the riders went to bed at two, had massages, and medical and equipment checks from four to six and dinner at seven. Lunch was a smorgasbord of raw carrots, onions, artichokes and beetroot. Unusually for the time Vietto banned wine and cigarettes. At eight thirty the riders played cards. At nine they were in bed. Cogan laughed, 'I'm getting younger every day.'

Albert De Wetter visited the camp at the end of January. Bernard Nehr told him Lucien Teisseire was in the right shape to win the Nice Grand Prix and to rival Fausto Coppi in Milan–San Remo. Apo Lazaridès was in fine form for the Cannes Grand Prix, José Beyaert was perfect for the start-of-season criteriums, and Lauredi and Lucien Lazaridès would be formidable in the pre-Tour de France stage races. Émile Teisseire, Apo and José were, De Wetter observed, 'of unalterable good humour'.

At the start of February Émile Teisseire won the Mont Agel

hill climb, a few miles north of Monte Carlo. It had been a team effort, although Teisseire explained, 'I owe everything to René Vietto.' José and Georges, then Roberto Vercellone, then Lucien Teisseire and Apo Lazaridès had been sent out to soften up the field. Nello Lauredi had made a dangerous attack, drawing counter-attacks from Bobet and others. Jean Dotto of France-Sport gained Lauredi's wheel, then launched himself into what looked like a winning attack until Émile Teisseire pounced, riding up to Dotto and, with one definitive acceleration, delivering the *coup de grâce*.

The win no doubt gave Vietto all the power he needed to run the team as he saw fit. However, despite the display of teamwork, all was not well at the camp.

José and Georges found that Apo Lazaridès could be sometimes infantile. Georges told me, 'He was difficult. He complained about the mechanics. He complained about everything. He'd won Nice–Paris, as it was in those days, not Paris–Nice. He'd won it and he believed he was really someone, Monsieur Apo Lazaridès.

'We went out training one day. Apo wanted to teach us to climb with our elbows out, one next to the other with Apo in-between, leaning on our elbows and getting a free ride up the hill. My brother could climb, as you'd expect. He told him, "If you can't get up on your own, you can stay down there. And don't count on my brother to help. My brother is here to help me, not you."

'Back at the hotel Apo made the mistake of closing in on my brother as if he was going to hit him. He didn't. Pum! One punch from my brother and it was over.

'Apo's brother came up, and my brother said, "You want one?"

'"No, no, no."

'Lucien Teisseire was there with his brother Émile. I was there with mine. If there was going to be a fight, it was going to be all of us. We didn't fight because everyone knew Apo was a bloody fool. Even his brother said so.'

The unheard-of Vietto who had smothered all-comers with unqualified agreement in December had reverted to the implacable, controlling Vietto everyone knew.

José told me, 'Vietto was an ass! He wanted everyone to do what he had done. If I did three hundred kilometres without eating or drinking while training, I was finished! He believed that what he'd done was right. And he took sides. We always had to ride for Lazaridès. Always for Lazaridès. Lazaridès was a good little rider; he had one or two formidable years. I always did the right thing by my team-mates. If another rider had a chance I gave everything for him. I was always equal to my sporting duties. But Lazaridès was a climber. Outside the mountain roads he couldn't follow me.'

Georges had much the same story: 'René Vietto was insane. With him, you had to ride long distances. He did three hundred kilometres so we all had to ride three hundred kilometres. But we're not all the same. He refused to see that. My brother couldn't do that. If he rode three hundred kilometres during the week he had no strength left when Sunday came. So we did our training on our own. Vietto set off with the team somewhere else. We went to ride the Ville d'Aix Grand Prix at Aix-en-Provence. My brother won. He was first, I was fourth and Vietto couldn't make any sense of it.'

José continued, 'Vietto wanted to show me the door. The Helyett boss told him, "Beyaert is our rider. He stays."'

6

José had never mastered the art of riding economically; his best results came when he expended energy with capricious abandon. So it was at the Avignon Grand Prix. Three riders gained a couple of minutes on the peloton. José, with his team-mate Lucien Lazaridès, the sprinter Robert Chapatte, the local rider Maurice Kallert and Jean Lauk, all good riders and team-mates with the Rochet-Dunlop team, gave chase and brought the peloton back together. Then José attacked again, gaining thirty seconds before he was reeled in. The intact peloton presented itself for the sprint. Chapatte and Kallert attacked early. Caput, the best French sprinter, made his move too soon. José used his slipstream as a sling and shot past him to take the win.

José was on the start list for Algiers Grand Prix but he notified the race organisers that he would not be there. It was perhaps a sign that he was acting more or less independently of René Vietto. Instead he went to Bordighera, a couple of miles east of Ventimiglia, for a circuit race. The event was won by Luigi Casola, an Italian sprinter who spent his later life in Mexico. The reigning Tour de France champion, Fausto Coppi, and the reigning world champion, Rik Van Steenbergen, were second and third respectively. José was unmentioned in the race reports.

He rode the Milan–San Remo on 19 March. The archives say he finished in the last big group of thirty-seven riders, a few seconds under twelve minutes after the winner, Gino Bartali. José said otherwise: 'I attacked on Capo Berta with a group. The breakaway got smaller and smaller and in the end I was alone. They caught me on the final straight. Bartali won the sprint. I was there but I couldn't sprint. Bartali won. I was given the same time and position as the rest of the peloton.'

The peloton was attributed ninth place and this is the position José claimed. It was the group in which his team-mate Nello Lauredi finished. Both men were criticised, rather harshly, by *L'Équipe*: 'José Beyaert and Lauredi were out of gas far too early for anyone to be satisfied with their transalpine sortie.' José's account no doubt compensated for his disappointment but the official results might very well have been wrong.

Back in France José rode poorly at the Critérium National on 26 March, but a week later he was one of the riders who, in strong wind and gathering rain at the Circuit du Midi Libre near Montpellier, led the chase behind two attacking Spaniards on the slopes of the Col du Minier. But later in the race he disappeared. The fact that Georges punctured on the descent and was unable to mend the puncture because of his frozen fingers may have contributed to José's poor showing. He rode badly in the cold. We know that much from Morocco. The same day Émile Teisseire won the race up Mont Faron, near Toulon.

A fortnight later José rode the classic from Paris to Brussels. His performance in the 326-kilometre race was nothing short of excellent. At Jolibois, after 310 kilometres, José attacked: 'I escaped alone. I reached Brussels with a two-minute lead, at Bois de la Cambe, where I thought the race finished. There were military processions and things in the city centre – something to do with King Leopold, the one who abdicated – and they had diverted the race by several kilometres. I arrived there with a two-minute lead: it's one thing when there's two kilometres to go, but after three hundred kilometres? In the distance remaining, they caught me.'

L'Équipe criticised the race for having too many entrants – there were 202 starters – and for being too long. If José had won that day his career would have taken off. '*Het Volk*, the Belgian newspaper, called me the moral winner. All the same, I lost Paris–Bruxelles.'

It was a breakthrough performance. Jean Bidot, the technical director of the French national team at the Tour de France, said as much to Albert De Wetter: 'Apart from Beyaert recently, no one else has really emerged [this season].'

Vietto's team, meanwhile, was falling apart. Apo Lazaridès was sick of living in a training camp. He told *L'Équipe*, 'The discipline René requires of us isn't new to me. I didn't prepare for the 1948 world championships by spending my days in the cinema, but the strictness was self-inflicted.'

Of the predictions Bernard Nehr made at Lorgues, little trace remained. There had been no big win and Vietto had withdrawn into silence. Instead of being his riders' intimate, he had become their slave-master. *L'Équipe* reported, 'He reacts to his riders' defeats with irony: "I could have done as well with one leg . . . You make me want to ride again . . ." when they might expect the consolation of a little encouragement.'

The Lazaridès brothers complained that they had over-trained. By imposing the same training programme and the diet on all his riders at Lorgues, they claimed, their team director had managed to destroy the first half of the season for many of them.

Vietto responded with an outburst that must have sorely disappointed his riders. 'With the exception of Lauredi,' he told Albert De Wetter, 'if any of them are selected [for the Tour de France], I will oppose their participation.'

After criticising Apo and Lucien Lazaridès for thinking only of the Tour, De Wetter commented:

> Émile and Lucien Teisseire aren't yet responding the way Vietto would like. The same goes for José Beyaert – and, by the way, René is wrong not to believe enough in Georges Beyaert. But it is understandable that a man who had believed his team was going to be distinguished not by weakness, but by panache, should be worried.

Still, when De Wetter telephoned Vietto with the news that Lauredi had been selected for the French national team at the Tour de France, Vietto was vindictive: 'Lauredi and Géminiani selected? Good! Apo rejected? Good!'

As the team readied itself for the Tour of Italy, its morale was at rock bottom. The Italian Tour hadn't been a happy destination for non-Italians in recent years. Belgian, French and Swiss riders tended to appear only as *domestiques* hired to assist Italian leaders with their sights set on victory.

The 1950 Tour had a rather different look. An international series called the Desgrange-Colombo Challenge had been organised by the newspapers *L'Équipe*, *La Gazzetta dello Sport*, *Het Nieuwsblad-Sportwereld* and *Les Sports*, bringing together the principal one-day classics, the Tour de France and the Tour of Italy. *L'Équipe* called the 1950 Tour 'a revolutionary Tour of Italy because everything has been done by *La Gazzetta* so that a foreigner can win'. As a result the organisers of the Tour assembled a more international peloton than in the past. Jean Robic led a formation in which Italians played the supporting roles habitually filled by foreign mercenaries. Ferdi Kübler was there. A foreign victory, considered practically impossible hitherto, had become a possibility.

There was Helyett's entirely French team, too, although things had changed rather for René Vietto and his team since Vietto had agreed to participate. Then he had been persuaded that winning the Tour would be a realistic objective for his riders. The season had not unfolded as he had envisaged and now the Tour looked like a last chance.

The race started in Milan on Wednesday 25 May 1950 at 11 a.m. A gale was blowing and within two hours the war between Vietto and his riders surfaced. There was a fall. Lauredi, Cogan and Apo Lazaridès hit the ground. The first two recovered quickly and sprinted after the peloton. Apo's rear derailleur was damaged. Ahead, team-mates of Coppi and Bartali seized the opportunity to distance a possible rival by acceleration. Vietto allowed Apo to chase alone for fifteen kilometres before telling his brother Lucien to wait for him. The chase would have been futile had not a level crossing held up the peloton twenty kilometres later and allowed the Lazaridès brothers to regain the group.

All the Helyett riders finished in the peloton that day forty seconds behind the stage winner, Oreste Conte. After the stage,

Lauredi complained about shoulder pain. *L'Équipe* singled José out for praise: 'Beyaert had a very good first day and finished among the leaders in the peloton.'

Meanwhile, in France, fourteen riders were named for the Tour. They included Roger Queugnet and Robert Chapatte but not José Beyaert.

Back at the Tour of Italy the mountain stages began immediately. Stage two took in the famous Raticosa on the road to Florence. Lauredi, pushing a gear that was too big, rode well until halfway up the climb, then weakened and in the end conceded 8 minutes 40 seconds to the stage winner. Apo stayed with the group containing the favourites until the final kilometre but he too suffered a physical crisis and conceded even more: 11 minutes 42 seconds. Cogan was worse: 17 minutes 55 seconds. José lost 21 minutes but still faired better than Lucien Teisseire (who conceded 26), his brother Émile and Lucien Lazaridès (both of whom lost more than 45).

From Florence to Livorno on the Tuscan coast, Livorno up to Genoa, and Genoa to Turin, there was little to report. But on stage six, between Turin and Locarno, as José finished safely in the peloton that finished in the same time as the second-placed rider, Luigi Casola, nearly two minutes behind the stage winner, Hugo Koblet, Lucien Lazaridès fell heavily. The next morning, he was unable to take the start. Vietto's comment to *L'Équipe* became a headline: 'I'm only really interested in Lauredi because he listens to me. The loss of Lucien Lazaridès leaves me cold.'

It may have been at this moment that the Helyett riders, who had no team-mate with any chance of a high finish, began selling their services as *domestiques* to other contenders, most likely Hugo Koblet, the Swiss race leader.

The morning before stage eleven, from Milan to Ferrara, Achille Joinard joined the French race *commissaire* Marius Dupin and Vincenzo Torriani, the race director and boss of *La Gazzetta dello Sport*, and went to see Vietto. Torriani wanted the Helyett team thrown off the race on the pretext that their contribution had been virtually non-existent.

Torriani no doubt offered Vietto the example of André Brulé, who had attacked alone after sixty kilometres of the previous day's stage to be joined two hundred kilometres later by three chasers. On the penultimate curve he attacked again but finished only third. Behind him Nello Lauredi had had a mechanical problem 230 kilometres into the 291-kilometre stage. He regained the peloton only after a rude chase by José, Pierre Cogan and Apo Lazaridès. Having restored Lauredi to the peloton, they relaxed. Cogan and José finished together, twenty minutes after Lauredi.

After a lecture from his old mentor Achille Joinard, José started the stage with every intention of imitating Brulé. But the peloton was tired and the heat draining and Gino Bartali had decided there should be no attacks that day. Each time José tried to trouble the somnolent group he was chased down by riders with no intention of contributing to a breakaway, as *L'Equipe* reported:

> He was joined each time by men who refused to work with him, and, surrounded by riders, some of whom even used their fists to get the message home, he had to accept defeat. In no way intimidated, José tried the impossible although he had later to ease up and go with his friends Teisseire, Cogan and Apo Lazaridès to the assistance of Lauredi, the victim, yet again, of bad luck. Lauredi, three and a half minutes behind the peloton, had to change his bicycle.

In mid-June José told the story of the stage to Jacques Augendre of *L'Équipe*. The version that made it into print reads as follows:

> It was very difficult for the French to try anything. We were marked oppressively. At times, when I was free of my *domestique* duties, I tried to attack to show myself a little. Immediately I found three or four Italians around me. Worse, I imagine Corrieri didn't like my face. Every time he threatened to launch me into the countryside.

The version José actually told Augendre was probably closer to the story he told me: 'There were cash prizes for intermediate sprints in each village and since I was a sprinter I wanted to profit from them to win a bit of money. But every time the sprint triggered breakaway attempts. It wasn't what Bartali wanted. So he sent Corrieri after me.

'"What are you playing at?"

'"I don't know about you. I'm taking part in the Tour of Italy!"

'"If you attack again, I'll punch your fucking face in."

'"Many have tried, very few have succeeded. Try your hand."

'At the next sprint I attacked all alone. No one moved in the peloton because they knew what was coming. Corrieri came to find me. He made the mistake of raising his hand. I saw it coming. When he raised his hand to punch me, boom! I ducked inside and threw myself at him and when I fell on him I caught him by the hair. I trapped his head against the ground and I put one on him. The peloton came past, slowly. No one said a thing. The journalists arrived.

'"What happened?"

'"I fell, he fell, we got tangled up."

'"And you?"

'"We got tangled up."

'Neither of us said anything.

'The next day in *L'Équipe*, it said "David and Goliath" because Corrieri was well over six foot. So in *L'Équipe* there was a quarter-page marked "David and Goliath" in which they tried to explain what had happened.'

This was an exaggeration: the day after, *L'Équipe* did not name Corrieri. He was identified only in Jacques Marchand's 19 June piece. Neither report made any biblical reference.

'So Bartali sent me someone else: [Adolfo] Leoni. "Gino would like to talk to you."

'"It's too late."

'So Bartali came in person.

'"Tell me what you're playing at?"

'"The Tour of Italy, same as you."

'"I don't understand you."

'"Exactly. It's because you don't understand that you come to see me. Have you thought that at the Tour of Italy the French teams have no rights? We've won nothing at all. Haven't you understood that we want to earn something? Today there are sprint prizes. Can I ride for them?"

'So Bartali said, "How many have you won?"

'"Three."

'"How many do you want to win?"

'"Six or seven."

'And he said, "Seven?"

'"All right."

'"And then you'll stop?"

'"Then I'll stop."

'So I sprinted through four more villages and then I stopped.'

José finished tenth that day.

René Vietto continued his venomous comments. On stage thirteen, from Rimini to Arezzo, Apo and Lauredi both tried to break away for a stage win but they were repeatedly chased down by riders who then sat on their wheels and refused to work. Vietto greeted Apo's return to form with typical sourness: 'It's not on stage thirteen you have to start pedalling, it's on stage one.' On the hilly stages José was consistently among the first to be dropped and among the last to finish in each stage, although in Naples at the end of stage seventeen he took fifteenth place. The following day the Tour of Italy concluded in Rome. The twenty-four-year-old José had completed his first three-week stage race, even if he did finish seventy-second of seventy-five and conceded two hours, fifty-two minutes and twelve seconds to the winner, Hugo Koblet of Switzerland.

In Rome Vietto attempted to justify his jeering brand of leadership to *L'Équipe*. He insisted that the contracts he'd given his riders made them 'the best-paid cyclists in France'.

He repeated his contention that no one except Lauredi had made the slightest effort and that his other riders had all ridden complacently. He said these things within earshot of José Beyaert. The newspaper account might very well have played down the argument that ensued:

At the moment Vietto pronounced these words, José Beyaert responded:

'But we all tried. For my part, I finished the Tour of Italy. For a first-timer, that's already something.'

'Something? You think it's something to have finished the Tour of Italy in last place but one?

'Kid, tomorrow, untrained, with nothing but willpower, I could finish the Tour of Italy seventy-fourth.'

Relations between the two men must have been severely strained. Vietto apparently sought to punish José by including him in Helyett's line-up at the Critérium du Dauphiné Libéré, a mountainous one-week stage race before the Tour de France.

José refused to go and informed the team that his brother, a climber, would be going in his place. 'I'm coming from one stage race,' he said, 'and riding another seems to me abusive.' His choice of words hinted at a simmering row with Vietto. 'I hope to be selected for the Tour and I wouldn't want to start completely empty. I prefer to maintain my present condition.'

After the train journey from Italy, José reached Paris on Friday 16 June. Georges met him at the station.

'We're doing Paris–Boulogne-sur-Mer on Sunday.'

'OK!'

The race attracted riders who had failed to qualify for the French national championship, which took place the same day. José had emerged from the torment of the Tour of Italy with tremendous strength and fitness for the type of event that Vietto refused to accept was his real speciality: hard, northern-style one-day racing. The 275-kilometre course had a number of abrupt rises and a difficult dénouement of forty kilometres. It suited him. *L'Équipe* made José joint favourite with Édouard Klabinsky.

But José almost didn't take part. At the race start at Le Bourget, only one 'Beyaert' appeared on the start list. Georges was turned away. José threatened not to ride but the organisers and *commissaires* refused to yield and José eventually took to the start line as Helyett's only representative.

Ten riders attacked from the start. Ten more quickly joined them. A hundred and thirty kilometres later, near Amiens, José made his move. Six riders went with him. They gained the breakaway with a lead of two minutes over the peloton.

Between Abbeville at kilometre 170 and Le Touquet at kilometre 230 the leading group thinned to ten. By kilometer 250 José had three men for company. On the Col de Cayolle in Boulogne he propelled himself away, alone. Behind him, Édouard Klabinsky, César Marcelak, André Brulé, Jean-Marie Goasmat and Robert Bonnaventure rode past the remains of the leading group but by then José had gone. Seven hours, four minutes and twenty seconds after the race started he crossed the finish line alone. His winning margin was one minute forty seconds over Klabinsky. *L'Équipe* reported:

> José, his face breathing health, no trace of fat weighing down his muscles, truly dominated the race ... He hopes to have done what he needed to in order to achieve the goal closest to his heart: his selection for the Tour de France.

Louis Bobet, now known universally as Louison ('Big Louis'), had won the French national championships that day after a titanic three-way struggle with the riders Antonin Rolland and Camille Danguillaume. The fight had become a duel when Danguillaume made contact with a motorbike carrying a race photographer. The fall put him in a coma. Eight days later he died.

On the day Danguillaume died Georges Beyaert fell on the descent from the Ventoux, bruising his face and, more importantly, damaging his bike beyond repair. He was forced to abandon the Dauphiné Libéré. On the day of the final stage, Georges rode the Circuit Pyrénéen over the Tourmalet, the Soulor and the Aubisque. He was hoping to pick up a last-minute place in the Tour but he could only finish fifth.

On Sunday 2 July the Dauphiné Libéré ended after unheralded dominance by Vietto's men. The winner was Nello Lauredi. Second was his team-mate Apo Lazaridès. Whatever Helyett thought of

René Vietto, his methods had borne fruit just in time for the Tour de France.

On Friday 23 June 1950 *L'Équipe* had published the news José had been waiting for, even if the announcement accepted that his selection to represent Paris at the Tour de France was open to criticism:

> His performance at the Tour of Italy was not exceptionally good. But let's not forget that the Olympic champion is young. He accepted the responsibility of starting the Tour with no experience and courageously finished it after commendable work as a *domestique*. Many cannot say as much. He deserved his chance. Furthermore, he won Paris–Boulogne-sur-Mer last Sunday.

Each of the selected riders was described in *L'Équipe* by an 'identity card' summarising his career so far. José's is of interest for the three words with which it concluded: *'La gaité personnifiée'* ('gaiety personified'). Days later a Tour de France preview in *L'Équipe* elaborated on José's personal qualities:

> José, the bespectacled rider, brimming with humour and pizzazz, smiling and streetwise, will be a first class team-mate. Alone he can sustain the morale of an entire team. [He] is a good climber and a formidable sprinter. He is an intelligent and remarkably well-balanced young man.

There was more the day before the Tour started. Despite the last-minute preparations with frequent interruptions by autograph hunters, José was 'permanently joyful'. Only talk of the first stage, a 307-kilometre marathon from the capital to Metz, could daunt his fresh demeanour. José called it 'a tough morsel and very long'.

The first stage through the Ardennes was so hard that even the French national team only managed to get two men, Marinelli and Géminiani, into the seventy-nine riders that finished seventy-eight seconds behind the stage winner, Jean Goldschmidt. José finished a minute behind that group with his twenty-two-year-old Paris team-mate Serge Blusson, his Helyett team-mate Nello Lauredi and the French champion Louis Bobet. Bobet had punctured and broken his wheel on the descent towards Metz. Lauredi braked, turned around and climbed back up the slope he'd just descended until he found his man. With José and Blusson, both of whom might very well have taken money for their efforts, Lauredi then led Bobet to the line.

Goldschmidt was a Luxembourger who normally rode in Gino Bartali's team and said he had learnt everything from his leader. The following day another Bartali man, Adolfo Leoni, took the stage. Stage three went to another Italian, Alfredo Pasotti; stage four to Belgium's Stan Ockers; stage five to the reviled Giovanni Corrieri; and stage six, an individual time trial, to Switzerland's Ferdi Kübler.

Through this first week José worked quietly for his team and lost time daily. He told me, 'I never looked at my results; they didn't matter to me. I looked at the results of the person who was paying me. It was business.'

In the time trial on stage six, saving energy for the ordeal to come, José finished eighty-seventh of 110 starters, only 104 of whom finished. Three of those who did not were José's team-mates Lucien Lauk, Maurice Quentin and Jacques Renaud. The following day another Parisian, Robert Dorgebray, abandoned on the day of the first stage win by a Frenchman (albeit one born in Italy): Nello Lauredi, who won at Angers.

It was a significant day for José on a number of counts. Two were causes for celebration. The stage winner, of course, was his team-mate at Helyett. Lauredi had been one of twelve escapees from the peloton. Behind him José himself had ridden a swashbuckling stage in a second chasing group of five, which he led home, outsprinting his team-mate Antoine Frankowski and, more importantly for José, his old Olympic rival, the silver medallist Gerrit Voorting.

The speed that day was high, so high it even prevented the usually amenable José from holding court on the road before *L'Équipe*'s journalists, who noted:

Beyaert, between *bidons*, was always ready to come alongside our car and regale us with funny stories.

This morning he suddenly dropped his nose to his handlebar and excused himself, saying, 'I'll be back in a minute to tell you the rest . . .' We didn't see him again for the rest of the day. It was fast!

After the stage he effused to Jacques Marchand:

I'm happy because I've removed a doubt. For two years, I've been hearing that I wouldn't have become the Olympic champion in London if Voorting had been alongside me in the sprint. The elbow-to-elbow I've been waiting for has finally happened, and taking thirteenth place in the stage means more to me than winning a stage! On top of that, I'm going well . . . I have a feeling I'm going to surprise you in the mountains.

José's enthusiasm was dampened by word of two more abandonments. One was Dorgebray. The other was José's friend Jacques Marinelli. A member of the French national team, Marinelli had been riding for several days with a steak down his shorts to protect his delicate skin from saddle sores. José told *L'Équipe*:

I suffered for him. I wish I could have taken his place. He has never been one to play-act. His suffering was painful to behold. He cried like a child and hid his face to hide his tears. It broke my heart.

Robert Chapatte was in the same unfortunate predicament and abandoned three days later. The Paris delegation was down to five riders.

The following day José's hopes of riding well in the mountain stages took a serious knock. Thirty kilometres from the stage finish a French rider named Raoul Rémy tried and failed to grasp two *bidons* with one hand. He fell flat on his face, bringing José down with him. Rémy was unhurt. José hit the ground hard and split one knee wide open. He remembered, 'The doctor told me, "You can't go on." He examined me to see if the kneecap was broken. But no, it was OK. The wound was ugly but nothing was broken so I started the next day. Obviously I was slobbering a bit because your knee bends more than anything else on a bike. So I dribbled with pain. But after I'd warmed up I was OK. It was mostly at the stage starts that I suffered.'

The Paris team director Jean Maréchal said, 'His open knee is going to hamper him considerably and he's going to suffer. But José is much more courageous than people suppose.'

Rémy was fined two thousand francs for his misdemeanour. Despite his pain José interceded on Rémy's behalf but the race judges insisted the fine had to stand.

At last the riders reached the mountains, where José's injured knee dashed his hopes of surprising the world.

After a seven-and-a-half-hour ride from Pau Gino Bartali celebrated victory at Saint-Gaudens. José reached the finish line more than half an hour later. One of many fallers on the descent from the Tourmalet, he had added rib injuries to his damaged knee: 'I ended up astride the guardrail and I still don't know how I didn't fall into the ravine. Blusson fell the same way at the same spot and we both set off with smashed-up knees.'

That same evening, citing a barrage of insults and physical threats from the French crowd on the Aspin, the Italian team withdrew from the race. The following day the new race leader, Ferdi Kübler, who had been in second place behind Magni, refused to wear the yellow jersey. It was perhaps not that day but on a later morning that José stole the yellow jersey. The laughter that ensued, captured in the famous photograph, is all the more poignant for José's pain. It is even possible that the theft of the yellow jersey took place on the very day José stopped the Tour de France for his dip on the shoreline in Sainte-Maxime. If so it was a day of mischief for him, a day he indulged his taste for shenanigans as an escape from the hell of dragging his mangled knee and hammered ribs through stages lasting nine and a half hours or more.

At Nice another team-mate, Antoine Frankowski, was eliminated. Two days later Dominique Forlini left the race. There were now just three riders left in the Paris delegation: Baldassari, Blusson and Beyaert. Free of team responsibilities, José found that the remains of the Tour held opportunities to boost his earnings. 'I was with Jean Robic on the Col de la Croix de Fer [in the Alps]. I caught him. Did you ever hear Robic speak? He was a friend of mine, Biquet.

'"I've punctured."

'He'd punctured. He was on his own. I rode gently and soon he was on my wheel.

'He said, "Who are you working for today?"

'"No one."

'"Why don't you work for me?"

'"OK."

'We agreed thirty-five thousand francs, as I recall.

'We were two minutes behind.

'"We'll get it back, easy," I said.

'I started to lead him. He even grabbed hold of me (that was what I was being paid for) and we regained the peloton. I remember in the final kilometres there was a little climb, the Col du Lapin. (It's funny, the name comes to me, just like that!) He rode off and caught the peloton.

'He came to pay me and he gave me twice what we'd agreed. I'd done more than I had to. I'd kept my word and more, and he saw that. Afterwards, I rode for whoever paid because there was no more team and no more moral obligations. Because I've never abandoned my moral obligations. The only obligation I had was to finish the race.

'That day,' José told me, 'my chain came off and I finished the stage on foot.' He picked up his bike and finished the stage jogging. The race photographers asked him to go back and make a repeat performance for their benefit. José obliged with a smile. His buoyancy was such that nothing could dampen his spirits. It was a truly extraordinary gift.

7

José finished the 1950 Tour with yet another fall. During the penultimate stage, between Lyons and Dijon, José was riding well. He even attacked, hoping to join the breakaway. However, just in front of the banner announcing twenty kilometres to go, he made contact with another rider and fell on his injured knee.

'I'm in some pain,' he said after the stage. 'Will I finish tomorrow? I don't know.' But José finished his first Tour de France. In Paris, as he headed for the changing rooms in the Parc des Princes, he quipped, 'Where do we sign on for the 1951 Tour?' *L'Équipe* asked, 'Is it really just a wisecrack? Haven't the three "babies" (Blusson, Baldassari and Beyaert) Jean Maréchal has shepherded into Paris become real mature road racers for the 1951 Tour?'

There is nothing like a public show of suffering to win popularity at the Tour de France. José was the living proof. The day after the race finish the newspaper *France-Soir* held a gala evening during which it presented the awards known as 'the Tour de France Oscars'. Raphaël Géminiani took the 'Best Team-mate' prize. José and Nello Lauredi were honoured for their courage. José also received a five-thousand-franc prize given by the wife of the automobile manufacturer Clément-Bayard for the Tour's most unlucky rider. At the end of the week José was mentioned four times in a poll of Tour journalists and riders: his was one of twenty names in the 'Friendliest Rider' (voted by journalists) category and one of sixteen in the 'Friendliest Rider' (voted by riders) list. He was one of nine 'Tour Philosophers'. He figured in another list too: the

'Almost Invisibles'. This last inclusion must have stung him: was he becoming a media sideshow?

On Sunday 19 August, the day of the world road-racing championships, José finished thirteenth at the Nouan-le-Fuselier Grand Prix, having missed the crucial breakaway. Still, apart from Dominique Forlini, he was the best Tour rider.

In mid-September, over a very flat, very fast course around Romorantin near Blois, José easily won the Grand Prix des Cycles Helyett et R. Lèvy. Then, in October 1950, José's father's old friend André Mouton, now the manager of the Vel d'Hiv, announced the revival of the legendary twenty-four-hour Bol d'Or race.

The first Bol d'Or had been held at the Vélodrome Buffalo in Neuilly, Paris, in 1894, in an age of insane endurance events including non-stop seventy-two-hour races and thousand-kilometre challenges. Constant Huret took the lead in the second hour and kept it to the finish, covering 737 kilometres in the allotted time. The last Bol d'Or had been held in 1928: Mouton had finished second to the great Australian rider Hubert Oppermann.

Within days of the revival's announcement entrants were flowing in. The winners of the last three editions of the epic race from Bordeaux to Paris, Ange Le Strat, Jésus-Jacques Moujica and Wim Van Est, were the first to sign up. Next was José. 'I want to ride the Bol d'Or,' he told *L'Équipe*:

> Everyone knows that the ex-Olympic champion, whose eyes glitter with mischief behind his glasses, is a man of impetuous resolutions.
>
> It's hard to visualise this excitable little chap, who can't sit still, starting a long-distance event that requires absolute self-control.
>
> 'Why's that?' he asks, without losing his sense of humour. 'There's plenty of evidence to suggest I can do a good Bol d'Or …I never get so bone-weary I can't stand up!' he says, punctuating his words with a burst of laughter. But he quickly becomes serious when he asserts he knows how to suffer and hang on when the going gets tough.

As José declared his interest in the Bol d'Or he made a comment that suggested soul-searching: 'It will help me discover my true way. I may be built for rude ordeals in which endurance, courage and willpower hold sway.'

As José ruminated news came through of the death of one of the Bol d'Or entrants. Late at night on 13 November 1950, as Jésus-Jacques Moujica and his training partner Jean Rey returned home to Avignon after a race in Saint-Étienne they were killed when they collided with a truck on Route Nationale 7 south of Montélimar. The two men were declared dead an hour after their admission to hospital. There is no way of knowing what impact their deaths had on José.

The prize for winning the Bol d'Or was two hundred thousand francs, offered by the tyre manufacturer Hutchinson. *L'Équipe*'s favourite was Antonio Bevilacqua, the Italian road-racing champion of Italy and the reigning world pursuit champion. Its front-page headline added, 'ALTHOUGH THE FEATHERWEIGHT JOSÉ BEYAERT CAN BLOCK THE ROAD AHEAD OF HIM'.

José was a surprising choice of outsider. The entrants included Fiorenzo Magni, who had won the Tour of Italy in 1948 and the Tour of Flanders in 1949 and 1950; Théo Middelkamp, the world road racing champion in 1947; and less conventional talents like the six-day specialist Raymond Goussot and his madison partner, Émile Carrara; or Rudi Valenta, the winner in 1950 of the 430-kilometre Vienna–Graz–Vienna behind a motorbike. It was the strength of José's character more than his achievements as a sportsman that attracted *L'Équipe*'s attention: 'His optimism, his morale are the characteristic traits of his personality and they will be valuable assets. Well prepared, resilient, he can do well.'

At 11 p.m. on Saturday 25 November Constant Huret, the winner of the first two Bols d'Or, started the race. With bonus prizes as an incentive the early pace was high. Six minutes after the start José called out to the race judge, 'How many laps to go?' The judge shouted after him, 'Another couple, my boy.'

Gaiety and laughter ruled the Vel d'Hiv, with José at its heart.

Carrara raced hard. José passed him and led at the end of the first hour (distance covered: 41 kilometres 502 metres). Carrara countered with Guy Lapébie. José fell with Middelkamp and Valenta but finished the second hour leading too (distance covered: 81 kilometres 262 metres). Then José slowed. Alvaro Giorgetti passed him with Le Strat and established a lead of one, then two laps. Giorgetti was the first to complete 100 kilometres (time: 2 hours, 28 minutes, 50 seconds). At the end of the third hour, he had covered 119.065 kilometres.

At 2.30 a.m. Magni made his move. Le Strat responded, Carrara attacked, then it was Giorgetti and Lapébie before Magni made a second acceleration that gained him and Lapébie three consecutive laps on the field. At 3 a.m., four hours in, Magni led (distance covered: 157.295 kilometres).

Raymond Impanis of Belgium fell badly. Valenta broke a wheel and chain. At four in the morning Goussot took the lead (distance covered: 191.687 kilometres). At 4.45 a.m., Impanis restarted, thirty-four laps down. He regained a lap. The pace slackened. After six hours of racing Carrara and Goussot led José and Lapébie by two laps. Magni and Giorgetti lay a further lap behind with the Belgian Prosper Depredomme, twice the winner of Liège–Bastogne–Liège, and the Frenchman Raoul Lesueur. Italy's Jules Rossi was seven laps adrift of the leaders; Le Strat, eight; Bevilacqua, nine; and Valenta, ten. Then followed Middelkamp and Walter Diggelmann, another lap behind, with the unfortunate Impanis, now thirty-two laps off the pace.

The seventh hour was calm. Fatigue set in. Distances covered: 252.513 kilometres in seven hours, 279.186 kilometres in eight, 306.105 kilometres in nine. Carrara led, then Goussot. At 8.30 a.m. Lapébie abandoned, paralysed by cold. At ten Impanis pulled out. José and Magni forced the pace. Goussot and Carrara led. After ten hours, 333.833 kilometres; after eleven, 362.647 kilometres. José, removing his jacket, entertained the crowd with a little gymnastics on his bike. Twelve hours in, Carrara and Goussot led. They had covered 392.184 kilometres. José and Depredomme trailed by two laps, Magni, Lesueur and Giorgetti by three, Rossi by seven, with Le Strat a lap behind Rossi, and Bevilacqua a lap behind Le Strat.

Depredomme and Magni launched another attack. Carrara and Goussot marked them closely. Then Bevilacqua awoke. In a temporary lull he gained a lap with Lesueur then joined Goussot, who took the lead outright. Goussot continued his attack with Magni, gaining two laps on Carrara, with Magni and Beyaert four laps back and Lesueur and Le Strat six.

At two-thirty that Sunday afternoon, Depredomme, with knee pain, stepped down.

Then the remaining competitors entered the final eight hours and the dernies, those small motor-assisted bicycles, entered the track. The race leader, Goussot, had covered 515.75 kilometres.

Lesueur ran out of strength. He dismounted twice but his *soigneurs* persuaded him to carry on. After an hour behind dernies, Middelkamp, exhausted, and Giorgetti, with knee pain, abandoned.

Distance covered: 561.750 kilometres in seventeen hours.

Goussot and Magni led. José trailed by six laps, Valenta and Bevilacqua by seven, Le Strat by thirteen. Of the sixteen riders who had started only ten persevered.

As Magni maintained his speed Goussot finally began to weaken. By 4.30 p.m. he was three laps behind Magni; by 5 p.m. he was seven behind. By 5.30 p.m. he trailed by eighteen laps. Carrara abandoned at 5.25 p.m. Rossi and Diggelmann were in difficulty.

The sturdy Valenta matched Magni's speed and maintained his deficit at eight laps. Raoul Lesueur, revived now, gained on the leader and moved to within fourteen laps. At six o'clock Magni had covered 649.020 kilometres. José was in a trough, forty-two laps behind him, although just five behind the former leader Goussot.

Then at 6.25 p.m. an exhausted Goussot abandoned, leaving eight men in the race. Valenta attacked, gaining a lap; Magni responded, winning it back. Le Strat shadowed them, twenty laps back. Bevilacqua, Rossi and Diggelmann all dismounted to rest. Lesueur did the same. An hour or so later, without remounting, he and Rossi withdrew from the race. Six riders were left.

At the stroke of nine o'clock, Magni had covered the prodigious distance of 780.466 kilometres. Still Valenti followed, eight laps behind. Le Strat was third, with a twenty-five-lap disadvantage.

José, fourth, was sixty-seven laps behind the leader, followed by Bevilacqua and Diggelmann, 109 and 165 laps back, respectively. Distance covered after 23 hours: 820.813 kilometres.

In the final hour Magni and Valenta fought doggedly and extended their advantage over the rest. Thirteen minutes before 11 p.m. Magni accelerated. He gained fifty metres on Valenta, who maintained the gap for a while then weakened. With five minutes remaining Magni flew past him. He finished very fast. In the last hour he covered 47.228 kilometres. In the twenty-four hours he had covered 867.609 kilometres. It had been an extraordinary spectacle.

Valenta was second, La Strat third, José fourth: ninety-two laps behind but still forty ahead of Bevilacqua and 158 ahead of Diggelmann.

All were heroes, lionised by the press. José made friends everywhere and was in great demand. In December, with the double world road-racing champion Briek Schotte, the brilliant Stan Ockers and the French national pursuit champion Paul Mattéoli, José completed a quartet who represented the Rest of the World at the Zurich track against the home riders Ferdi Kübler, Hugo Koblet, Armin Von Buren and Jean Brun. José was as famous as a cyclist could be in France and elsewhere. Left to his own devices as his Helyett team fell apart, he capitalised on his fame in the winter; although, after riding the draining northern classics, the whole of the Tour of Italy and the Tour de France from start to finish and then the Bol d'Or, what his body needed was not the winter on the track but an extended period of rest.

The clash between René Vietto and Apo Lazaridès had come to a head in September, when Vietto made still more public criticism of his former protégé:

> Apo Lazaridès was paid fifty thousand francs a month in 1950. What did he achieve? Thirty-third in the Pneumatique and second in the Critérium du Dauphiné Libéré. So I've decided to replace him myself as a member of the team. I'll be more use there than in a jeep.

115

In October Apo and his brother Lucien Lazaridès rejoined the France-Sport team. By the end of November Vietto claimed he'd ridden four thousand kilometres in four weeks and planned to ride Milan–San Remo. In January he was training with the rest of the Helyett team down on the south coast. His riders now included Raoul Rémy, the man who brought José down at the Tour de France, and Robert Chapatte.

In February José failed to start the Nice Grand Prix and failed to finish the Avignon Grand Prix. He did not follow up his brilliant Paris–Brussels in 1950: Helyett did not enter. Only at the Rouen Grand Prix in the middle of April, won by his team-mate Lauredi, did José, ninth, show a flicker of life. The following week he was ninth again in the gruelling Circuit du Morbihan. By then the Helyett riders were openly defying René Vietto. They accused him of refusing to pay their travel expenses. At the Tour de l'Est in April they abandoned as one. Vietto asked the French national manager, Marcel Bidot, to replace him at Helyett, although the answer was no.

Exhaustion may have been behind José's wretched luck. At the Noveltex Grand Prix he crashed and did not finish. On stage one of the Tour de l'Oise in mid-May he attacked repeatedly. Twice he had punctures. Twice he rode back to the breakaway. After the third puncture, there was no way back. On stage two, ten kilometres after Crévecoeur, he darted out of the peloton with the previous day's winner, Pierre Lagrange. They gave chase to three leaders who had a lead of over two minutes. Four more riders joined them. José and Lagrange lost a little ground. The seven disputed the sprint. José had to be content with winning the sprint of the chasing group. On stage three he had two mechanical problems and abandoned.

Taking part in the second-string calendar – he was not even entered for the best races – he had nothing to show for the first half of the year. In *L'Équipe*, mid-month, he came clean:

> I got off on the wrong foot. I hadn't recovered from last year's efforts . . . I'd certainly have been better off resting for more of the winter, but isn't it through our mistakes that we learn?

My goal, like every rider, is obviously to ride the Tour de France. I only ask one thing: that the selectors wait for Paris–Limoges to judge me.

In Paris–Limoges, though, José was anonymous. On 27 June *L'Équipe* announced José's inclusion in the Île-de-France North-West team for the Tour de France. He certainly had Jacques Marinelli, one of the team's leaders, to thank for his selection. Two days later the series of deaths among riders continued when Fausto Coppi's brother Serse, whom José referred to as a friend, was killed in a crash at the Tour of Piedmont.

The 1951 Tour de France started in Metz on Wednesday 4 July. At 12.15 p.m. the peloton of 123 set off into a violent headwind. José's second team leader, not Marinelli but Attilio Redolfi – another very Italian-sounding Frenchman, this one born in the north-east of Italy – attacked with six others after fifty kilometres. *L'Équipe* described the action behind them:

> Protecting Redolfi's breakaway, the Île-de-France riders, often with good humour, put the brakes on the attempts by the France and Italy riders to counter-attack. Marinelli and José Beyaert proved themselves the most capable in this task.

However, the story of the day was a breakaway by one of the big favourites, Hugo ('Ugo', as *L'Équipe* always wrote) Koblet:

> Soon after Somme-Suippes, less than 50 km from the finish at Reims, Ugo Koblet, who had until then been riding conservatively, accelerated powerfully in pursuit of the six riders at the head of the race, led by his team-mate Giovanni Rossi.

Koblet gained thirty seconds on the peloton before Fiorenzo Magni and the Italians accepted responsibility for the chase. Eighteen kilometres from the finish line Koblet was caught. *L'Équipe* published a photograph of José chasing hard with Fausto Coppi and Raphaël Géminiani.

The following day's stage took in the famous Mur de Grammont, the crux of the Tour of Flanders. José was at the front again. This time *L'Équipe* dedicated an entire column to his performance:

> It has been some time since we last saw José Beyaert ride as brilliantly as in yesterday's stage.
>
> Pedalling easily, he was always in the right place at the key strategic points. And in the heat of battle, he showed no signs of weakness. Yesterday, he reminded everyone that he is still the Olympic champion.
>
> 'I'm too young to look to the past,' he said after the stage finish. 'What counts for me now is to play my part in the team.'

Years later José span one of his tall tales about that day. It painted a rather different picture of the stage. 'I attacked just before the Mur because Marinelli had said, "There's certain to be an attack there. If one of us can get a lead there'll be a chance of getting into a breakaway."

'The rider who reached the top of the Mur and shot past like an arrow was Koblet. I managed to catch his slipstream and there I was, breaking away with him. A little later one or two journalists came alongside me. One of them asked my name.

'"Napoleon."

'He disappeared, then came back to tell me I wasn't allowed to attack and that was an order . . . I couldn't help Kübler . . . I pretended I didn't understand. I didn't see why I should sit up when I was so strong. This time Jacques Goddet himself came alongside and signalled for me to stop working with Koblet.

'Koblet turned to me, saying: "If you ignore them, they'll destroy you. You won't be able to ride."

'"Keep riding, old man. If I stay on your wheel, I won't challenge you for the stage win."

'Then Koblet himself desisted. "I think we've done enough for today."

'He asked me for water. I gave him a *bidon*.'

Koblet washed his face and combed his hair, and the two men waited to be caught.

'Only four riders joined us: Bartali, Magni, Coppi and Marinelli.'

Magni, José recalled, won the stage in a sprint. José finished at the back of the group. 'Considering what had happened, it didn't matter.'

Georges Beyaert told me, 'Cycling was a dictatorship. You had the big stars like Koblet and the rest. You had to do what you were told and José was never one for obeying orders.'

The problem with José's story is that no attack by Koblet was noted in the newspaper reports for the stage, which was won not by Magni but by the Luxembourger Jean 'Bim' Deiderich. He seemed to have conflated the first two stages into one and added an altercation with the race director that perhaps never happened. Jacques Goddet was also the director of *L'Équipe*, and *L'Équipe* missed no opportunity to praise José. I wondered if something else was at play.

José rode strongly through the first week of the 1951 Tour. But in the time trial on stage seven he was devoid of all energy. He finished ten seconds outside the time limit and was eliminated. Eleven other riders suffered a similar fate.

Then, abruptly, almost inexplicably, José's career in European professional cycling ground to a halt. He took part in a number of smaller events: the Nouan-le-Fuselier Grand Prix at the start of August, the Circuit de l'Indre and the VIII Grand Prix des Alliés on the Joinville-Champigny circuit towards the end of the month. He achieved nothing. He never raced again in Europe.

8

Issues of nationality, and clashes of it, were common in cycling during those years. During the 1950 Tour of Germany three Italian riders abandoned rather than continue riding for German teams. In 1947 a rider named Paul Neri, Italian-born but brought up from early childhood in Marseille (he had been French amateur road-racing champion in 1942), won the national road-racing title for professionals. There was a dispute concerning his nationality. Neri believed he was French but he could produce no documentary proof of his naturalisation so he was stripped of his title. This sort of confusion over national identity was not uncommon in cycling during those years, especially in France, with its sometimes porous borders.

Midway through the 1950 Tour de France the foreign names that made up the Paris team became the subject of mirth. The Dutch had been faring even worse than the depleted Parisians and by the end of stage thirteen their team had been reduced to one rider. The Dutch car was removed from the race and their last contender, Wim De Ruyter, was attached to the Paris team for material support. The team director, Jean Maréchal, joked: 'Frankowski, Baldassari, Forlini, Beyaert . . . and now De Ruyter . . . That's Paris!'

But the demands of French bureaucracy could make life for immigrants, even second-generation immigrants who had won Olympic medals for their adopted nation, bitterly frustrating.

Georges told me the story of how his father had acquired French nationality. 'He wanted to change nationality in 1936. You had to get your papers at the Prefecture of Paris and in those days it wasn't easy. You needed four or five documents. When he took them there they said, "Sir, these documents are no good. They're out of date." He had them dated and signed but by the time the last document was ready the first one was out of date. He was fed up, absolutely fed up, and he told them, "You know what? I'll stay Belgian.'"

Then in 1939, when war was declared, the gendarmes came to the house.

"'Monsieur Beyaert. Beyaert, José?"

"'That's me."

"'You applied for French nationality."

'My father said, "Yes. In 1936 I applied for French nationality."

'And they said, "Well, here are your papers. You are French. Here are your marching orders. You're leaving for the front today."

'My father burst out laughing. The Germans were in Belgium and that's where he was being sent. But he spent the war in Pantin. He never left.'

Ten years later the Olympic champion had a brush with the system that left him with a smouldering grievance. It was 1949. 'I'd earned a bit of money,' he told me. 'My father didn't have any; he was a shoemaker. There was a *bar-tabac* for sale in Pantin: it's still there, for that matter. We went to have a look. We had money and credit and we reached an agreement with the owner. All we needed was to sort out the paperwork.'

To sell alcohol, tobacco and official stationery the Beyaerts needed a licence. José paid a visit to the Prefecture with Georges, on leave from his military service in Morocco. They imagined it would be a simple matter of paying an administrative fee.

"'I'm sorry, sir. You can't buy them."

"'What do you mean we can't buy them?"

"'You're not French."

'My brother and I looked at each other. "We're not French?"

'My brother, the soldier, wasn't French.

'Me, the Olympic champion, decorated by the President of the Republic, and all that fuss, gold and bronze Olympic medallist, wasn't French.

'"You have one generation born in France. You need two."

"What?"

"It's the Napoleonic Code."'

Fifty-five years later José told me, 'I was angry. I'm still angry. When I talk about it, the first thing that comes out is—'. And he released a sudden explosion of breath.

Georges told me the same story. 'My brother, the Olympic champion who had just shaken the hand of the Duke of Edinburgh. Me, in the French army. And we weren't French.'

Sometime in the aftermath of the 1951 Tour de France – José said it was September but his memory for dates was unreliable and it might have been earlier – a letter arrived for him. Georges told me his father opened it, read it and put it in his pocket for a fortnight. The only record of the letter is in *L'Équipe*. José had, it says, received 'an invitation from the Colombian government for him to give the South American country greater familiarity with European cycling'. With this in mind, José Beyaert, the reigning Olympic champion, was hereby invited to be the special guest at the inauguration of the velodrome in Bogotá.

José told *L'Équipe*, 'I was contacted by letter one day, when nothing led me to imagine such a journey. The contracts were signed by correspondence. I received my return ticket . . .' José's new passport was issued on 12 September 1951 in Paris. He kept quiet about the trip but as it approached word got around. On 25 September *Le Parisien Libéré* wrote, 'José Beyaert and B. Loatti will fly to South America'. Bruno Loatti, a track sprinter from Castel Bolognese in Italy, had spent the war in Argentina. He had even won Argentina's national sprint title in 1941, 1942 and 1943. He too had been invited to the opening of the Bogotá track so the paper had got it half right although Colombia wasn't mentioned. 'Several contracts await them,' the article says, 'and they will very probably take part in the Tour of Mexico that is held in November.' That bit, at least, was wrong.

Three days later, *L'Équipe* was talking about Georges:

'I'm in talks with [the bicycle builder] Monsieur Colomb, on my brother's behalf too. But I'm confident we'll agree terms soon.' Moments later, Monsieur Marcel Colomb, the manufacturer of the marque that carries his name, confirmed to us that he will sign the two brothers for 1952 and that he was still waiting for other Belgian riders.José left Paris knowing he had something to come back to.

L'Équipe also asked Georges about his brother's South American trip: it was, he told them, 'a tour of Colombian and Venezuelan velodromes lasting several months. He [would be] joined by two Italians and two Swiss riders.'

José's name disappeared from the start list of Paris–Tours. Instead, he said, 'I'll take part in eight competitions, track and road, including the Tour of Colombia, from 15 November, which has fourteen stages.'

This was either misinformation from Colombia, whose national tour was scheduled for January, or, more likely, an insertion by the writer, who was still thinking of November's Tour of Mexico. José continued:

'I've decided to leave my family in France, and to rejoin them at the start of December after reaping a good harvest on the other side of the Atlantic . . . Like Columbus . . . I'm going into the unknown to try something new, to learn, and to try to earn my living as an adventurer.'

His words had a definitive edge that *L'Équipe* picked up on. The report it published the day after José's flight is distinctly valedictory:

José Beyaert, Olympic road champion in 1948, polyglot, is a good road racer, but his professional career didn't produce the results expected of him. It is said of him, 'He's too cerebral to succeed in a sport where you have to show so much heart.' And José knows he can, in another branch of the sport, get on by virtue of his intelligence and versatility.

'I felt I was vegetating here,' he told us, 'so I accepted the offer from Colombia . . . I'll learn and keep my eyes open there. If I see that I can find interesting work, I'll tell my wife [to make the journey] and I'll stay there.

'For the moment, my sponsor M. Colomb provides my bicycles and expects me at the start of the next road season. But will I come back?'

José left the question hanging in the air.

I collected the story of the letter from an old South American rider I met in Medellín, Colombia, named Roberto Serafín Guerrero. You might call him an active eighty-five year old. He still uses the track bike made for him in 1948 by Brambilla, the Italian frame builder. He rides it on rollers, half an hour a day, longer on a Sunday. And he still races the thirty-two-year-old Mini Cooper he bought when his son Roberto José was competing in British Formula 3 in the 1970s. Seven years after his son Roberto José Guerrero became Colombia's youngest-ever national go-kart champion, aged thirteen, Roberto Serafín Guerrero became Colombia's oldest-ever national go-kart champion, aged fifty-five. He told me these things as he showed me the bike and the Mini ('I brought it in illegally through Curaçao') in his Medellín basement. The thirteen-year-old champion had a future in Formula 1, and then at the Indianapolis 500, where he finished runner-up twice. His fifty-five-year-old father had a past as an Olympic cyclist but not in Colombian colours.

Born in Buenos Aires on 10 October 1923, Roberto Serafín Guerrero travelled to the 1948 Olympics as a member of Argentina's pursuit team. His participation in the 1948 Games lasted 5 minutes, 17.1 seconds. If he had been 3.3 seconds quicker Argentina might have beaten the Swiss and made the second round. Instead he spent the rest of the Games as a spectator. From London the Argentinians stayed in Europe for the world championships in Holland, where José finished eighth in the world road race. Then Guerrero and another Argentine cyclist, the sprinter Jorge Sobrevila – thirteenth in the thousand-metre time trial – went to Italy.

'I made friends with a member of the Italian pursuit team called Anselmo Citterio and he made the introductions and got us into the post-Olympic tour.' It was during the two-month spectacular around Italy that Guerrero got to know José Beyaert. 'I'd spoken to him in London but we really made friends during the tour, riding on the track. José was a madman. He was always climbing things, jumping over things, vaulting fences.'

After the tour Guerrero went back to Argentina. His Italian friend Anselmo Citterio gave him a package: 'Gold was very cheap in Italy so he said: "Take these two kilos of gold to Argentina and send me the money," and because of the gold our friendship continued.'

As well as his cyclist's legs Citterio had a good business brain. In London he had seen pocket spring mattresses. He brought them back to Italy, opened a factory and made his fortune. Guerrero, meanwhile, continued his career as a cyclist, which meant returning to his training rides around Buenos Aires with another national rider named Julio Arrastía.

It was too late for me to speak to Julio Arrastía. In 1992 he had begun to lose his memory and was forced to retire from his second career as a sports commentator on Colombian national radio. In 2003 he died. But in his prime Arrastía had been a legendary broadcaster who used his experience to shape the races he was paid to describe by telling the protagonists when and where to attack and then predicting their moves in his commentary. Arrastía was even better known as a horse-race commentator and there are stories, unconfirmed, of his involvement in horse doping. He was, in short, a man more alive than most, and Guerrero adored him.

'We were more than brothers. For three or four years we used to train in the mornings and then meet up in a bike shop in central Buenos Aires in the afternoons. When we came [to Colombia] we shared a hotel room for six months in Bogotá and for four years in Medellín. You'd never do that with a brother.

'I met Arrastía before London. He was five years older than me and he'd been very good when he was twenty. He was Argentine sprint champion and everything. Then he retired and spent ten years without riding. He drove a taxi and lived it up at night and eventually had some health problems, so he started riding again to see if he could get his strength back and that was when I met him. We started training together and then he started racing again.'

The two friends raced for their country in Uruguay, Chile and Brazil. On their travels they kept their eyes peeled for money-making schemes. 'When we went to Chile we used to take bicycles, wheels and tubular tyres to sell.'

Javier Buitrago, a former colleague with the Radio Cadena Nacional station (RCN), knew Arrastía well in later life. He told me the Argentine had always been a first-class hustler. 'They made good money on those Chilean trips and when they went home they took gold coins known as Chilean escudos with them. It wasn't legal but in Buenos Aires they sold them for thirty Argentine pesos a piece.'

Argentina was the leading cycling nation in the Americas and Guerrero and Arrastía decided there might be money to be made by selling themselves as coaches. 'The cycling federation in Trinidad and Tobago made us an offer but Julio told me, "In March the Pan-American Games will be here. We'll make some friends there." He was right.'

The Latin American delegations had come up with the idea of four-yearly Pan-American Games at the 1932 Olympics in Los Angeles. Buenos Aires was eventually selected to host the inaugural competition in 1942. These had to be postponed until the end of hostilities. However, the plans were revived at the London Olympics in 1948, and in February 1951 more than two and a half thousand athletes from twenty-two countries were in Buenos Aires for the first ever Pan-American Games.

Roberto Serafín Guerrero wasn't one of them. He had ruptured his spleen in a motorbike accident. But he spent the Games trackside with Arrastía, making friends, according to plan. One of the friends they made was Guillermo Pignalosa, the coach of the Colombian cycling team, who was also the president of the Colombian Cycling Association and the chairman of the cycling league in the Bogotá region.

'When the delegation was leaving we said, "Guillermo, we want to go to Colombia."

'And he said, "OK, I'll invite you for the next Tour of Colombia."

'This was March. I said, "When's the next Tour of Colombia?"

'"January."

'"But we want to go now."

'Well, we went to the centre of Buenos Aires every day to see if a letter had arrived from Pignalosa but there was no letter, so one day we went to a stationer's and bought paper and an envelope and sat in a café and wrote our own letter, and our letter crossed their letter in the post. They told us that in two weeks we had to take a ship from Valparaíso and Julio said, "We won't make it." The next sailing was three months later. The ship had to go to Italy and back. So we packed our things and left.'

They set off westwards for Valparaíso in Chile, to meet the *Reina del Pacífico*, the ship that would take them north to Colombia.

'We arrived in May 1951 and we're still here.' And Roberto Serafín smiled, forgetting for a moment that his soulmate was dead.

They reached Cartagena on Monday 28 May 1951 after a seventeen-day voyage. From the Caribbean coast they flew to Bogotá, where the national press and radio covered their arrival. Guerrero and Arrastía arrived with an enormous crate full of bicycles and spares to sell. And more: Arrastía had somehow laid his hands on the plans of the President Juan Domingo Perón Velodrome.

Javier Buitrago confirmed this to me. 'They had spoken to Arrastía about the possibility of building a velodrome in the capital and he brought with him the plans of the Buenos Aires velodrome. So the Bogotá velodrome was built under Arrastía's direction.'

The velodrome was commissioned by Santiago Trujillo Gómez, the Bogotá mayor from October 1949 to July 1952. It was named after him, although everyone knew it by the Bogotá district where it was built, 'The First of May'. The opening ceremony for South America's third velodrome (numbers one and two were both in Buenos Aires) took place on 8 December, meaning the twelve-thousand-seat stadium was built from scratch in barely six months.

Guerrero and Arrastía spent some of that time planning a prestigious inauguration meeting. Guerrero inevitably thought of his old friend José Beyaert, the reigning Olympic road champion. With Pignalosa's approval a letter was dispatched.

On 2 October 1951 José boarded Pan Am Flight 117/02. With his round showman's glasses, his athlete's physique dressed in the dandiest of styles and that brilliant, outgoing personality, he must have been quite a presence. But José Beyaert, Olympic champion, Tour de France cyclist, was not the only celebrity on board or the only showman. The passenger manifest lists Cole Porter's address as Waldorf Astoria Tower, NYC, one of the most exclusive on earth. The veteran songwriter turned sixty in 1951 and to celebrate, Cole Porter Nights attracted vast crowds to Seattle, Chicago, the Yale Bowl, the Hollywood Bowl and elsewhere. Porter had written his most successful show, *Kiss Me, Kate*, just three years before, and his most recent, *Out of This World*, had been a critical failure but a popular success. Even so he was suffering insomnia, appetite loss, depression. He had been in almost constant pain since a riding accident in 1937. In 1958 his right leg would be amputated.

In 1950 Porter had written to the American art historian Bernard Berenson saying, 'I haven't been [to Paris] since 1937 and I constantly pine for it.' Late in September 1951 he flew there for a six-week holiday with his valet, Paul Sylvain. Seven days later Porter was suffering lethargy and delusions and Sylvain was afraid he might attempt suicide. They flew back to New York on Beyaert's flight.

It is hardly likely Porter and Beyaert met. If they did no trace of their conversation has survived. What the Olympic champion and the crippled songwriter might have said to each other we can only imagine. With a voice all agreed was charming, might José even have sung a chorus or two to one of the most famous musicians on earth?

In the days before José left, Colombia had been in the news in France.

IN THE JUNGLE, SLICED IN TWO BY THE RIDER THE
UPPER-ORINOCO EXPEDITION HAS MET THE
MOST PRIMITIVE MEN IN THE WORLD

The explorer Joseph Grelier and his team had cabled *Le Parisien Libéré* to update France on their quest to find the source of the Orinoco and their encounters with the Waika Indians. Grelier's adventures, later described in his book *Aux sources de l'Orénoque* ('To the source of the Orinoco'), followed on from those of another Frenchman, Alain Gheerbrant, who at the end of September 1949, travelling up the Fruta river, a short tributary on the Colombian side of the Orinoco, had made first contact with another forest people, the Piaroa. If Colombia was this – Stone Age tribes using the poison curare as currency – what strange adventures lay in store for José Beyaert?

TWO

COLOMBIA

9

Larbi Benbarek had never worn football boots so he played his first game as a professional in sandals. Against the mighty US Marocaine, three times the winner of the North African championship in recent years, Benbarek scored twice.

After leading Casablanca's Ideal Club to the Moroccan Cup he made the Moroccan team, played France B and got noticed. Olympic Marseille signed him up in June 1938. Five months later he played his first game for France against Italy in Naples. The longest international career in French football – fifteen years, ten months – started in a cacophony of racist whistles.

Like so many great sportsmen and so many of Beyaert's colleagues – Bartali and Coppi, René Vietto, the boxers Marcel Cerdan and Théo Medina – Benbarek's athletic prime was taken by the war. Not being French, and therefore exempt from military service, he spent the war years at home in Casablanca. In 1945 he moved to Paris to play for Stade Français. In 1948 Athletic Madrid took him off Stade's hands for seventeen million francs, despite one journalist's pleas: 'Sell the Arc de Triomphe or the Eiffel Tower, but don't sell Benbarek.' With Athletic Madrid Benbarek won two Spanish league titles and scored over fifty goals. Such was the threat he posed that Athletic's city rivals Real Madrid combed the earth looking for a player to match him. They settled on Alfredo Di Stéfano, an Argentine who played his international football for Argentina, Colombia and Spain. With Di Stéfano Real Madrid built perhaps the greatest football team in history.

For many who played against him Larbi Benbarek wasn't just the first great African footballer: he was the greatest footballer, full stop. Pelé is reported as having said, 'If I'm the king of football, he is its god.' Yet by the 1990s Benbarek was so isolated and forgotten, even in his homeland of Morocco, that his body wasn't found until a week after his death.

But in April 1950 Benbarek was on the front page of *L'Équipe*. It was an article the Beyaert family might well have read and discussed. The Moroccan was jockeying for higher wages and threatening a move elsewhere. 'What happens if Athletic Madrid doesn't reach an agreement with a French or foreign club to transfer you at the end of the season?' the newspaper asked. Benbarek replied:

> Well, even if I'd be reluctant to travel so far, and also to step outside the international regulations, I'd go to Colombia. No one could stop me. But let me say it again: it would only be an extreme solution. I've received promoters from that country, not affiliated to FIFA, with offers that go far beyond anything I could earn anywhere else! Fifteen thousand dollars for a one-season contract, plus five hundred dollars a month and bonuses. It would be well worth the sacrifice for one or two seasons, after which I would retire definitively in Morocco, my playing career over. I have two projects: to open a sport-goods store and also a brasserie in Casablanca.

Colombia, in the world of football, meant no FIFA wage cap, so it paid huge wages by European standards.

In 1945, Humberto Salcedo Fernández, the president of América de Cali, had proposed the creation of a professional football league in Colombia. He called it Major Division Football: 'Dimayor' for short. He had government support too: during the violence that followed a high-profile assassination in 1948 it was thought that the distraction of Major Division Football might help calm nerves and restore public order. Soccer's sole regulating body in Colombia, recognised by FIFA, was the Colombian Football Association (CFA), so in June 1948 Dimayor informed the CFA of its intentions and asked for approval. The CFA provisionally accepted Dimayor on the condition that each team affiliated to Dimayor become a legal entity by adopting articles of incorporation, submitting a list of all the players enrolled in the tournament and paying the association a hundred pesos up front and then 3 per cent of the gate of every game, which later became 2 per cent.

The tournament began on 15 August 1948. There were only ten teams but it was a massive success and Dimayor's wealth soon far overshadowed that of the cash-strapped CFA. A power struggle inevitably followed and in March 1949 the CFA expelled Dimayor and refused to authorise any further Dimayor events. It also suspended Dimayor's representatives for five years. As a result Dimayor was no longer bound by FIFA rules. This presented an opportunity. The second Dimayor tournament started in April 1949 with five new teams. Colombian teams began to invest large sums to bring the best players from overseas, in violation of FIFA regulations and irrespective of the contractual rights of their official clubs. The piracy soon known as 'El Dorado' began.

A players' strike in Argentina played into the rebels' hands. The first player contracted was the Argentine Adolfo Pedernera of the team Huracán. He asked for five thousand dollars in hand and a two hundred-dollar monthly salary. The boss of the Bogotá club Millonarios agreed. He told the board: 'I propose that we hire him. If we go bust I'll pay Pedernera.'

Pedernera reached Bogotá on Saturday 10 June 1949. The following day he was presented at the El Campín stadium. He wore a suit and tie but his mere presence attracted fifteen thousand spectators for a gate of twenty-two thousand dollars: five thousand dollars for Pedernera and seventeen thousand for the club. El Dorado was underway. Pedernera proposed bringing more Argentines, given their physical and technical superiority – and given the players' strike there. At the end of the 1949 tournament he returned to Argentina, and on 11 August 1949 he landed at Bogotá with Néstor Raúl Rossi and Alfredo Di Stéfano, the latter considered the fastest player in South American football.

Given the breaking of contracts FIFA expelled the CFA from its organisation, isolating Colombian football. Millonarios contracted top international players from many nations and created the team known as the Blue Ballet. In 1951 Millonarios played with players from nine countries, although English players Bobby Flavell and Billy Higgins never arrived.

The piracy began to break down in 1951, when the South America Football Confederation backed the so-called Lima Pact, an agreement that would lead to the return of all the non-Colombian players in the country to their original clubs by October 1954. It affected about three hundred players from all over the continent.

Little wonder that in May 1951, when Roberto Serafín Guerrero and Julio Arrastía left for Colombia, the press in Argentina feared another exodus, affecting the country's cyclists, this time:

> Part two of the action plan will be put into operation, that is, the contracting of Argentine cyclists, considered the best in the continent.
>
> Our first cycling deserters are Roberto Guerrero and Julio Arrastía, who do not arrive with written contracts to ride but have a verbal agreement to work as cycling coaches, race organisers and advisors to the Colombian directors as they reorganise the sport there.

And in Colombia *El Siglo* could not resist relating their arrival to that of the great Argentine football stars. They became, according to the headline, 'los Pederneras del Pedal' – 'the cycling Pederneras'.

As José Beyaert considered the possibilities Colombia might offer he surely thought of Larbi Benbarek, El Dorado, and the huge sums of money that were pouring into Colombian sport.

South America was supplementing cyclists' earnings too. In November 1949 *L'Équipe* reported:

> ROME: We learn officially that Gino Bartali is in the course of preparing a great tour in Latin America, which will start on 1 December and finish at the end of January.
>
> Bartali will take six other Italian riders with him, with whom he will ride in Argentina, Brazil and Uruguay. He has reportedly

demanded a guarantee of twenty-four million lire, ten thousand of which must be paid before his departure, and a percentage of the receipts.

Two weeks later the project had grown:

FLORENCE: It has been announced that a group of sixteen Italian riders including Gino Bartali, Fiorenzo Magni, Fausto Coppi and his brother Serse will take part in two meetings to be held on 7 and 8 January near Caracas (Venezuela).

According to the final contract, the organisers have reportedly agreed to pay 2.5 million lire to the Coppi brothers, 2 million to Bartali, 1.5 million to Magni and 400,000 lire to the other riders on the tour.

The up-front payments, it would appear, never materialised. In December 1949 the Coppi brothers rode in Algeria and Tunisia before heading to Paris for a night at the Vel d'Hiv. Three other Italian riders, Antonio Bevilacqua, Vito Ortelli and Erminio Leoni, – fine riders but not legends like Bartali and Coppi, José might have reflected – did make the trip to Caracas.

South America might have meant something else in France at the start of the 1950s. France retained an outpost in the Americas sandwiched between Dutch Guiana and Brazil: French Guiana. Attempts at colonisation had led only to sorrow and disillusionment: in the 1760s fifteen thousand men, women and children from Alsace and Rhineland-Palatinate had accepted the promise of land, liberty and a new life in Guiana. Within two years the tropical humidity and an outbreak of smallpox had killed three quarters of them. The founding of the penal colonies added human brutality to the hostility of nature. Partly modelled on the British camp at Botany Bay, the open prisons in French Guiana were established in the 1850s. Their extreme cruelty came to fascinate writers, journalists, poets, composers, playwrights and filmmakers. The penal-colony prisoner with his ball and chain and striped uniform became a stock figure of fun. French parents told naughty children *'Vous êtes sur la mauvaise pente, celle qui mène au bagne!'* ('The slope you're going down leads to the camps!') or '*Si tu continues, tu iras casser des cailloux sur les routes de Guyane!'* ('Carry on like this and you'll be breaking rocks on the roads of Guiana!') And the idea of the man with the unbreakable spirit, unjustly imprisoned and banished to a far-off hellhole with nothing to lose, his only thought escape, began to seize the public imagination.

The escape routes led from the camps to Albina and Paramaribo in Dutch Guiana; the island of Trinidad; Georgetown in British Guiana; Venezuela, especially Caracas; and then neighbouring Colombia, a country of vast landscapes where a man could disappear and, more importantly, with which France had no extradition arrangements.

Colombia was on the itinerary when Prisoner 27307, Henry Marcheras, made his first escape from Guiana, perhaps in the late 1800s:

> I worked as a logger all over Paramaribo. I shined shoes in Demarara. I was a barman in Panama, the manager of a bar in Colón, and a gold-prospector all over the place. In Mexico, I joined Francisco Madero's men to fight Francisco Díaz. That lasted a month. Then I joined Francisco Díaz and fought Francisco Madero. I was a convict who became a pirate. I was a merchant, too: in Bogotá I sold ice creams. Also in Colombia I tried my hand at the emerald mines, where your workmates are murderers, stranglers and swindlers. An intelligent man isn't bad for the fun of it, but you have to maintain the façade of freedom and a pistol shot is easily fired of an evening, if saving your skin depends on it.
>
> I looked for oil in Venezuela. I bled balata trees for sap and made rubber. I went to Imataque, sixty kilometres into the interior, and made good money with gold-bearing quartz.

On 8 April 1919 H.-Aymé Martin, the French *chargé d'affaires* in Colombia, wrote to Paris, 'For some time now, Bogotá has been the theatre of audacious robberies, most committed by escapees from Cayenne.' In December 1934 Henri Charrière, the future author of *Papillon*, was arrested in the Colombian port of Barranquilla. He had crossed from Curaçao to the Colombian department of La Guajira, where he claimed he lived months of sensual bliss with his Indian wives, fathering a number of children.

In May 1935 Prisoner 46635, René Belbenoît, was also captured and imprisoned in the Barranquilla. During the six months he spent in captivity he wrote a memoir before escaping to New York, where his book, *Dry Guillotine*, was published in 1938.

On 17 June that year, Gaston Monnerville, Deputy for French Guiana, complained to the French parliament:

> The very existence of a penal colony in France's only colony in the Americas brings France's good name into disrepute in Latin America and even in the North. Escaped convicts all over Brazil, Venezuela and Colombia form dangerous criminal nuclei that bring suspicion on all our compatriots.

The decree-law signed hours later sounded the death knell of the infamous camps by abolishing the transportation of French convicts. But the Second World War interrupted the decommissioning process and the penal colony was still a functioning French prison as late as 1951. By then Corsicans and Frenchmen fleeing justice – ex-*bagnards*, wartime collaborators and *carlingues* (members of the French Gestapo) – were notorious for the secret gambling dens, nightclubs and brothels they ran in Caracas and Bogotá.

José can hardly have been unaware of the penal colonies. On 27 June 1924 the newspaper *Le Petit Parisien* published perhaps the most famous report in cycling history, in which the author, an outspoken investigative journalist named Albert Londres, compared the cyclists of the Tour de France with the prisoners of the penal colonies in Cayenne, from which he had recently returned and about which he had published a series of damning special reports.

The article is a brilliant account of Londres's interview with the brothers Henri and Francis Pélissier after their abandonment at Coutances on stage three. Its publication overshadowed the 1924 Tour de France. The headline was: 'LES FORÇATS DE LA ROUTE' ('Forced labourers on the road'). Henri Pélissier seems to have invented the moniker, and it stuck. Even today the expression is used to describe professional riders.

Londres had started by asking Henri Pélissier why the brothers had abandoned the race. Pélissier replied:

> – This morning, at Cherbourg, the *commissaire* approached me and, without a word, lifted up my jersey. He was checking whether I had two jerseys. What would you say if I lifted your jacket to see if you were wearing a white shirt? I didn't like his manners, that's all.
> – What could he have done if you'd had two jerseys?
> – I could have fifteen of them, but I'm not allowed to start the stage with two and finish it with only one.
> – Why?
> –Those are the rules . . .

Pélissier then sought out Henri Desgrange, with whom he had a heated exchange:

> – I can't throw my jersey onto the road, then?
> – No, you can't throw away your sponsor's material.
> – It isn't my sponsor's, it's mine.
> – I'm not discussing it on the road.
> – If you're not discussing it on the road, I'm going back to bed.

Which Pélissier did, taking his brother with him. He told Londres:

> – You have no idea what the Tour de France consists of . . . It's a Calvary – except there are only fourteen stations of the Cross. We have fifteen. We suffer on the road, but do you want to see how we cope? Look . . .
> He took a phial from his bag.
> – Cocaine for the eyes and chloroform for the gums.
> – Liniment to warm your knees, said [Maurice] Ville.
> – And there are pills. Do you want to see pills?
> They took out three boxes each.

– Basically, said Francis, we're on dynamite.

Henri carried on:

– Haven't you seen us washing at the finish? It's worth paying to see. Under the mud, you're white as a sheet. You're drained by diarrhoea, your eyes roll in water. At night, in your room, instead of sleeping you twitch like someone with St Vitus's dance. Look at our shoelaces: they're made of leather – and they still don't always hold, they break. And it's tanned hide; at least, I think it is. Imagine what happens to our skin. When we get off our bikes, we're hanging out of our shoes and britches, and nothing will stay on you.

– And your toenails, continued Henri. I've lost six out of ten. They fall off, one by one, on each stage.

There was another tale of the penal colonies with a cycling connection. It may very well have circulated in the professional peloton: the story of a brilliant cyclist scouted by the all-powerful Alcyon team after the First World War who was arrested on his way to sign his contract and dispatched to Cayenne. If José felt he was stagnating in France the opportunities for adventure that Charles Hut's experiences revealed might have proved inspirational.

Born in Longwy, where France meets Belgium and Luxembourg, to parents from each of the cross-border countries, Hut lived in France but acquired French papers only late in life. His obsession was the Tour de France. In 1910, when Hut was sixteen, he saw the Tour de France pass:

> I felt my legs itch. I had only one ambition: to become a champion, too – one of those giants of the road, as they were known at the time. Straight away I went to the Longwy Cycling Union where, two years later, I had become one of the best, if not the best, riders. A first-category independent, professional in 1914, a protégé of Alcyon, the winner of something like twenty regional races and one international event.

Before the First World War he had become a cycling prodigy appreciated by François Faber, Lucien Petit-Breton and Henri

Desgrange. Faber was a Luxembourger who considered himself French but is credited as the first foreigner to win the Tour de France, in 1909. Petit-Breton, a Frenchman, although he was raised in Buenos Aires, became the first to win two Tours in 1908. Desgrange was the director of the Tour de France, who, in Hut's words, 'introduced me as a future world champion'. But with a misguided robbery that led to thirty-five years of imprisonment and hard labour in French Guiana, Cuba and the United States, Hut threw away his cycling career.

It was during a visit to Paris in 1920 to sign his professional contract with the great Alcyon cycling team, at his hotel near Porte Maillot, that Hut was arrested for the theft of a hundred thousand francs from the Ministry of the Liberated Regions in Longwy. He was questioned at the Paris police headquarters at Quai des Orfèvres, imprisoned at Nancy, examined at the psychiatric hospital in Maréville and tried at the assizes by a judge who 'had awarded the prizes after two races I rode and won at Trieux and Mancieulles in 1913'. In February 1920 Hut was sentenced to twelve years' hard labour, then shipped to South America and the inhuman regime of the penal colony as Prisoner 43963. The penal colony extended beyond the confinement blocks to forest clearings, where convict labourers cut timber, and public spaces, where they were employed to clean the quays, load and unload ships, and shift the ill and the dead due to heat and sickness. The locals were allowed to employ convicts for domestic work, on payment of a fee to the Navy and a heavy fine in case of escape. Convicts ran small portside workshops selling shoes and trinkets or repairing clocks. There were convict cobblers, convict chefs, even convict teachers.

Like many with no fixed trade Hut moved from job to job: a butcher's assistant at Saint-Laurent-du-Maroni, a fisherman on Île Royale, a telegraph supervisor in Cayenne, all the time fantasising of escape:

> I didn't want to stay in this hellhole for ever. I wanted to see my family again, and return to my bicycle.
>
> If I regained my freedom, I'd go to the United States and

ride the Six Days of New York. I'd do as well as Wampst and Laquehay, the 1927 winners.

His early escape attempts were bungling and led only to betrayal and the extension of his sentence. To pay for the equipment and favours necessary to plan an escape, Hut broke into a department store in central Cayenne with an accomplice and stole several kilograms of jewellery, which they buried in the forest. But his accomplice confided in a fellow convict, who informed the police. The accomplice was sent to the islands, where he contracted leprosy, lost his sight and died obsessed with his treasure, perhaps still interred in the Guianan jungle. Hut was condemned to five more years of hard labour in a logging camp, where he raised money for a future escape by trapping highly prized butterflies.

> There were rare butterflies the locals paid a high price for . . .
> I hunted them day and night. I had a technique many envied. And especially to capture the Blue Morpho, that large and magnificent butterfly in a striking metallic blue that earned me very good money (it is known that the wings of these butterflies are used in the manufacture of American dollars).

Once, he noted, he captured fifty Blue Morphos in a morning. Hut's earnings financed one of the most sensational escapes from the penal colonies: in 1937 he crossed the Caribbean to Trinidad in little more than a rowing boat, then, on the SS *Caribia*, stowed away to Cherbourg. Longing to see the son with whom he had spent only a few hours before his arrest, and to reach his sick mother before her death, he was defeated by the telegraph. At Cherbourg the authorities were waiting for him and he was arrested before disembarking. Then began a bizarre two-year Tour de France of French prisons – from Cherbourg to Caen, Le Mans, Nantes, La Rochelle, Angoulême, Limoges and Riom, before his transfer to Saint-Martin-de-Ré for shipment back to Guiana.

Four years later Hut and eight others stole a thirty-foot sailing boat from the prison authorities and embarked on a sixty-day odyssey. The voyage took them to Georgetown in British Guiana, then to Santo Domingo after encounters with a German supply ship, a U-boat, a cataclysmic storm and near starvation. After unhappy stops in two small Haitian ports, they received supplies from two US cargo ships and then beached their vessel in Asseradero in the Cuban Sierra Maestra, where they were duly imprisoned.

Hut made it to Miami only to be arrested and returned to Cuba. On the island he traded in drugs, grew marijuana and brokered a deal between Cuban revolutionaries and the crew of a French ship carrying clandestine arms to Venezuela. His commission made him a wealthy man, temporarily, at least. In the Prado nightclub he was introduced to Charles 'Lucky' Luciano, the chief architect of the post-war heroin trade, whose cooperation with US military intelligence during the Second World War had earned him exile as an alternative to prison. The mobster asked to hear Hut's story. Days later they were due to meet. Luciano didn't show: undesirable in Cuba, he had been deported to Italy. 'I never saw him again,' Hut said, 'which was undoubtedly best for him, and for me.' Hut made and squandered fortunes and then, after seven years in Cuba, five of them in prison, he joined the crew of a cargo ship, the SS *Robert*, whose master secured him a French passport.

The final, Hemingway-esque, touch to Hut's adventures was added by his friendship with a fellow crew member called Al Brown, an indebted former prizefighter already suffering from the illness that would eventually kill him:

> But Al Brown was ill, very ill. Suffering from tuberculosis, he had coughing fits and spat blood. During one stop at Brooklyn, as his health declined, he insisted I go with him into town. We toured the nightclubs: each time someone recognised him, he bought them a drink. Everyone took advantage of the old prizefighter. One night, he didn't come back. He'd been robbed of what little he had left . . .
>
> Soon afterwards, we heard he had died penniless in New York. Poor Al, who'd never again ask for a ten-dollar advance.

Brown, it would appear, was the Central American bantamweight known as Panama Al Brown, who in 1929 had become the first Hispanic boxer to hold a world title.

Hut's macho storytelling was pure Hemingway – the Hemingway of the early short story 'The Battler': '"What made him crazy?" . . . "He took too many beatings, for one thing."'

And during his Cuban years Hut's friends encouraged him to visit the author in San Francisco de Paula and invite him to publish his adventures.

> I pulled the cord to a large bronze bell and the door opened on a vigorous, bearded man with a look that suggested judgment, goodness, but also firmness. Ernest Hemingway was before me. A tiny kitten huddled in his muscled arms.
>
> Stepping forward, I pronounced my name and nationality. Those two words were enough to break the ice. The fine figure of the Master was enlightened.
>
> – You're the famous captain of the boat of escapees from Guiana. You're welcome here!
>
> Then, looking me straight in the eye, he sized me up from my feet to my head and asked:
>
> – Do you want to know what I make of you?
>
> And without leaving me time to reply, he continued: – Have you heard of Tarzan? Well, the Tarzan of the twentieth century is you, Mr Hut . . . You and your companions were remarkable. I haven't yet seen – and God knows I've seen plenty – a man like you.

It was probably a heartfelt compliment: when Hemingway was fifteen Edgar Rice Burroughs, the author of *Tarzan of the Apes*, had moved to his neighbourhood, Oak Park, and may well have provided the future Nobel laureate with an early role model. And, 'For a man like me,' said Hut, 'who believed himself permanently banished from society, his compliments were a great comfort.'

With two books on the go – *Across the River and Into the Trees*, perhaps, and either *The Garden of Eden* or *Islands in the Stream*

– Hemingway declined Hut's invitation to write his story. But he did continue to welcome his new friend:

> Each time the Master, who asked me to call him 'Papa' like all his close friends, gave me a Bank of Canada cheque.
>
> The last time I went to see him was the night before my clandestine embarkation on board the *Saint-Malo*.
>
> – Champagne? asked Papa, and then, when he knew I was finally certain I could board her, he wanted to give me all the French and Belgian money he had left after the war: five thousand-franc notes, and a hundred Belgian francs, as well as another cheque for several hundred dollars, but Papa also had another thoughtful gift. He went to find a bottle of Pernod and another of Champagne.
>
> – Drink them on board, to my health. You'll have a foretaste of France! How I envy your return to Paris . . . Ah! Paris!

The SS *Robert* finally took Hut back to the country of his birth, where, after a long search, he found and was accepted by his wife and son.

The French journalist René Delpêche heard what he called Charles Hut's confession in Germany, at Frauenberg and Lahn, in August and September 1955. Their book *Parmi les fauves et les requins* ('Among the beasts and the sharks') was published later the same year.

> My great sadness today, after thirty-five years of atonement, is that I failed in my career as a sportsman and just as foolishly wasted my life . . . Despite twenty years in the penal colony, six years of solitary confinement and the rest, I have maintained a certain physical vigour. When the opportunity presents itself I still ride my two hundred and fifty or three hundred kilometres in a day.

Hut's story didn't end there. In 1967, aged 73, he was again imprisoned for a series of burglaries. But there is every reason to believe that by the time José Beyaert was considering his South American adventure, Hut's story, or the start of it, had become part of cycling's rich oral culture. The Alcyon team still existed and its legendary *directeur sportif*, Ludovic Feuillet, remained in his post. Francis Pélissier, whose brother Henri had been an Alcyon rider before the Great War, was the *directeur sportif* of the team La Perle. Lucien Petit-Breton's son Yves was his counterpart at Automoto.

José Beyaert landed in Bogotá on 4 October 1951. A photograph of him with his urbane good humour and his well-cut tweed suit appeared in the newspaper *El Siglo*. The description conveys a sense of disbelief that 'the famous French Olympic world champion . . . the first world champion to visit Colombia' had actually arrived:

> The people of Bogotá will witness a spectacle in the history of Colombian sport on 11 November next at the inauguration of the first velodrome to be built in the country. The date of the inauguration, initially fixed for 2 October, was postponed to allow famous international cyclists to be present. Enthusiasm for the big day is growing every day, especially yesterday when the famous rider José Beyaert, the Frenchman who won in the World Olympics in London with a performance that marked him out as among the best cyclists of the moment, arrived in this city. At the end of the present month and the start of the next the arrival of other outstanding riders . . . will be announced.

This, in a city that drawn-out mob violence had recently devastated after the assassination of a populist leader named Jorge Eliécer Gaitán.

José would have hated the man. He disliked politicians ('Show me a poor one,' he once challenged me) and he would have detested anyone capable of railing about 'the Liberal oligarchy' and 'the Conservative oligarchy' – he would have asked what exactly 'oligarchy' meant – and anyone he heard saying, as Gaitán did, 'I'm not a man, I'm a people', he would have held in utter contempt. 'I met peasants who couldn't read or write who were Liberals,' José told me, 'although they didn't know why and they were prepared to kill or be killed by other people who were Conservatives, although

147

they didn't know why either, just because of their grandfather or father or mother-in-law or God knows who . . .'

Still, Gaitán had been a rousing speaker who could play a crowd well enough to earn comparisons with Mussolini and Hitler. His eloquence allowed him to become Mayor of Bogotá, then Minister for Education, then Labour Minister and finally the leader of Colombia's Liberal Party. Enormously popular among unionists, left-wingers and Colombia's poor majority, Gaitán terrified the Establishment, for whom politics meant cordial conversation and personal agreements, and he found it curious that 'the men of the two parties profess the same ideas, and men in the street kill each other in defence of the same ideas'.

In 1946 Gaitán was one of two Liberal candidates for the presidential elections. With the Liberal vote split the Conservative candidate, Mariano Ospina Pérez, took the prize. Ospina Pérez's presidency was marked by a surge in political violence. By the end of 1946 fourteen thousand lives had been lost in violence between party supporters. In 1947 there were nineteen thousand deaths.

Gaitán became leader of the Colombian Liberal Party in 1947. He would very likely have been elected president in 1950. Instead, at 1.05 p.m. on 9 April 1948, shortly before a meeting with a Cuban student leader named Fidel Castro, Gaitán was assassinated.

Gaitán had been unique in Colombian politics. His personal magnetism did not lend itself to institutionalisation. When he ceased to exist the structures built around him, all of them centered on his style and popularity, became useless and the lumpen masses he had mobilised began to sack the city. Shops were pillaged, government ministries and public offices attacked, religious buildings burnt, prisoners freed. Every symbol of social order and public power was attacked. Cars and trams were seized and destroyed. The Capitolio, with more than a hundred overseas diplomats inside, was sacked. Fidel Castro likened the insurrection to the storming of the Bastille.

A state of siege was declared that lasted ten years. The destruction of Bogotá city centre was so complete that visiting diplomats who had seen Europe after the Second World War compared Bogotá to European cities destroyed by aerial bombardment. In the year of Gaitán's death there were estimated to be forty-seven thousand political deaths in Colombia. The 1950 figure was fifty thousand. The inter-party violence continued in the countryside and in the cities. In 1952 Conservative militants set fire to the offices of the Liberal newspapers *El Tiempo* and *El Espectador* and to the homes of two prominent Liberal leaders.

But Colombia was a land of paradoxes. One of these was the Tour of Colombia, a national cycling race created against this violent backdrop and first held over ten days in January 1951 to astonishing popular acclaim. On the basis of its success the institutions of Colombian cycling had begun importing expertise with governmental support. The European and North American centres of world sport were worlds apart. Confusion reigned over José's achievements as a rider (little-known amateur races like Paris–Briard and Paris–Cayeux were mentioned in the same breath as the Tour de France) and the terminology used to describe them (he had won 'the Olympic championship'). The Bol d'Or was described as 'the most demanding event in the world', as if it were incontestable. Still, José's arrival was part of the effort being made to reduce the distance between Colombia's fantasies of the cycling world and the reality.

The inauguration of the First of May Velodrome was postponed again, from 11 November to 8 December. In the meantime José rode a number of city-centre races. He was not always victorious, partly because it was also the time of year when European riders needed to rest and partly because every other rider was out to take the Olympic champion's scalp. José also faced one or two very good riders who simply had no opportunity to compete in the European scene. One was an Argentine named Humberto Varisco. Third in the road race of the Pan-American Games in 1951, Varisco had been invited to compete at the inauguration of the First of May Velodrome and then to ride the Tour of Colombia in January. After he defeated José in the Tenth Avenue Circuit in central Bogotá on 1 November, José knew who the man to watch was.

149

10

'Where did you finish?'

'Second.'

'What about so and so?'

'Last but one.'

'Last but one? That's not so good. But second . . . !'

Edmund Mathieu Bougaud added, quietly, 'It was just the two of us,' and waited for the penny to drop.

As well as training and taking part in occasional races, José began to meet other Frenchmen who lived in Colombia. Edmund Bougaud was probably one of the first.

Edmund's father, the brother of a quarter-mile champion – a world champion, if Bougaud family history is right – had been the owner of a prosperous Parisian sports store called Unisport and the manager, either side of the First World War, of the Parc des Princes velodrome in Paris. His boss at the Parc was a man named Henri Desgrange, who, late in 1902, partly to fill the stands of his cycling track and partly to sell his newspaper *L'Auto*, had created a fantastically successful sales gimmick: the Tour de France. The first sixty Tours finished at the Parc, until 1974, when it was demolished to make way for a bypass.

It was during his military service that Edmund took a silver medal in the French military track championships. Soon afterwards he had a training accident. While he was in hospital Hitler remilitarised the Rhineland and as international tensions built Edmund's mother decided her only son would miss the next world war. In Cali the

French consul, Edmund's son Georges, told me, 'My grandfather had contacts in Morocco, Uruguay, Venezuela and Colombia. He was told Colombia had the brightest future and he put my father on a ship in December 1936 with money and instructions to set up a hat business in Colombia. My father had worked in a hat factory and knew the industry.'

In January 1937 Edmund reached the port of Buenaventura on Colombia's Pacific coast. Within minutes of landing his plans changed. At Buenaventura he met another Frenchman who would shape José Beyaert's life in Colombia: a wealthy hairdresser living in Bogotá named Georges Alric, whose mother had arrived on the same ship. Bougaud and the Alrics took the train to Cali, then travelled by road to the capital. Ample time to swap life stories.

Alric had come to Colombia four years earlier, at the invitation of another French coiffeur named Fernand. When Fernand abandoned chilly Bogotá for warm Medellín Alric bought his salon. He introduced French hair lacquer to Bogotá and thrilled the ladies of the *haute bourgeoisie*. A local hairdresser tried to achieve the same effects by fortifying his clients' hair with starch and water. As his ladies celebrated Bogotá's most precious social events, their hair dried and contracted, stretching their faces into so many deathly grimaces. Alric's competitor fled across the border to Panama.

The Frenchman and his lacquer attracted the wife of the president of Colombia, Enrique Olaya Herrera. She introduced him into Bogotá's high society. Alric's fortune was made. Within two years he had enough capital to return to France and establish his own business in Paris. There he began to build up his clientele. He groomed the author Colette before she joined the SS *Normandie* for its maiden voyage in 1935. She gave him a horseshoe charm he kept for the rest of his life. But Alric grew restless and in 1936 returned to Colombia.

When they reached Bogotá Edmund stayed in touch. Edmund spent some of his money, was robbed of the rest and wrote home asking for more. Georges told me, 'His father told him, "You're twenty-three, you have to stand on your own two feet. I can't help you any more." So, following Alric's advice, he started selling hair products to beauty salons all over Colombia.'

In 1942 Edmund abandoned cycling, left Georges Alric and moved to Cali. He bought a beauty salon, the Madrileña, and renamed it Recamier. The business grew into one of Colombia's largest producers of hair and beauty products. In the 1960s José worked there.

Then, in January 1938, as if hats and hair products weren't French enough, Edmund's mother arrived with a shipment of Automoto bicycles and he resumed training.

Georges told me, 'One day my father was out riding when a car pulled alongside and a man asked him if he would mind stopping. It was General Arámbula Durán, the president of the Colombian Cycling Federation. He said, "We're looking for a coach. I know you're French. Would you like to coach the Colombian cycling team?"

'My father said, "Where do I sign?"'

Edmund's son Georges still has the commemorative plaques from the 1938 Bolivarian Games, where the Colombian cycling team finished third, riding Automoto bikes and directed by his father, Colombia's first national cycling coach.

In Cali Edmund met another Frenchman, Georges Oganessof, whose son André was a competitive cyclist. Oganessof, once a competitive swimmer, and Edmund, the former cyclist, became race officials. Oganessof used Edmund's contacts and began importing Automoto bicycles from France into Colombia. The two men founded the Cali section of the French cultural organisation Alliance Française.

José and Georges Oganessof probably met in Bogotá. On 18 November 1951 José took on Julio Arrastía, Guerrero Varisco and the best local riders in Cali. His appearance fee was paid for by the Automoto Club, the team sponsored by Bougaud's and Oganessof's business. Six weeks later, on 11 January 1952, José started the second Tour of Colombia wearing the colours of the famous Automoto team that had, in Europe between the wars, won every major honour: the Tour de France, the world championship, the French national championship, Bordeaux–Paris and most of the other classics with pre-war riders Ottavio Bottecchia, Lucien Buysse and the Pélissier brothers.

Whether José's former sponsor Helyett or his present European contractor Colomb had thoughts about his decision to ride for a sponsor that had a major European counterpart, we do not know. The world was that much bigger in 1952.

In theory a considerable obstacle stood between José and his participation in the 1952 Tour of Colombia: his licence as a professional cyclist. Colombia's events were for amateurs only, officially, at least. The issue had recently come up in Argentina: there, an Italian rider named Antonio Bertola had been allowed to ride on the track but was banned from competing in road races.

José did not give up his professional status. 'I was riding the Tour of Colombia to prepare for riding [in Europe],' he told me. Instead the issue was simply ignored.

News of José's impending participation prompted the following startling headline in *L'Équipe*: 'JOSÉ BEYAERT IS GOING INTO THE JUNGLE'.

The race started in Bogotá on 11 January. The first stage dropped from the high altitude of the capital to the town of Honda on the River Magdalena. José told me, 'I was a good descender so I attacked, but it was hard. After the Alto del Trigo the sun came out and it was so strong I got sunstroke. I had blood coming out of my nose. There was a waterfall. I stood underneath the icy water coming down from the mountains to refresh myself. I watched the riders pass. With me were two or three Frenchmen who lived in Colombia. I said, "If I abandon, I won't damage my career."

'Cyclists were going past on bikes like bedsteads, and the Frenchmen were telling me, "We've taken our holidays to be with you."

'"They're going to be short holidays."

'I was feeling fresher and we were almost at the top of the climb and I thought, "Hell, I need to abandon with more elegance. I'll fall on the descent." So I got to the top of the Alto del Trigo and when I started the descent I realised it was rock and mud and I thought, "I won't have to invent anything here!" I wanted to abandon but it was too dangerous to risk it. I began to pass cyclists and cars, and fifteen kilometres from Honda the road disappeared into a river.

'I stopped. The people accompanying me stopped too. I said, "What do we do now? The road stops here and there's no other route. Where did we go wrong?"

'We started wondering whether there was a fork in the road back up the hill. Then another cyclist arrived. He'd got it wrong too. Without even looking at us, he picked up his bike and plunged into the water. I'm not joking! He crossed the water and got back on. A huge rock had fallen down and blocked a stream, flooding the road. We hadn't seen that it continued on the other side towards Honda. We looked at each other.

'"*Merde!*"

'I crossed too. I realised it was good to wash off the sand from the road and from then on I profited from each water crossing to wash my arse. I got to the car park. I finished the first stage twenty minutes down, in fourth place.'

The stage winner was Humberto Varisco, the excellent Argentine. That night José and his entourage lay in their beds sweating in Honda's oppressive heat.

'I was in a small, cramped room. There were four beds. You couldn't walk between them; you walked over them. A door, four camp beds but no windows. In Honda, where it's still hot at midnight! *Merde!* I was sleeping next to the door.

'Someone spoke. It was still dark. I looked at the clock: 4 a.m. I couldn't speak Spanish but I said, "What are you doing, coming in here at this hour to piss me off?"

'There were two of them.

'"It's the priest."

'"What do I care about the priest? What does he want?"

'"He wants you to go to Mass."

'I'd never been to Mass in my life!

'"You wake me at four when I only got to sleep at one and you come and piss me about at this hour because you want me to go to Mass? Get him out of here!"

'My friends argued with the priest. He threatened to excommunicate me.

'I said, "Fuck you a hundred times. I don't believe in God. Don't argue with me. I respect you. Respect me."

'He said, "All right, how do you explain all those miracles at Lourdes, in your country?"

'"My country is like any other: it's full of idiots."

'"But the miracles?"'

And, at four o'clock in the morning, after a sleepless night, with a terrible mountain stage in prospect, José found himself in a theological argument. The mental workout seems to have done the trick. José won the following day and the day after that, and again on stages six and eleven. He told me, 'The priest was Father Efraín Rozo. He had ridden for Colombia. He was a good type!'

Humberto Varisco countered with wins on stages eight, ten and twelve. The race became a hard-fought duel between the two men. For José it was about more than the results. As each day passed he grew more and more enchanted with Colombia and its people. The examples he gave me suggested an almost spiritual process of discovery.

'The tubulars had to be repaired during the stage and by the time we got to Medellín I'd had so many punctures I had no more tubulars.

'A rider came up to me: "What's up?"

'The Frenchmen with me explained the problem. And the guy said, "Take my bike, my friend. You need it more than me."

'He didn't know me, I didn't know him. At the stage start we barely saw each other and by the time he reached the finish I was already in bed. He'd given me his bike, an old bike but well maintained, to allow me to continue in the race. That evening, I went to my team car and asked for a bike that was in more or less good condition. I took it to him and said, "Here, take this. If you can keep up with me on that old bedstead you might beat me on this."

'He didn't understand me very well but the next day he rode the bike I'd given him. I crossed the finish line first, carrying my bike in the mud as night was falling. It was at Riosucio, I remember. We were lodged with families – there was no hotel – and at ten o'clock at night someone came for me.

'"There's a señor who wants to speak to you."

'It was the rider who'd brought me the bike. Arevalo he was called, from Pasto.

'I said, "What are you doing here? Don't you like the bike?"

'"Oh yes. I rode it today and I climbed really well," and so on.

'He had the bike with him. He'd cleaned it up and everything.

'"So why are you giving it back?"

'"It's yours."

'"No, I've given it to you. For keeps."

'He thought I'd given it to him for a stage!'

The prizes were of so little value that it didn't cost José to be generous with them as well.

'At Ibagué, the prizes were little cups: no money, but little cups. A kid on the pavement came up to me and said, "I'm a cobbler."

'I said, "I'm a cobbler too."

'I looked for something to give him but all I had was the cup. I gave it to him. Twenty-five or thirty years later I was in Ibagué and he saw me. He introduced himself and he told me he still had the cup.'

Humbled by the warmth of Colombia's poor, José was like a man in love. If, in his rage, France had become the focus of his outrage and contempt, Colombia came to represent life stripped down to the essential, the projection of everything he desired and imagined.

On the eve of the thirteenth and last stage José led the race but victory was far from certain. It was Roberto Serafín Guerrero who gave me an astonishing revelation about the finale of the 1952 Tour of Colombia. 'The final stage,' he told me, 'was over roads of sand.'

'Varisco knew how to ride on that sort of surface. He was used to it from Argentina. José won the penultimate stage but he was exhausted so he went to see Varisco and gave him a thousand dollars to let him win. Varisco took the money.'

This version of events is confirmed in a memoir by a man who befriended José many years later. Auguste le Breton, a small-time crook who became a bestselling crime writer, speaks in *Ils ont dansé le rififi: memoires*, one of his many autobiographical works, about an old friend from the Montmartre underworld named Didi.

Didi had travelled there in 1951 as José's *soigneur* and followed him on the 1952 Tour of Colombia. As he remembered it, the war for victory was total. He accused Varisco, José's Argentine rival, of climbing with the aid of a wire connected at one end to a motorbike and at the other to a cork stopper that he gripped in his teeth. Didi threatened to go to the press about it. Varisco's men stopped him: 'If you grass, you'll take a bullet.' At Ibagué, after stage eleven, a group of fans accused the stage winner Beyaert of climbing with the aid of a car. Others denied it. Fighting broke out. One of the naysayers was stabbed to death. One night, when Didi was asleep, an intruder entered the room and switched off the alarm on his expensive Boucheron watch so that José would miss the stage start.

As the denouement approached, Didi confirmed Roberto Serafín Guerrero's account. José was capable of winning the race but so too was Varisco.

Didi resolved the matter. He reached an agreement with the Argentine's agent. 'You have the ten thousand pesos, we'll have the Tour. OK?'

'OK,' came the reply. And José crossed the finish line the winner, beating the Argentine in the final classification by seven minutes and the third-placed rider by . . . six hours.

Back in reality, Didi's six hours were six minutes twenty-four seconds. To ensure José's win it was probably money well spent. Victory in the Tour of Colombia was an excellent way of opening doors, and by the time the race had finished José had decided he was going to stay.

News of his decision reached *L'Équipe* in the form of a letter giving colourful details of the race. The roads were in such a state, he said, that he had had eighteen punctures on stage five alone. The previous year's winner had suffered fifty punctures in all. José missed his old companions Marinelli, Blusson, Chapatte, Caput and Guégan, and of course his brother Georges. He congratulated his old Olympic team-mate Jacques Dupont on winning Paris–Tours. Then he broke the news: he was planning to spend two or three years in Colombia. In Bogotá, with government assistance, he would open a cycling school.

The news came as no surprise to Georges. 'They offered him a well-paid contract. He said, "A foreigner is a foreigner. If I'm a foreigner in France . . . I might as well stay in Colombia." That's what finished his career here.'

That and a meeting with a politician for whom sport was an integral part of development. There were votes in sport: the transcendental popularity of the Tour of Colombia proved it. 1952 was an Olympic year too and Colombia's absence from the Games in Helsinki was commented on in the national press. Invitations had been sent out to seventy-nine countries. Colombia was one of just eight countries to send no delegation.

José always said that the decisive meeting took place after the Tour of Colombia. He said he had his bags packed ready to return to France. In some tellings he stopped off on his way to the airport. It was a good story but considering his letter reached France in time to be published on 18 January, seven days into the thirteen-day Tour, the encounter with the national president, Roberto Urdaneta Arbeláez, must have taken place early in the Tour of Colombia if not beforehand.

'For coffee. He spoke French better than me! What would you call it? an aristocratic French! He made me a proposition. He said, "Monsieur Beyaert, in your opinion, do you believe Colombia has good cyclists?"

'I said, "I'm sure of it. I've seen riders here who could stay with me without proper training."

'He said, "You wouldn't consider staying in Colombia as a coach?"

'I didn't know what to say.

'"Colombia needs men like you. Tell me, how much do you earn a month?"

'In my epoch you earned nothing as a cyclist, or very little.

'"I don't know. It's not always the same month by month. There are rich months and poor months. It depends on the place, the conditions, results, all that."

'"But give me an average."

'I came out with a number – a big number. I just wanted to be more interesting than I really was!

'And he said: "I'll double it!"

'I didn't think twice.

'"In that case, you've just found yourself a coach!"'

I asked José if he ever regretted ending his career in Europe. Regrets were not his style.

'I never missed it. I knew that it was difficult to earn a living in Europe so I had to be realistic. I had an opportunity and I took it.'

On 29 January 1952 Louisette sailed into Cartagena on the SS *Amerigo Vespucci*. José went to Cartagena to meet her and was mobbed.

'The Tour of Colombia hadn't had a stage to Cartagena. There'd been no riders from Cartagena. *Merde!* I was more popular in Colombia than in France. In France even my neighbours at Pantin didn't know I was Olympic champion.

'We went to the hotel for breakfast. It consisted of a coffee with a tortilla. Well, to show my wife I could speak Spanish, I said, "*Me trae un perico, por favor.*" ("Bring me a *perico*, please.")

'In Bogotá, a *perico* was a little *café au lait*. I'd never drunk *café au lait* in my life, I only asked for it to show my wife I spoke Spanish.

'"What did you ask for?" asked Louisette.

'"A *café au lait*."

'"Oh."

'He brought me an omelette. I ate it. I said to Louisette, "I must have pronounced it badly. He didn't understand."

'"Can I get you anything else, sir?"

'Everyone just wanted to be helpful!

'"Now, sir, I'd like a *perico*."

'He looked at me.

'"Right away, sir."

'He brought me another omelette.

'The French consul arrived. He wanted to arrange a car for me, as if I was the Pope. I said, "How do you say omelette?"

'"*Perico.*"

'"Yes, that's what the waiter told me. I've eaten three of them."

'"A *perico* is a little *café au lait*, but only in Bogotá."

'"Oh, *merde*! And I still haven't got one."

"'Anything else, sir?"

"'Yes." My wife looked at me. "A Coca-Cola."

'She burst out laughing. I'd eaten three omelettes just to prove I could speak Spanish.'

The Friday after Louisette reached Colombia she and José were invited to *El Siglo*'s offices to be interviewed. They had become Colombia's celebrity couple.

Despite his early difficulties José was a natural, quick linguist who learnt languages first through his ears because of his constant necessity for understanding people and for communicating. This natural ability was assisted by his work on a 'Popular Cycling Course' for the newspaper *El Siglo*, published under the title 'Make Yourself a Champion, by José Beyaert'. The series, in twenty-three parts, with another seven parts responding to readers' letters, was published in February and March 1952.

The series made the latest cycling wisdom from the French heartlands available to Colombia's fledgling cyclists. 'My work was very difficult at the start,' José told me, 'because they had false ideas that I had to fight against. I created cycling schools in Cali, Pasto, Cúcuta, Barranquilla, all over. I spent months in each city getting to know the veterans and I tried to select the most intelligent of them.'

José turned his newspaper articles into a book, which he dedicated to the president, personal acquaintance with whom must have greatly simplified life. José's visa was a handwritten note in his passport dated 14 March 1952 and his accommodation came with the job. José and Louisette were given a large house in a comfortable Bogotá suburb.

However, José's book was never published: 'When the new president was elected, my book disappeared.'

José's training sessions were open to everyone and advertised in the national press. By July *El Siglo* noted, 'The Frenchman Beyaert's training is beginning to show' in the young Automoto riders with whom he was working.

In March 1952 Georges joined José in Bogotá. In his first race, the Circuit of Aces in the capital, he and José sprung a trap. José attacked on lap eighteen. A small group formed behind him, giving

Light, powerful, toned: José the boxer in 1941, when he was fifteen.
Surprising that he wears his glasses in such a photograph.
(courtesy of the Beyaert family)

'I love my little club.'
Theatrical in his bold black
glasses and his JPS shirt.

Second! The first
surviving image
of José on a bike,
6 September 1942.

Windsor Great Park: riding away from Breakheart Hill and a tired knot of riders, José has a winning lead. (Olympic Photo Association)

Le Bourget airport, the day after José's Olympic win: top to bottom, Moineau, José, Rouffeteau, Dupont. (*France-Soir*)

Front row: Jean, Georges, Louisette, José, his mother Marie, his father José.
(© Offside Sports Photography Limited)

L'Equipe front page, 10 June 1949. (© Offside Sports Photography Limited)

The 1950 Tour de France: José in the stolen yellow jersey, with
Ferdi Kübler, Jean Maréchal (middle) and Jean Coussy (left).

Home at last to a welcome kiss from Louisette.

'I stopped the Tour de France': but where is José?
(© Offside Sports Photography Limited)

José at the 1951 Tour de France beside two legends: Fausto Coppi (left, dark glasses)
and Raphaël Géminiani (middle). (© Offside Sports Photography Limited)

Jose at the 1952 Tour of Colombia, with
Humberto Varisco (middle) and Julio Arrastía (right).

The emerald trader. (courtesy of the Beyaert family)

MINISTERIO DE MINAS Y PETROLEOS

Válida hasta el 31 de
Diciembre de 1.971.

PATENTE D E INSCRIPCION

COMERCIANTE INSCRITO BAJO EL No. 569
(Artículo 7o. - Decreto No. 293 de 1.964)

Nombre y apellidos   JOSE BEYAERT   Cédula 29864 Ex. de Bogotá

Ciudad - - - - - B O G O T A - - - - - Departamento C U N D I N A M A R C A

Dirección. Carrera 4a. No. 54-88   Teléfono - 49-61-56

Firma autógrafa del Comerciante,

Interventor de Salinas y Esmeraldas Jefe de Fiscalización Jefe de la División de Minas.
y Vigilancia

The harrowing chaos of Georges Julliard's funeral in January 1975. (courtesy of Olga Cecilia Rangel)

Gil Roberto Garzón, aka 'El Bobo Gil'.

Olga Cecilia Rangel.

Mario Arroyo Caamaño, aka 'Ñerito'.

Carlos Morales, aka 'Tachuela'.

Doting over his daughter.
(courtesy of Mayerly Beyaert Vallecilla)

At La Rochela.
(courtesy of Mayerly
Beyaert Vallecilla)

José in his other life with Esperanza
and their daughter Mayerly Carolina.
(courtesy of Mayerly Beyaert Vallecilla)

José in San Andrés with
Marcel Plazz-Lartigau, *circa* 1990.

chase. Georges slipped into it. Then, when they reached José's wheel, he flew away alone to a stunning solo victory.

In his spare time Georges worked in Georges Alric's salon.

'Everyone crowded around Georges Alric because he paid for everything: the restaurant bill, drink, the hotel. He earned money easily, he wasn't married and he had no children. I did a bit of hairdressing myself out there. I enjoyed it. Georges Alric said to me, "After cycling, what do you plan to do?"

'"I don't know."

'"Learn to cut hair."

'So I began to cut a little in the salon. We put adverts in the press: "*El francés*" ("The Frenchman"). Women came in.

'"Who would you like?"

'"The Frenchman."

'The girls shampooed them, then I came in, put in the rollers and put them under the drier. When the moment came to cut, the telephone would ring. Every time.

'"Georges, the president would like to talk to you."

'"Excuse me, madame. This sounds important."

'Someone else took over while I hid behind the curtain. When they had finished, I came back and combed them.

'"I do apologise, madame. It was the Minister . . ."

'But I still got the tip.'

Georges brought his fiancée, another Pantin girl, like Louisette, to Colombia and married her in Bogotá, 'with my brother and sister-in-law and a few friends', he told me. 'It was 20 September, the same day Édith Piaf married Jacques Pills in New York.'

Races were still relatively scarce and the only one for which sponsorship was in any supply was the Tour of Colombia. In 1953 Georges rode in support of his brother. *L'Équipe* published sporadic stage results. After the twelfth stage it noted that with three stages remaining and José lagging twenty-seven minutes behind the race leader, a young and devastatingly good climber called Ramón Hoyos, his chances of victory had dissolved. Four days later the final classification was published, with José second and Georges sixth. Georges told me, 'My brother fell and fractured his left hand, so in his second Tour of Colombia he was only second. I was always with him to help him climb and bring him drinks because he had to finish, come what may. You do, when you're the national coach. He was second; I was sixth. I perhaps had a chance of winning but, well . . . I've never had any regrets. What's done is done.'

But Georges's account of the Tour of Colombia did no justice to Hoyos's exceptional gifts. He had won no less than eight stages of the fifteen and taken overall victory by a margin of one hour, six minutes and seventeen seconds over José. He was Colombia's first true cycling talent. At the end of the Tour of Colombia José announced he was considering his retirement from competition to devote more time to what *L'Équipe* mistakenly called 'the hairdressing business run by his brother Georges'.

Days after the race a plan was announced to take Hoyos to compete in the Tour de France. A group of industrialists persuaded of their compatriots' abilities had agreed to fund the trip, which would be led by José.

The adventure was ill-conceived from the start. Hoyos had started his national service and was no longer in training, and when *L'Équipe* heard of the plan it sounded a wise word of caution: 'Without doubting the merits of Colombia's road men, it seems that this first essay . . . would be better directed at sending them to lesser international events where Hoyos and the other riders can test their qualities.'

José argued that it was too soon to expose Colombia's cyclists to European racing. He told me, 'There was too much time between races. The riders who were in form for one race had lost it a month later, so it was difficult for anyone to shine. Team selections were always made on the basis of the Tour of Colombia, which meant the leaders were always climbers. That's why time-trial specialists and sprinters never emerged. I knew some very good ones but they could never shine because there were always two climbs before the finish, which meant they arrived thirty seconds or a minute back. No one ever talked about them because they never won.'

Another tendency on the part of the Colombia media annoyed José: 'Whenever they had a champion they immediately compared him with Fausto Coppi. But how could I criticise them when Coppi was all they knew about cycling?'

All this was self-evident to a former professional rider like José but in Colombia it was not understood. So, towards the end of April, a Colombian national team was enrolled at the Route de France, the amateur cousin of the Tour de France. As the only man in Colombia with any experience of European cycling, José was placed at the head of the delegation.

He flew to Paris in advance of his riders. When the six riders landed at Orly airport three days later, *L'Équipe* was taken aback to see among them what it called '*un solide pilier [nommé] Mesa, un «coloured man» [sic] trapu et puissant*' ('a solid pillar named Mesa, a thick-set, powerful coloured man'). The reversion to English is arresting: black cyclists, rare even today in Europe, were not at all unusual in Colombia.

José complained, 'I was the trainer. There was a doctor, a mechanic, two secretaries . . . More directors than riders. And no bicycles. And no money. I had to find bicycles. Helyett helped me. Everyone got a bike but they'd gone three weeks without riding.'

José was exaggerating, of course.

'The directors went to England to see the coronation of the new Queen,' he told me. 'We didn't see them again.'

They were expected to start the hardest race of their lives three days after the first long-haul flight of their lives, jet-lagged and unadapted to the climate, the food and the lack of altitude.

Surprised by the high speed of the stage start and utterly incapable of riding into gusting sidewinds on treacherous cobblestones, the Colombians were in trouble from the beginning. Two of them fell within fifteen kilometres of the start and lost time to mechanical repairs. Hoyos was incapable of sustaining the pace. The one rider who managed to keep with the peloton, a man named Fabio León Calle, was then involved in a fall with two others. The Colombians crossed the finish line at Saint-Quentin an hour and two minutes after the stage winner. 'José Beyaert,' wrote *L'Équipe*, 'lowered his straw hat over his eyes.' The race judges agreed to allow the Colombians to start the next morning. On stage two, riding towards

Ostende on the greasy cobblestones in a storm of rain and hail, Efraím Forero, the winner of the first Tour of Colombia, crashed out of the race and had to be hospitalised. By the end of the day the five remaining Colombians filled the last five positions in the race classification. The next day the seventeen-year-old Mario Montaño, the youngest of the Colombians, abandoned. The rest left the race during stage four. José took them back to Paris, where they resumed training. José told them that if they could earn enough in local weekend events to pay their expenses they might be able to extend the trip and achieve something to be proud of.

'They didn't stay in a hotel. They stayed with my father. He had a café – *I* had a café, L'Olympien, that I later sold. It had a big room on the first floor with billiard tables. We moved them and put mattresses on the floor and they slept there. Friends supported them by selling me food at cost price. One of them was a butcher who sold horse meat. They sold me the meat and my mother cooked it. Three or four months later, when we were about to leave, the riders came to see me.

'"Since we're in France we'd like to taste horse meat, José."

'"Ah *bon*! Tomorrow."

'The following day I took Roger Rioland with me.

'"Where are we going?"

'"To buy meat."

'We went into the butcher.

'"Beef steak, please."

'Rioland said, "But they want to try horse."

'"I've brought you with me so you'd see it was beef."

'"Ah, *bon*."

'They ate it like this.' (José pulled a face.) 'I left them to it for a while. Then Rioland told them, "It's not horse, it's beef."

'"What?"

'"José bought beef, not horse."

'They looked at each other.

'"But we wanted to try horse."

'"You've been eating it for four months."'

Mesa was invited to take part in the Grand Prix de France time trial in Limoges but crashed in training and could not compete. He and Hoyos finished ninth and tenth in an amateur event around Nanterre at the end of May. Two weeks later they were entered for a race between Paris and Verneuil. The United Press news agency circulated a report according to which the Colombians had stayed in bed. The Colombian Ministry for Education was outraged. The delegation was ordered to return home immediately. José protested: 'My riders decided they were tired and that they needed to rest, that's all. They came here to gain experience and now they have it. And they've performed well in new and difficult circumstances.'

José was right to defend his men. On 21 June Fabio León Calle became the first Colombian to win a race in Europe: a 110-kilometre event ending at Châtillon-sous-Bagneux in west Paris. Montaño was fourth.

Days later they were due in Cannes for the voyage home. José told me, 'The directors had disappeared so I paid for the train to the Mediterranean coast. There was no money for a hotel so we slept in a park. By the time we reached Colombia the government had changed. I was never reimbursed.'

In March 1953 the Liberal Party and the moderate wing of the Conservatives had advised their supporters to abstain from voting in the presidential elections. With the country in chaos and political violence on the increase, the commander-in-chief of the Colombian armed forces, General Gustavo Rojas Pinilla, seized power in June 1953 after a bloodless coup. Rojas Pinilla's four-year presidency saw none of the vicious atrocities of military dictatorships elsewhere in Latin America. The inter-party violence largely abated. This allowed the country's development to take giant steps.

Race reports and cycling news shared the national press with items on industrialisation and economic development. Technical change in agriculture received extensive coverage. Industrial development was an everyday theme.

The contributions of overseas scientists and advisors were given exhaustive coverage. In July 1952 a study of rubber tree species by a US botanist spread over three pages. The following week a report about a survey of Colombian cacao varieties by British botanists included thumbnail biographies and photographs of each of the researchers. There were also reports about cultural relations with other, more developed nations. At the end of July 1952 the French ambassador and the Colombian Chancellor signed a Franco–Colombian cultural convention. José – Frenchman, Olympian, Tour of Colombia champion, national cycling coach – was in some way present in all of this. As Colombia worked its way into his identity he too became part of Colombia as it slowly moved towards modernity.

However, at the 1954 Tour of Colombia José's contempt for officialdom resurfaced. This time it brought his entire future in Colombia into jeopardy.

After the fifth stage the riders faced a transfer from Socorro, on the fringes of a great expanse of forest known as the Opón-Carare, to Santiago, 291 kilometres to the west by road.

'You cannot know how the roads were,' José told me. 'They were tracks made of mud. It took two days to get to Puerto Olaya, on the River Magdalena.

'There were boats but there was no bridge across the River Magdalena. There were barges, but only one or two of them. Every rider was followed by a car and there were forty or fifty riders and then journalists and others, so with only two or three cars per barge we spent all night crossing the river. The only hotel was still being built, so at midnight we lay on the ground in the open air and tried to sleep. The following day we had to travel by train from Puerto Berrío to Santiago because there was no road, so we had to load all the cars onto the wagons.

'When we got to Santiago the directors said, "Hurry up, boys, there's less than an hour to go before the departure."

'I said, "Hurry up? We've hardly even slept. And we're not all here."

'"What do you mean 'we're not all here'?"

'"I haven't seen any of the Antioquians yet, and no one from the armed forces team."

'"They've been here for two days."

'"What?"

"'They came by air."

'They had gone in secret.'

The race regulations said nothing about how the teams should travel, so Arrastía and Guerrero, who managed the teams from Antioquia and the armed forces, had chosen to avoid the draining journey through the jungle. Flying allowed them to reach their destination quickly, sleep well and even enjoy a gentle training ride on the rest day. José flew off the handle.

"'What about the people who haven't even eaten? Let's rest today and we can ride tomorrow. That way everyone gets to rest a bit."

"'No, no, no."

"'OK. I'm not riding any more. You don't understand anything about cycling, you are *desgraciados*, all you care about is having your portrait done." I told them.'

But all the rest said José was right and didn't ride. 'The only people who rode were the people who'd travelled by plane.'

José's story amplified the facts although the embroidery served to convey the sheer frustration he and the other terrestrial travellers must have been feeling. The number of riders who made the exhausting journey was probably around seventeen. The rest was true. The Colombian newspaper *El Tiempo* reported, 'The other riders spontaneously converted [José Beyaert] into their leader, because they credited him with the greatest authority and the greatest ability to articulate their unhappiness.'

With José at the helm thirteen of the seventeen withdrew. The stage from Santiago to Medellín started without them. Of the twenty-four riders who carried on only four had travelled by land. The rest of them reached Medellín by car and bus. When they arrived the authorities were waiting for José.

'They sent a sergeant with two military police.

"'Señor Beyaert?"

"'That's me."

"'I have orders to detain you."

"'Why?"

"'Sedition."

"'I'm not going anywhere."

'Then he said, "I'll take you by force."

'"Then there's going to be a fight."

'I was with a couple of mechanics.

'"Don José, you're not alone."

'"That makes three against three. When shall we start?"

'The sergeant said, "OK, I'm leaving, but I'll be back."

'He returned with two truckloads of soldiers. They began to arm themselves with bars and pieces of wood and all that sort of thing. I had all the riders who'd abandoned with me, but I told them, "There's no point in this. I'll go with them."

And they took me to the Hotel Nutibara to be judged by the governor of Antioquia.

'He said, "You're a . . ."

'He had to look for the word.

'". . . Communist."

'"I don't even know what a Communist is!"

'He talked and talked. I interrupted him.

'"You're talking too much, governor. You're drunk. You do no honour to the uniform you're wearing."'

I interrupted the flow: 'You said that?'

'You don't know José Beyaert!'

I stood up, went to the door and opened it.

'Let's let the whole world hear this nonsense.'

For once the situation was worse than José's description. The evening of the rebellion a race official from the Colombian Cycling Association declared that the body would seek José's expulsion from the country.

'Rojas Pinilla was in Medellín at the time. He got me out of it. I was in a meeting with him the next day and he said, "What's going on?"

'I said, "You'll have heard bells ringing, General, but I doubt you've heard the truth." I said, "Do you play tennis?"

'"Yes."

'"Good. What happens if we go and play tennis together, the two of us, you with a broom handle, me with a racquet."

'"You win. You can't play that way."

'"That's it. If some fly and others go by foot, or by car and then barge and then train, you can't play that way. Either we're all equal or it doesn't work."

'The General looked at the governor.

'I said, "Today he's sober but yesterday he was drunk."

'The president asked the governor, and the rest of them, "What do you know about sport?"

'Nothing.

'"Don't you see this gentleman is trying to teach you something? And you imprison him and expel him without waiting for any explanation?"'

José and the other protesters were invited to rejoin the race. The ambassador of France had travelled to Medellín. José told him, 'This is ridiculous. How can I rejoin the race when I've missed a stage?'

'He told me, "You're going to have to rejoin the race anyway, after all the president has done for you!"

'Everyone had finished together, so they gave all the protesters the same time as the peloton, and added a ten-minute penalty. Except me. As a punishment, they gave me I don't know how many hours!'

The rebellion made José hugely popular in the country at large. *El Tiempo* wrote, 'The Frenchman has taken part in three Tours of Colombia and in none of them has he aroused so much devotion as now, after the incidents at Puerto Berrío and Santiago.'

He was carried out of the hotel shoulder high and was feted as a symbol of equality for all. 'At Caramanta, Riosucio, Cartago and Cali, he received greater ovations than the stage winners.' This was despite his modest position in the race. He finished it twelfth overall after conceding more than five hours to Ramón Hoyos.

The following year, in his last Tour of Colombia, José made sure he won the stage finishing at the town of Melgar, in front of President Rojas Pinilla's house. Then he ended his career as a cyclist.

'I stopped riding for a reason,' José told me. 'I was professional but the races were too far apart so there was no money to be made.'

José became a man with no metier but many schemes. One of these was a textile factory in Bogotá, on a second floor near the bullring at Carrera 70 and Calle 12. He sank a great deal of his fortune into the business.

'We had machines that made tubes. They worked for twenty-four hours a day without supervision. If the wool broke the machine stopped. We'd arrive in the morning, rethread it and start it up again. The business started well. I was a supplier to Sears.'

One morning José opened the factory door and the machines had gone. It was widely believed that one of José's business associates had stolen the machines himself.

The German occupiers who had stripped France's factories during the war had nothing on the Colombian thieves who had robbed José. The loss left him ruined and disorientated.

His brother Georges had returned to France in 1955, largely because of his wife's homesickness. In 1957 José and Louisette followed in their footsteps, not knowing if they would ever return to Colombia.

THREE

FRANCE

11

It was nine o'clock one winter's morning either late in 1957 or early the following year. It was dismal and cold out of doors. A man walked into the small bar-restaurant at 64 Avenue Gallieni, Bondy, south-west of central Paris: José's father's establishment.

'Beer.'

José pushed the drink across the bar.

'Another.'

The man turned towards the door.

'And the money?'

'You pay.'

The former gymnast vaulted the bar and was on him before he reached the door. ('I was an athlete,' he told me, as if I didn't know.)

'You should take your coat off.'

He looked at me.

'It's going to get dirty.'

('He was Polish,' José told me. 'A Foreign Legionnaire.')

It was winter and the market square was stained with a gritty, sodden slush.

'It's dirty outside and I'm going to wipe the square with you, so take your coat off. You'll need it later.'

'I saw him come towards me,' José told me. 'I hit him in the balls. Pah! I lifted him off the ground with my knee. Ping! And I took his coat off. Then I threw him through the window. It was the first time I'd broken the glass. He landed in the street. The market traders, who had been too afraid to come into the bar, turned around to watch. I dragged him through the dirt. I'd made a promise. Thirty feet I dragged him. Then I threw him to the ground, looked up at the marketplace and said, "No one help him. I don't want anyone to help him."

'No one helped him. The Foreign Legionnaire hauled himself to his feet and limped away.'

Afterwards, José told me, some of the market traders came into the bar.

'Are you the new owner?'

'Yes.'

'It looks like things are going to change around here.'

'They already have.'

That night, the Legionnaire returned. José saw him come in.

'So you remembered your coat? It's on the rack.'

Sheepish: 'Will you serve me a beer?'

'You know how much it costs?'

José pulled him a glass. The Legionnaire drank it down.

'Will you have one with me?'

'OK.'

José pulled two more beers and they both drank. Then he pulled two more, and pushed one towards the Legionnaire. They drank again.

'How much do I owe you?'

'Two beers. The first two. The third one is on the house.'

'And the two from this morning?'

'You've already paid for them.'

In Bondy José started again. This time he was no longer a French migrant alone (but for his wife and son and legions of French friends) in Colombia. This time it was José against the world.

'I had to take a taxi because of the suitcases I had with me. I told the taxi driver, "I don't know how much this is going to cost but when we get there they'll pay you." My father paid when I arrived.'

José always played down the effect that financial ruin had had on him and accentuated his resilience but it seemed to me probable that he felt humiliated at having to retreat all the way back to France and his father and that these feelings came out in the self-serving stories of often meaningless violence he told me about the bar. A runaway machismo is everywhere in them, and a preoccupation with the delinquent and the outcast.

The bar stood beside a market, he told me, in a working-class district. A local gang of full-grown men, José stressed, not adolescents, had adopted it as their meeting point. By the time José's father bought the place they were the only patrons. Then José arrived.

'There was a fight there almost every day for three months. I'd call the man who replaced the windows and say, "The door on the left."

'"I'll be straight over." He knew the measurements by heart.'

The gang members came three at a time, a table here, a table there.

'Ladies, gentlemen?'

Louisette was in the kitchen. 'José, careful.'

The first table. 'What can I bring you?'

Everyone wanted something different. Coffee, wine, beer. The second table was the same. They drank and talked and then a young man in a cap on the first table called José over. 'I'll pay their round, but not the guy with the hat.'

The man in the hat called him over to the second table. 'I'll pay their round, but not the guy with the cap.'

José was writing it all down.

Then, 'The bill', and, all at the same time, 'I didn't have this', 'I'm not paying for that', 'Such and such was on him . . .'

'You know what? You can pay later. Don't worry.'

Quietly: 'You've come here looking for trouble. Why didn't you tell me when you came in? There's something here for all of you. Who's the tough guy? You?'

The gang members looked at each other.

'You decide. This is what you came here for.'

'The night before,' José told me, 'I'd beaten up two gypsies who'd dragged my father away from the counter by his tie. I grabbed one of them and smashed his face against the counter. They spoke Spanish, so I told them in their language, "Pay the bill, get out and don't come back." Now these guys had come looking for trouble too.'

He raised his voice. 'I'm the man you've been looking for all your lives.'

José's father and Louisette were watching from the kitchen and whispering, 'Easy, José.'

'But I was twenty-five or twenty-six' – he was actually thirty-one – 'and I could dead lift a hundred kilos. How many men do you know who can dead lift a hundred kilos?'

José was shouting now, 'If you haven't got the balls, don't come looking for me. The day you're feeling man enough, come and get it!'

José opened a drawer behind the bar and pulled out a pistol and a knife.

The gang fell silent. Then, 'How much do I owe you?'

José looked at his pad. 'The hat, so much. The cap, so much. The scarf, the pipe . . .' and so on.

'There were no more arguments. They paid what they owed, and came back every day. There was no fighting. I put my tools away.'

'The Legionnaire fought for me,' José told me, 'and we cleaned up the bar. No more gangs. Businessmen, normal people. Soon you couldn't get to the bar, it was so full.'

His stories brought together his favourite elements. He had humiliated a thief and befriended a foreigner. He had taken on and defeated a small army. He had imposed his personality on the situation and through his own brand of violence made peace. In his stories he was Cyrano de Bergerac in glasses.

There was easy money to be made too.

'I spoke everything: Spanish, Italian, even a bit of English.'

One day a table of customers called him over.

'How many languages do you speak?'

'Seven.'

He was joking.

'We want to talk to you.'

José was taken aback. 'I kept a gun under the counter,' he told me. 'I wasn't afraid of anything. Anything!'

'We work for Thomas Cook and we need linguists urgently.'

José smiled. 'They took me on the next day for a good wage. Easy work: I went on trips around Paris and did virtually nothing. They paid me well and I more than doubled my wages in tips. Then Avianca came looking for me.'

Otherwise supremely confident, even charismatic, José always felt a basic longing to be wanted, not just emotionally but professionally too. It had mattered to him greatly to be selected for the Tour de France. When the president of Colombia had asked him to stay it was surely the flattery as much as the money that persuaded him to do so. Late in life he admitted he had always hoped the Colombian authorities would give him Colombian nationality without him having to ask. It was an irrational desire, of course, a naïve hankering that was destined to be frustrated. It goes some way to explaining his later withdrawal into the rainforest. He couldn't be found in the jungle, meaning that if no one came knocking on the sawmill door with pitches and proposals for the Olympic champion it was not because no one wanted him any more, it was because he had made himself unavailable.

So when an agent of the Colombian national airline Avianca came to Bondy on a headhunt with an offer, José heard him out.

'Do you want to go back to Colombia?'

'That's my dream. But how?'

'Señor Farías, the director of Avianca, has sent us to find you wherever you are. We want to make you the *directeur sportif* of our cycling team, and to justify the wage we're offering, since you speak several languages you'll hold the rank of international flight steward.'

The sport Beyaert had helped establish in Colombia had gone from strength to strength. In January 1958, his old fellow professionals Fausto Coppi and Hugo Koblet, thirty-seven and thirty-two respectively, had taken an off-season tour to Colombia. Tens, hundreds of thousands turned out to welcome them. They filled the velodromes and even agreed to an exhibition race on the roads around Medellín, where Ramón Hoyos soundly beat them on a day of crushing heat and humidity. The tour ended in controversy when its promoter disappeared with the stadium takings, leaving Coppi and Koblet out of pocket. But by the time they had left, cycling was more popular than ever.

Riding this wave of enthusiasm, Avianca had decided to sponsor a cycling team and they wanted José to direct it. Outside the racing season he would work for Avianca as cabin crew. There was only ever going to be one answer. His vanity stirred, José prepared to go back to Colombia. Most likely steady work and a regular income held little attraction for him but Colombia, cycling and regular international travel promised what José most missed: an opportunity for expanding his repertoire of anecdotes.

'So I went back to Colombia. And my father said, "What am I going to do now?"

'I said, "I'll go for a couple of months, then I'll be back."'

I wondered whether his father had encouraged him to take the job to get him out of the bar and put an end to the trouble José seemed to attract.

But there was something missing from José's account. He had started a new passport on 24 January 1958. It recorded his new profession: sleeping-car conductor with the Compagnie Internationale des Wagons-Lits. The job entailed regular trips into Germany. The first entry in his new passport was a German visa dated 28 January, allowing multiple entries for a year. It looked like a new job too: his company identity card was issued on 3 February 1958. The job didn't last.

On 7 May he received a permit to export three hundred US dollars, withdrawn from the Comptoir nationale d'escompte, Paris. Two weeks later he presented himself before the Colombian Consulate in San Antonio del Táchira on the Venezuelan border, which gave him permission to enter Colombia after a cable from Avianca. On 23 May José entered Colombia again, to stay this time.

He left behind him a nation in crisis. Hostilities in Algeria had become total war in 1955. On 13 May 1958, as José packed his bags, rebel elements in the French army seized power in Algiers. Hoping for a strong approach to the Algerian question, they demanded the return to power of Charles de Gaulle. For a few hours paratroopers were expected in Paris. The threat was enough: on 1 June 1958 de Gaulle became premier and was given emergency powers for six months.

By then José was in South America again and the Tour of Colombia had started with a stage win in Bogotá for Pablo Hurtado of his team. It was the perfect start. It was also Avianca's last moment of joy in the event. Ramón Hoyos dominated with two crushing stage wins and a final advantage twenty-three seconds short of eighteen minutes over the runner-up. His team, coached by Julio Arrastía and nicknamed the 'Antioquian liquidiser', filled four of the first five spots in the final classification. This wasn't what Avianca were paying for. Beyaert's best defence was that, contacted at the last minute, he had had no time to prepare his team. There must have been relief in climbing the stairway and joining one of Avianca's fleet of Super Constellations and DC4s as an air steward, although there, too, danger lurked.

'One day over Lake Maracaibo we entered a low-pressure hole and dropped like a stone, four or five hundred feet. I was stuck to the ceiling until it stabilised and I was thrown onto the backs of the seats. Two broken ribs.

'Another time we'd landed at Medellín when there was someone crossing the runway on a horse, towing some cows. The pilot had to brake so hard that the stewardess, who was already on her feet attending passengers, was thrown down the aisle and into the cabin door. An arm and a leg broken. I was OK because I was still sitting down.'

Or at Cartagena: 'Customs: "We need everyone off the plane." I set to work until there was only one passenger still on board, fast asleep. I gave him a shake: "Everybody off." He was dead!

'Another time we were flying to San Andrés when two of the four engines broke down. The captain called back, "Get rid of any excess weight." I opened the door and started throwing things into the sea: sacks of potatoes, cauliflowers, bundles of newspapers, suitcases. Everything I could lay my hands on. Everyone was praying. In Colombia people pray. That's what they do. We made it to the island, just, and put her down on the beach. For the onward flight we changed planes. Three quarters of the passengers stayed on the ground. So did the co-pilot. Nerves shot to pieces.'

It wasn't the flying but the riding that ended José's Avianca excursion. The 1959 Tour of Colombia was a disaster. No stage wins, no riders in the top five, domination by a new young rider from Pereira called Rubén Darío Gómez. The Antioquians finished second, third and fourth. For Avianca, no stage wins, nowhere in the final classification. José Duarte was one of José's riders. He told me, 'José was intelligent as well as being a former rider and the winner of a Tour of Colombia. Not everyone can say that. He had been an agile, thinking rider and he was a strict director. You had to do what he said. Even so, the sponsors pulled out the same year because they wanted victory and we couldn't deliver.'

FOUR

COLOMBIA

12

By the late 1950s José was importing Helyett bikes branded 'Beyaert'. 'I opened a bicycle shop in Bogotá, 'Bicicletas Beyaert', next to where the Tequendama hotel stands now. Helyett helped me, they exported frames painted 'Beyaert' to start me off. But they were all stolen.

'They took everything: a hundred and forty bicycles, the telephone, the waste-paper bin, everything. They ruined me. I didn't have a cent. There were other swindles by a few dishonest people. I can't complain about it. It was my fault for trusting too much. I thought of returning to France but Edmund Bougaud said, 'Why don't you come and work with us?' He made hair lacquer. The only manufacturer of lacquer in Colombia.'

The Beyaerts left Bogotá for Cali, where they began to work for Recamier, José as a salesman, Louisette as the factory supervisor. After Bogotá, Santiago de Cali was another world. Seven hundred thousand strong, some of the fastest urban growth on earth had left the city bursting at the seams. The abolition of slavery in 1851 had created a free black peasantry, which was reduced over the years to casual labour by ill-advised property sales and brutal land clearances. By the 1950s agroindustrial sugar production was forcing up population flight to frantic levels. The arrival of so many forced migrants of African origin quickly transformed Cali into the blackest of Colombia's great cities.

Refugees arrived with little but the clothes they stood up in, but even they brought rhythms and dances, some blending the European and the aboriginal, others of African origin, many compatible with the Cuban music that had been spreading throughout the Caribbean, carried by the sailors who passed through Havana even before the first fragile gramophone records. These languages of movement and dance mingled in the city and even though Cali was five hundred miles south of Cartagena, on the Caribbean coast, Cuban radio stations still had better reception than local stations. Songs that might even have been dangerous to play in Bogotá – lilting tales of love, Negroes, slavery, sugar cane and tobacco – spread euphoria through Cali, which quickly became a dancer's paradise.

A journalist named Guillermo García told me that José was at one stage a candidate for the post of regional cycling coach. 'I objected. José was my friend but he was a lover of drink, women and the Cali nightlife, and I didn't think he would be a good example to our young riders.'

The Olympic champion started selling lacquer and shampoo. He was an instant sucess. José told me, 'At the end of the year Bougaud held a seminar for his salespeople from each department. "Now, José, explain something to us. In five months you've sold more than anyone else in a year." He wanted me to explain my techniques so the others could profit from it.

'I said, "I haven't got a technique. You might be a better salesman than me. You can't have less experience than me. But I'm José Beyaert. I go into a beauty salon:

'"No thanks."

'I give them my business card.

'"You're José Beyaert? Have a seat. Coffee?"

'"They bought from me not because of Recamier but because I was José Beyaert."

'They named me chief of personnel. I became a director.'

José was dispatched to Paris to find a hair scientist. He found one at the offices of the French Cycling Federation, an amateur cyclist named Marcel Plazz-Lartigau. Plazz-Lartigau told me, 'I'd gone to collect the race calendar. I knew who José was and we started to talk and we became friends.'

Plazz-Lartigau was the man José had been looking for. Born at

Châteaufort in the Alps, his grandfather, Marcel Lartigau, was a French Basque who had opened the first import firm bringing French beauty products into Colombia. The family fortune had been lost during the Second World War, and Marcel's grandmother, Josephine Lartigau, had taken the family back to Colombia.

'Eveything had gone. It had all been stolen. We didn't have the money to go back to France, so we stayed, although later I was sent to France to study.'

Marcel Plazz-Lartigau went back to Colombia with José and began working for the Bougauds in Cali. Years later, with José's encouragement, Plazz-Lartigau left Recamier and founded his own cosmetics firm called Marcel France. It made him a millionaire. He always credited his success to José, and in times of need José could always call on him.

Bougaud had opened a small factory in Lima. In August 1963 he and José flew into the Peruvian capital.

Bougaud's son Georges told me, 'One evening in front of the factory my father got out of a car at the very moment a bus was passing. His clothes got caught in the bus and he was dragged under it. The bus stopped in the nick of time, with the wheels between his legs, although he suffered road rash all over his legs. José was travelling with him. He helped lift the bus.'

José told much the same story: 'The bus stopped at the bus stop, and Bougaud was stuck with a leg between the two rear wheels. The driver said, "Shall I move, or not?"

'"Don't do anything."

'"But to get him out?"

'If he went forward, he'd crush his leg. And backwards, the same thing. So I got in and took out the key.'

'"Sorry! Let's have a good look first."

'These people didn't think. I kept the key because these people didn't care about the guy. No one got out, so I ordered them: "All of you, off the bus, and the men are going to help me lift the back of the bus."

'The men got off. We lifted the bus, and Bougaud, when he felt the weight diminish, pulled his leg out. It wasn't broken but it was crushed, all the meat here. It oozed pus for months. But when they saw the man move they let go of the bus. I shouted "No!"'

José was left holding the bus in the air. Only the Olympic champion's tremendous strength kept the vehicle from crushing Bougaud as he extricated himself. But not even José's robust frame could withstand the pressure.

'I felt a wave of heat cross my back, and heard: "Crack!"'

José had suffered a hernia near the spine.

José's right arm began, slowly, to wither. He could still arm-wrestle twenty-five years later but José's physical decline began in 1963, when he was nearly thirty-eight.

Since José's departure France had changed. The Algerian War of Independence had taken many casualties. The constitution was one of them – France's fourth republican constitution, adopted after the Second World War and now held responsible for a succession of weak, short-lived governments and the failure to deal with the Algerian question. On 13 May 1958 French paratroopers under General Jacques Massu had seized Algiers. Massu had led calls for the return to power of the tall, gaunt form of Charles de Gaulle, still towering over French politics at the age of seventy-seven.

De Gaulle had his own terms: emergency powers for himself and a new constitution for France, giving the president strong executive powers and a seven-year term. He had his way on both counts. The French settler community in Algeria, whose cause had brought down the previous regime, was elated. With a military man calling the shots they expected a more robust approach to the Algerian rebellion. They had not understood de Gaulle, whose military experience was European, not colonial, and his *Weltanschauung* was just that: a world view that saw the French empire in a global context rather than regarding it as an end in itself. So, on 13 February 1959, the Algerian Sahara saw France's first A-bomb explosion blast the nation and its president into the exclusive atomic club.

The atomic age was also the age of decolonisation. Morocco and Tunisia had been independent since 1956 and between de Gaulle's appointment in summer 1958 and the end of 1960, Guinea,

Madagascar, Mali and Senegal and then French Cameroon separated from France. De Gaulle's Algerian policy took shape over the same period and along the same lines.

When General Massu, the man who had led the campaign to restore him to power, expressed his frustration with de Gaulle to a newspaper reporter, the president recalled him. For some in the French armed forces it was the final straw.

Six years earlier the French Expeditionary Force had returned from Indochina in a state of shock. The French army had been totally unprepared to confront the Communist world in Vietnam, Cambodia and Laos, and in May 1954 the French army had surrendered at Diên Biên Phu, Vietnam. After that defeat dozens of officers swore: 'Never again!'

In November the same year Algerian militants seized the town of Messali and triggered off an uprising. The Algerian War began. On Saturday 20 August 1955, at the mining centre of El-Halia, a maddened crowd had fallen on everything that was French. Thirty-seven Europeans, including women and young infants, were tortured, mutilated and murdered. French reprisals were ten, a hundred times worse. War became total war. By January 1961, after many years of fighting in Algeria, the army felt compromised: why continue to fight if the outcome would be an independent Algerian republic?

On the night of 21 April 1961 French commandos and parachutists seized Algiers in a full-scale putsch. As in 1958 there were rumours of a massive attack on Paris by elite army troops. In Algeria the putschists controlled the capital but their attempts to extend the movement to Oran and Constantine met with resistance. De Gaulle took to the television, caught the public mood and sealed the putschists' fate.

In the meantime, a new acronym began to appear on walls in Algiers: OAS. The Organisation armée sécrete was not an army organisation although it had grown partly out of associations of Indochina veterans and other disaffected elements in the French military. It was a strange hybrid of politicians and paramilitaries, uniting ex-Communists, fascist hardliners, former Second World War Resistance heroes and ex-army mercenaries. Its leader was a distinguished ex-army officer named Raoul Salan. Salan had been the commander-in-chief of French forces in the Far East during the Indochina War. But the OAS was also financially linked to the criminal underworld, using prostitution and bank jobs for finance.

The Delta units, authentic OAS commando units, were made up of deserters from the Foreign Legion and the paratroop divisions, trained in counter-terrorism during their military careers. And the organisation had sympathisers and informers in the public administration, the police, the army and the intelligence services. It received lists of members of pro-de Gaulle organisations and forced them to leave Algeria with threats of violence.

Just as the Front de libération nationale (FLN) used every means to shock its French adversaries into submission, the OAS did the same. There were bombings: forty in Paris between May and July, thirty-four more on mainland France and a hundred and eighty in Algeria between 18 and 30 September. There was every other form of rural and urban terrorism, with torture, mutilation, massacres. And there were attempts on de Gaulle's life: the strafing of the president's car with machine-gun fire on 22 August 1962; a bomb in a bucket of sand beside Route Nationale 19 on 8 September 1961, which sent a wall of flames across the road but left the presidential convoy unharmed; a sniper in a window opposite the presidential balcony, intercepted by the French police – Frederick Forsyth's inspiration for *The Day of the Jackal*; another roadside charge on Mont Faron in August 1964, which failed to detonate – or, rather, detonated thirteen days late. The OAS always identified its main enemy as de Gaulle and his followers, not the FLN that was fighting and winning the war of independence.

In June 1962 the French electorate approved Algerian independence by an overwhelming 91 per cent. Overnight the OAS became a spent political force, less than a year and a half after its creation. French police successes sent its militants into prison or exile. All told, 3,682 militants would be condemned for their involvement in the OAS in France and Algeria.

There were OAS men scattered throughout Europe, with groups

in Spain (they set up training camps in Madrid, Alicante, Mallorca, the Basque Country), Italy (aided by the extreme Right), Germany, even Brazil. And, as ever, Colombia was a favourite place to run to, for all the familiar reasons. In 1964 France complained to the Colombian government that more than a hundred Frenchmen with OAS connections were circulating freely in the country.

The issue came up as de Gaulle prepared to tour South America. He had already visited the Soviet Union's satellite states, encouraging them to pursue independence from their hemispheric giant. He planned to take the same message to South America. France could be a good friend, he told them, and Europe could act as a buffer between the United States and the USSR.

Massive and complex security arrangements had to be made. De Gaulle's visit attracted no end of possibly imaginary threats. A Hungarian named Iván Edelény approached the Colombian police, offering his assistance in the security operation, only to disappear when police began to ask questions. The French security services were looking for a mysterious French woman 'who changes names in every town and passes herself off as an artist or traveller'. A Haitian named Félix Jeannot who 'figured on a black list of potential assassins' was arrested in Bogotá. And more than two hundred former members of the FLN were scattered over South America.

But the former OAS men were uppermost in the minds of de Gaulle's security staff. According to intelligence reports they included one of the organisation's most senior leaders, a former army general named Pierre Château-Jobert. A veteran of the Second World War, when he fought with de Gaulle's Free French Forces, and Indochina under General Raoul Salan, Château-Jobert joined the army general staff in Algiers in 1953 before taking command of the Second Colonial Parachute Regiment based in the Algerian town of Constantine. He sympathised with the April 1961 putschists and in January 1962 he deserted. In Algiers he rejoined Salan, who sent him back to Constantine to take command of the local OAS forces.

In June 1962, as the tide turned against French Algeria, Château-Jobert fled North Africa, reaching France in a cargo ship, then crossing the border into Spain, where he continued to agitate. In 1964, three months before Charles de Gaulle's visit, he appeared in Bogotá.

An iconic-looking portrait of Château-Jobert, with beret, shorn head and goatee beard, looking like a fascistic equivalent of Che Guevara – a French anti-Che – was published on the front pages. *El Tiempo* called him 'de Gaulle's Enemy Number One'. The caption read: 'Château-Jobert, the terrorist who, according to *France Observateur*, represents the greatest threat to the life of General Charles de Gaulle, will have "the most terrible opportunity during the General's tour of South America".'

On 20 September 1964 de Gaulle flew to Venezuela. Two days later, as he boarded the presidential Caravelle in Caracas heading to Bogotá, the problem was still looming. *Le Figaro* commented:

> The only shadow in the picture: it has been necessary to make a number of arrests among the 'OAS exiles', as they call them here, who are rather numerous in Colombia. A hundred and fifty suspects are at present in custody . . .
>
> Colonel Gutierrez, one of the three officers in charge of security for General de Gaulle said yesterday: 'The former colonel Château-Jobert has been living in Bogotá for the past three months using the name Gillot. He is wanted by police.'

At 5 p.m. on 22 September de Gaulle became the first European head of state ever to visit Colombia. French was still the main foreign language taught in Colombian schools and French republicanism was regarded as a model for the Colombian constitution. Even if the visit was scheduled to last just thirty-nine hours, ecstatic celebration greeted him. The roads from the airport were lined with cheering crowds and, later that evening, a dinner was held in de Gaulle's honour for a hundred and thirty guests in the San Carlos Palace.

The following day an appeal was made with two telephone numbers for the public to call to report sightings of Château-Jobert. The appeal perpetuated *El Tiempo*'s chronic inability to get its names right:

Jobert [*sic*] has been residing in Bogotá for the past three months using the false name Monsieur Guillot [*sic*, not 'Gillot']. The terrorist is a man of athletic build with prominent cheekbones, blond, green eyes and aged over forty . . . He has recently been seen wearing beige trousers and sweater and carrying a large suitcase.

It was inconceivable that someone as strikingly Nordic and blond as Château-Jobert could pass unnoticed in Colombia and on 24 September *El Tiempo* reported the security services' conclusion that he was no longer in the capital. By the time Bogotá had digested breakfast de Gaulle had been and gone. At 8.45 a.m., de Gaulle arrived at El Dorado airport. The presidential Caravelle flew out at 10.55 a.m.

José had a curious anecdote about de Gaulle's coming. He claimed he had a conversation with the French president. He was introduced as the Olympic champion; de Gaulle asked for more details, José mentioned London 1948, the memory coalesced in de Gaulle's mind and he told him: 'It was important for French morale during the Reconstruction. You should have had the *Légion d'honneur*.'

The meeting might even have taken place. Not, perhaps, at the dinner on 22 September, even if José had been invited, unlikely for a humble cyclist, even an Olympic champion. The following morning, however, de Gaulle visited the Louis Pasteur Lyceum, where, after a rousing chorus of 'La Marseillaise', he received members of Colombia's French community.

It was the first and last time the honour was mentioned although later it became one of José's standard tales. He even told strangers he had received the medal.

The evening after de Gaulle's departure a French television programme called *Coulisse de l'exploit* ('Backdrop to achievement') asked: 'What has become of France's fifty-two individual gold medallists at the Olympic Games since their revival in 1896?' The programme was previewed in *France-Soir*, opposite the newspaper's own reports from Bogotá. José Beyaert (road, 1948), had become a coach, it said. In Argentina.

There are many versions of José's departure from Recamier. In José's account he was busy transforming the company with ingenious technical improvements and gigantic increases in productivity when a series of arguments with a fellow employee, perhaps envious of José's closeness to Edmund Bougaud, led to a showdown. José was vague about who it was: he said, 'He didn't want a Frenchman to be one of the directors,' suggesting someone without French nationality. I later suspected José of conflating a number of rivals into a composite enemy.

José told me he had come up with the solution to one of the major problems facing the business: the management of the flow-resistant lacquer. 'I invented a machine using shock-absorber springs. You pressed a pedal, let it go, the liquid was forced through and filled two bottles waiting under nozzles with four ounces of lacquer. The liquid was transported by compressed air into a glass vessel and from there through a pipe into the bottles. I changed the compressor head and doubled production. The machine reduced the workforce by fifteen.

'I also invented a gigantic hopper operated by a wheel, which meant that instead of filling a thousand bottles, we filled ten thousand. That was why we had to change the compressor head. There wasn't enough air—' José made the hissing sound of air escaping. 'It removed another two workers.'

It seemed to me the inventor of such a contraption should be able to explain it in the simplest of terms, from first principles. But José's description was deeply confusing.

Edmund Bougaud's son Georges – the French consul in Cali and now the director of Recamier – has a rather different opinion of José's activities with the company.

'In 1964 my father bought a plastics company called Tecnoplast. It still exists: it's the largest manufacturer of plastic packaging in the region. Injection moulding and plastic-blowing machines are complex. At the time they were very high technology. José hadn't studied and he couldn't have invented a machine like that. You needed engineering skills, and more in those days than today because there was less technology. When we bought the factory they were already blowing and injecting bottles. If José had done what he says, he would have invented injection moulding!'

José told me he had made his innovations at a time when Edmund Bougaud was in France for three or four months.

The increased output meant more precursor chemicals had to be bought. There was a tremendous argument over the purchase of large quantities of industrial alcohol.

José was summoned to the acting director's office.

'Explain yourself.'

'I bought it with my own money. I also bought suspension springs for a machine you don't know about.'

'Ah yes?'

('He looked at the machines and he was surprised by my invention,' José told me.)

'But I don't have any orders.'

'I spoke to my sales team and we've doubled, tripled sales. Have you looked?'

'No.'

('He didn't do anything,' José told me. 'His work was rubber-stamping things all day. That's the sum total of what he did.')

Matters came to a head when José accused his acting boss of needling Louisette: 'If you carry on pestering my wife, because you haven't got the balls to do it to me, not to my face, there'll be trouble. And don't come looking for a fight with me. You know how I am. If you rile me, you know I'm capable of it. If you want to fire me, fire me, but don't fuck with me. And you'll have to pay me what you owe me.'

'After I'd confronted him,' José told me, 'he wouldn't come anywhere near me.'

When Edmund Bougaud returned, José and the acting director presented their cases to the old man.

'This guy went to meet him at the airport and force-fed him his version of events. Then I was called in.

'I had to justify myself. I gave him my side of the story. Well, I could see he didn't know any of this. "You didn't know all this? Of course. He's only told you his version. Tell me what he's done? Tell me what he does?" I said, "He does nothing except rubber-stamp things. Any idiot can do what he does."

"'OK . . .' The patron wasn't a fool. "What do you say to this?"

"'It's impossible for us to go on working together, the two of us. So I can't go on working with José Beyaert. You decide."

"'In the interests of the factory, in view of the output that's been achieved in five months here, more than doubling the sales, the production, all that, Señor Beyaert is very necessary here."

'The acting director stood up. "In that case, I'm leaving.'"

José's claims that Louisette was mistreated in the factory were contested. I met sources who claimed that if anyone had mistreated Louisette it was José. A specific story about José's infidelity that came from one of his closest friends. Marcel Plazz-Lartigau told me José had fallen in love with a girl from Pereira who was in Bougaud's care. José had run away to Peru with the girl. When the passion cooled they returned to Cali but the incident made it impossible for José to stay.

José's passports show a visit to Peru and Ecuador between 15 August 1963 and 26 October 1963. During at least some of this trip José was with Edmund Bougaud in Lima. However, there was another journey: from 28 January to 29 February 1964 José was travelling in Ecuador and Peru. If the story about absconding with the girl is true it was during this period of time. Shortly afterwards José and Louisette left Recamier and Cali.

'You worked on there for a while?' I asked José.

'Yes. Until I got bored! It was work that didn't suit me. I said, "I'm dying here." I'm not made for an office.'

It was a turning point in his life, a moment of self-illumination he would refer back to for the rest of his life.

One day he told Edmund Bougaud, 'I'm off.'

'Where are you going?'

'I don't know.'

'What do you think you'll do?'

'I have no idea.'

Georges Bougaud told me, 'My father sacked him because he got up to all sorts of madness here. He lived behind the factory in a house that belonged to my father, and we realised that he was passing crates of lacquer from the factory to the house and then selling them on his own account, so my father sent him packing.'

But José's vocation was to speak a great deal, to invent and to amuse. If the truth lent itself only to melancholy he felt absolutely free to dispense with it.

I came across other rumours too, persistent ones, lacking in details and impossible to investigate, that José had killed a man. He had murdered his lover's husband. I did not know what to make of it. By the mid-1960s there was certainly enough animosity surrounding José to generate unflattering stories. But murder seemed to me to lie beyond the province of everyday office resentment.

13

At Bondy in 1957 Louisette had worked in the kitchen, cooking the meal of the day. In Bogotá Georges told me, 'She ran a family pension. I can't remember what it was called. There were lots of petty criminals there. I brought sachets to make pastis for one of them, and he made it in my brother's office and sold it to the French community.'

There were other forms of cheating the law. Georges said, 'I sent a 2CV car for my brother. He needed a car and I sent him an entire car, piece by piece, in suitcases, to avoid tax.'

Louisette was hard-working, independent and an excellent cook. Perhaps at Georges Alric's suggestion, she opened a restaurant in his house in Chapinero Alto, at the time the most exclusive and chic area in downtown Bogotá. The house stood in the folds of the Western Sierra that flanks Bogotá, between Carreras 3 and 4. The entrance to the salon stood on Carrera 3. Carrera 4 and the restaurant entrance are lower down the hill, effectively in the basement of the building. José, Louisette and their son, also José, lived on the first floor. As close friends of the wealthy Alric they paid rent neither for their apartment nor for the restaurant. Instead they fed the ladies who worked in Alric's salon.

The establishment was called Chez Louisette. In 1970 a national newspaper described it as 'a fabulous restaurant located in an uncommercial area, where the best cuisine is served':

So exclusive is it that there are scarcely half a dozen tables in a welcoming setting, with a hearth that keeps the temperature perfect and dedicated, attentive, knowledgeable staff . . . The proprietors are José Beyaert, who cooks as well as he rode a bicycle a few years ago, and his enchanting wife.

One of José's closest friends in Bogotá told me, 'On Friday nights José had to be in the restaurant. He was charismatic and people went to meet him and talk with him.' Another of José's intimates said, 'Chez Louisette was one of very few French restaurants in the country. The food was very good and the restaurant was famous.'

The staff included two brothers, Fernando and Henry Londoño, who waited; Louisette, who cooked; and her assistant, Lola, who laundered for the salon and the restaurant. Lola worked with Louisette for four or five years. She told me, 'I cleaned the salon in the morning and in the afternoon I prepared food for the next day: cutting mushrooms, washing potatoes. Louisette was wonderful to me. She was very pretty and very engaging. She did all the cooking. It was a small, exclusive restaurant with six to eight tables. José was the host because he didn't work in the evenings. He helped a little behind the bar. But Louisette ran the place. José never issued orders or anything. I helped her. She was very organised.'

Even so, José told me, 'It wasn't a restaurant where you were going to earn anything. She was too absorbed in what she was doing. If she made *Entrecôte bordelaise* it had to be with wine from Bordeaux, not Chile.'

In December 2008 I visited the restaurant's successor, La Poularde, which occupies the same physical space although the old building has been torn down and another erected in its place. The dining room was tiny: I was surrounded by well-dressed businessmen and diplomats with elegant wives. The filet mignon was tender and caramelised, and the chocolate mousse was a mud of cacao finished with turning cream, the way Colombians like it. On the next table three besuited politicians discussed the future governorship of the Department of Boyacá, with Édith Piaf in the background. It was easy to imagine Chez Louisette was very much the same.

José told a story that, if true, gives Louisette's establishment an important role in contemporary Colombian history. According to the tale, two delegations of politicians met there on the evening of 19 April 1970, a date with notorious connotations for Colombians. It was a day of presidential elections. Early results suggested victory for the populist Alianza Nacional Popular (ANAPO), or People's National Alliance, led by Rojas Pinilla, the military president of the 1950s. By the morning of 20 April the National Front candidate, Misael Pastrana Borrero, had clawed back the lead by less than fifty thousand votes. According to José, ANAPO and National Front functionaries spent the night negotiating around the tables of Louisette's restaurant. A sum was agreed and the presidency was sold by ANAPO to the National Front.

Victory was announced to accusations of corruption on the part of the National Front alliance. Fifteen years of political violence followed. But, if José's story is true, the corruption was collective and the pretext for violence that shaped Colombian politics for the next decade and a half was a false one.

With Louisette ensconced at Georges Alric's place, José began to spend time with a Swiss watchmaker named Mauricio Brand. Brand had been brought to Colombia in the 1950s by a prominent watch and clock manufacturer named Alfonso Huerta and Company. But Brand dealt in more than timepieces. It was said that after a shoot-out between rival emerald dealers in central Bogotá Brand had found a bag of stones belonging to one of the dead. The stones had funded his entry into the emerald business, although he didn't travel to the mines; he merely sold the gems from the repair shop.

The green stones are a national symbol. In 1964 President Valencia had presented Madame de Gaulle with a 2.5 carat emerald ring on the occasion of the first visit by a European head of state. After conversations with Alric and Brand, which can hardly not have centred on the dangers lurking in the emerald fields, José made up his mind.

'I said, "I'm going to Muzo."'

* * *

Smothered on all sides by pillows of humid forest where the orchids reek of decomposing flesh, the notorious emerald fields lie not a hundred and twenty miles from central Bogotá yet they belong to a different world.

In those far-off days when José the cyclist was rarely out of the newspapers, the report of a murder ('Emerald trafficking in a far-off settlement in eastern Boyacá caused the blood of a miner to be spilled . . .') conveyed this sense of removal by providing a beginner's guide to the emerald business:

> For many years emerald mines have been exploited at a site known as 'Chivor' in the municipality of Almeida, Boyacá department. A private company exploits the mineral wealth . . . the company contracts individuals who know the region, and these agents hire workers to mine the seams in the property. When a precious stone is found, the value is shared. Half goes to the company and half is divided between the tunnel boss and his workers . . .
>
> Contraband emeralds abound in the market. And for this reason negotiations, often involving large sums, never take place in public places.

The report described how the culture of secrecy among the emerald workers hindered investigations into the disappearance of a twenty-eight-year-old emerald dealer named Agustín Vaca Mondragón. He had travelled to Chivor in March 1952 with ten thousand pesos and a revolver and vanished. When the missing man's father received word that a worker at one of the Chivor emerald seams was carrying the missing man's watch and pistol, he informed the police. Two men were quickly apprehended. Under interrogation they cracked.

The killers had met Vaca Mondragón to negotiate a price for his pistol. On an isolated track they had bought the weapon and turned it on its former owner. They stripped the body of cash and valuables, rolled it into the undergrowth and went to work. They returned that evening, bound the dead man's wrists and ankles and threaded a pole between them. Then they carried the remains to a grave they had opened in advance. The investigators stood by as the killers dug up their decomposing victim.

It was a story José may very well have read thirteen years before his first visit to the mines. In May 1965, perhaps shortly before José's first trip to Muzo, little had changed:

> According to information received by Cundinamarca police headquarters, at 5 p.m. last Tuesday [11 May 1965], an armed incursion took place at an emerald mine named 'El Diamante' in the Gachalá area. Twenty men carrying revolvers and rifles invaded the mines and announced that 'for better or for worse' they will exploit it.

The intruders fired more than fifty rounds at police, who sustained one light injury. To avoid bloodshed police used tear gas to dislodge the gang:

> Information from Gachalá states that the intruders were from the settlements of San Pedro de Jagua, El Engaño and Mámbita, led by a notorious bandolero from the eastern plains named Fonseca, and an accomplice named Hernán Solano, several times indicted in the Guavio region for cattle theft.

The bandoleros were peasant rebels who took refuge in inaccessible regions to distance themselves from established society and to attack it. There were bandoleros of every political hue, some of them proto-communists, others serving landed interests. Most depended on the cooperation of local peasant communities for their security. This made them extremely hard for the forces of state to track. A popular mythology spread. One bandolero was said to be able to transform himself into a tree, a banana palm or a phantom. Another could assume the form of a white horse. A Conservative bandolero from the department of Santander named Efraín González could become a tree or a stone.

Little can be said of the bandoleros that is verifiable except the dates of their invariably violent deaths. 'Chispas' ('Sparks'), said to have perpetrated six hundred murders, was shot down on 22 January

1963. 'Capitán Desquite' ('Captain Revenge') followed on 17 March 1964. 'Sangrenegra' ('Black Blood') died in a battle with police on 26 April 1964.

Efraín González is said to have witnessed the murder of his father by soldiers and then enrolled, with three of his brothers, in the Mafias in the settlements of Muzo and Otanche. There, in the 1960s, he tried and failed to unify control of the emerald region.

In June 1965 police learnt that González was holed up in the Bogotá suburbs. Hundreds of military personnel, supported by cannon, machine guns and tanks, surrounded the building. Seventy thousand rounds were unleashed to destroy its sole inhabitant. It is as if the soldiers believed in the legends of his mutability. By the time of his death Efraín González had been condemned *in absentia* to prison sentences of more than two hundred years.

The operation was broadcast live on national radio. To genteel Bogotá the radio commentary, like the mythology that surrounded the bandoleros, was both fascinating and terrifying. To José it may have been an irresistible call to adventure. He boarded a bus and began the journey to a Colombia he had never seen.

Intense heat, frequent driving rain and regular seismic movement mutilate the roads and make for a bone-shaking ride to the villages where vast transient communities of fortune-hunters assemble before the final push towards the mines. The seams are fifteen kilometres beyond and below the village. Above the road stand the needles of Fura and Tena, two lovers who, in punishment for their transgressions, according to an indigenous myth, were turned into mountains and separated by a river, the Rio Minero, the River of the Mines. After one late battle between the doomed Muzo Indians and Spaniards now certain of their conquest, a Spanish officer threatened a dying Indian with dogs. Blind fear loosened his victim's tongue and the officer learnt that the Muzos stored their finest emeralds on the peaks of Furatena's twin needles. The holy treasure was looted and shipped across the Atlantic.

The official mines stand on high ground. There two hundred men use hand tools to perform sometimes intricate operations on the working seams. Fifty bulldozers pile the barren slag at the site's edge.

When the slag piles reach a certain size a siren sounds and the area is cleared. Higher up the mountainside the sluice is lifted on one of a number of small lakes dammed for the purpose. The flux engulfs the knolls of broken slate and calcite and churns them into a sludge. This coats the waiting valley and settles. Even before the all-clear is given, thousands of fortune-hunters wade in to sift the sodden gravel for jewels the official miners have missed. The slag is called the *guaca*; the workers are *guaqueros*. The mud and gravel stain their clothes and become ingrained in their skin. Everything is either green or grey in this sprawling landscape. No other colour can subsist.

José told me, 'If you found a stone, you put it quickly in your mouth and carried on. You had to be alone before you could look at what you had found. Otherwise . . .'

In Muzo he asked around and quickly found himself buying a few small stones. 'They were already cut. I didn't really realise you don't cut them at the mines. I should have taken them to Bogotá and had them cut there. The dealer fooled me. And they were very dear. When I reached Bogotá I went to see some cyclists I knew who worked with emeralds. A man named Jaime Valencia looked at the stones I'd bought and asked, "José, how much did you pay for this?"'

José told him.

'"They aren't worth half that." To get my money back I had some cufflinks made of gold with the little emeralds and a tiepin with tortoises, the same as the cufflinks. They were pretty. I sold them to French visitors. I didn't earn anything but at least I didn't lose anything. Then I said I was going back to Muzo.

'"You're crazy."

'"No. I want to do this."'

In the meantime José had been learning about emeralds by taking his coffee in the Furatena café where the *esmeralderos* went.

'Here's a story that's a movie,' José told me.

'I arrived at Muzo again. There was only one bus a day so there was a line of people waiting. I was getting out of the bus but the moment my foot touched the floor I saw the man who'd sold me the emeralds. His name was Silvano. And at the moment I saw him, he saw me.

'"Ah, my client."

'I looked him in the eye. "You cheated me once. You won't cheat me twice."

'Silvano was taken aback. The people in the square began to back off.

'"What? Did you say I robbed you?"

'"Take it any way you like."

'"There's a bad smell around here."

'I still had one foot on the bus,' José told me. 'Imagine the scene. He hadn't foreseen this, but nor had I. The guy was like this' – José held his hand over his hip like an old-time gunslinger – 'but his gun was back there and covered by his shirt.' He indicated the small of his back. 'By pure chance, my pistol was here,' José said, pointing to the front of his belt.

'I said, "If you're very fast you might have a chance but you'll have to be very fast. I don't think you're going to make it."

'He looked at me and then he looked at his friends. I thought this was to distract me but I didn't come down in the last shower of rain. I didn't take my eyes off him.'

Recognising the hopelessness of his situation, Silvano smiled.

'"No! I got the gringo wrong. He's one of us."

'"I'm not a gringo. I'm French."

'"He's not gringo, he's French. He's a gringo *francés*"' – a French gringo.

'And that was the name I became known by: the French gringo. It all ended with a beer although I never bought from him again and he never offered. People who weren't in the square when it happened heard about it afterwards. They told the story among themselves and afterwards, in the outback, I'd hear, "It's the French gringo." It made my name there and allowed me to join the emerald community. No one swindled me again. Never. They sold me raw emeralds, uncut, to take to Bogotá.'

José had entered the lawless, murderous world of the emerald trade, and it suited his talents. He took from the emerald sellers: '"José, if you like, take these. We want so much."

'If I couldn't sell the stones I took them back. When I sold them for more I paid them more than we'd agreed.' He seemed to be remembering Jean Robic's generosity at the 1950 Tour de France. 'The extra, we divided. I never cheated them. Never! I never bought when groups of dealers had come to Muzo to buy stones, I waited until they'd finished. I didn't buy large stones or many of them. I bought only what I needed. I never had any problems. I was always civil and I think that was my way in. Being correct and punctilious.'

These were years of bloody factional wars for control of the mines. Many lost their lives but José always moved unscathed surrounded by violence. Looking back with me, many years after the events he was describing, he returned to the meeting in Muzo square with Silvano, as if reciting the words of a favourite script: '"You cheated me once. You won't cheat me twice." "If you're going to draw, you're going to have to be fast." That made an impression on everyone.'

Blood has always flowed around the green stones. They were said to craze the men who chased them. The handful of novels on the subject make much of this superstition. Flor Romero de Nohra's *3 Carats, 8 Points* is set in the official mine. Its list of characters includes a priest who deals in emeralds and carries a pistol in his cassock. This was no fiction. José told me, 'In my day even the priest was a *guaquero*. At 9 a.m. Muzo was empty. Women, children, the priest, the police – all sifting the sludge for emeralds. Green fever contaminated everyone.'

José used his position between two cultures to make Colombia's treasure available to his compatriots. He supplied visiting French diplomats and businessmen and brought writers and journalists to the mines.

'I sold only to the French – people on business trips and so on. The people in the French Embassy and the official offices knew me. Every so often I'd get a telephone call: "We have a client to see you." A representative from the French Chamber of Commerce one day, an engineer the next. Tourists. Anyone who came. I had this many clients' – and José made a hand gesture meaning 'more than I could handle'. 'When they called me I asked, "How much does he want to spend?", so that I didn't bring stones that were too dear or too cheap.

'At times I wasn't working but I went to the Calle 13 or 14 anyway to take coffee and see my friends. It was my office for twenty years. I lived well. I could go two months without selling anything but then there'd be two months when I sold emeralds every day. I enjoyed it. I had no boss. I did what I liked.'

'It sounds like an adventure,' I said.

'That's it. *Fantastique!'*

José told me he felt more comfortable talking to me of his life in the emerald trade than to other interviewers because I had visited the area several times, although his assumption that I was some sort of emerald insider was quite wrong. My interest had been in the transformation of an emerald village called Buenavista. I had visited Buenavista with an agronomist named Gabriel Cúcuta from the regional town of Sogamoso. Gabriel told me about his first experiences of the emerald territories in 1988, in the middle of a bloody war for control over the area that lasted from 1984 to 1990. He pointed to the gutters and told me, 'They was a permanent red stain here from the blood of dead *guaqueros.'*

In those days the village was a lawless dormitory town of macho emerald hunters where dreams of fabulous wealth blinded the miners to their squalor and gunfire deafened them to reason. Gabriel had immediately recognised that Buenavista's real treasure was not the emerald wealth that spelt misery for the great majority but the fertile soils and microclimate of its hills. It was a paradise for tropical-fruit production. Initially terrified by the harvest of roadside corpses – miners murdered for stones they'd sought to sell – and dogged by local incredulity, Gabriel had a vision of his own. He brought UK agronomists to town, funded by a Whitehall grant, and by uniting British know-how and resources with Colombian passion, took ten years to convince villagers that their future lay in farming. The Buenavista I visited was a peaceful garden village with full employment and negligible crime, which was exporting organic fruit around the world.

The emerald fields I had seen were not as José knew them. A newspaper cutting among José's papers could hardly be more explicit. It is dated June 1973, perhaps eight years after José began to frequent the mines, but the picture it paints can be justifiably backdated:

REVENGE KILLINGS AMONG ESMERALDEROS

In revenge for the murder of José Vicente Ardila (also known as 'El Flaco' ['Skinny' or 'Bones'] Ardila) on 27 March, an ambush on the night of Tuesday 29 May took the lives of three *esmeralderos* and a woman unconnected to emeralds. There were ten wounded.

Ardila had died with two others in an attack in the early hours on a road leading to the mines at Coscuez near the village of Borbur. 'As a result of this homicide,' the report goes on, 'a fresh vendetta between *esmeralderos* began. In thirty days more than four hundred deaths have been registered, most of them the victims of unreported massacres in the emerald region far from the capital. There is no list of names.'

Soon after this spate of killings police occupied the mines at Muzo, Coscuez and Peñas Blancas. To pacify the region the leader of the principal armed faction, a strongman named Humberto 'El Ganso' ('the Goose') Ariza was picked up and jailed and a precarious calm descended on the area.

Two years later a visit by Colombian parliamentarians to Muzo, the best known of the emerald villages, led the national press to characterise it as a paradox: the world's wealthiest village but also its poorest. Its three to four thousand fixed residents were swamped by at least five thousand transient workers and prostitutes. There had been no electricity for two years; the water main, when it worked, served only two-thirds of the town; violence was rife and the army reported daily arrests of dozens of unlicenced miners looking for gemstones.

It was lunchtime on 9 April 2008 at the crossroads of Carrera 7 and Avenida Jiménez, in the heart of Bogotá. For half a century this street corner has been associated with violence. Fifty yards away, sixty years ago to the hour, Jorge Eliécer Gaitán was assassinated. Sometime after Gaitán's murder the emerald traders began to gather here.

I was here to meet an old friend of José's, an emerald dealer who might, if I played it just right, allow me a glimpse into the secret, dangerous world of the *esmeralderos*. For more than twenty years it had been José's world too, years of shocking violence that had long since passed when I started my investigations.

My contact gave me coffee. I explained myself. He eyed me cagily, then gave me a list of names. We shook hands and I began a long round of telephone calls and street-corner conversations that eventually led me to a tiny café on the Plazoleta del Rosario in central Bogotá and, at last, two of José's *esmeraldero* colleagues, Guillermo Robayo and Gonzalo Perrilla. They used to meet up with José in Brand's workshop at Calle 14 and Carrera 8.

Robayo told me: 'We were all close friends. We finished work at six or seven then we met there to play cards. José was a good friend and a good person. Very sociable. He was easy to get on with. Euphoric. Enthusiastic. He never said no to anything. He was strange that way. His personal life was disorderly and he loved to gamble. He gambled every day.'

I learnt something else that day that ran directly contrary to everything José had told me.

'José went to Muzo frequently but it was for the adventure. He didn't take money. He was driven by a kind of madness. He was what we call a commissioner: he commissioned stones. He used to call and ask for two carats and I'd get him a nice piece. He knew about cycling, yes, but he didn't know about emeralds.

'We used to take the stones to the restaurant for José's buyers. He'd buy a ten thousand-peso stone and sell it for twelve. He made good money.

'In those days very few Colombians travelled to France and very few French people visited Bogotá. José translated for French visitors and everyone bought an emerald.'

The visits to the emerald fields that José had described to me as a necessary part of his involvement in the industry had more to do with his thirst for adventure and risk-taking than with making money.

Among the papers José lent me was a cutting about yet another *esmeraldero* murder. It was undated and I could not find it in any of the newspaper archives. It seemed to me to evoke the early 1970s.

MUSICIAN KILLED IN BAR 'EL BUEN GUSTO'

A young Bogotá musician working in a central bar was murdered by an *esmeraldero* who did not like the song he was singing.

At one o'clock this morning, when the waitresses were collecting bottles and clearing tables in the bar 'El Buen Gusto' at Calle 16 No. 19–49, Rodrigo Zárate Mejía, 21, the singer in a trio that worked in the bar, began the final piece of the evening. It proved to be the last one of his life.

Accompanied by maracas, the musicians and two guitarists performed a song dedicated to a young woman, which, it appears, was not to the taste of a man drinking at a table in the company of one Carlos Arturo Olaya.

The man argued with the young musician, pulled out a .22 calibre pistol and fired several shots. Two bullets penetrated the musician's body, one in the shoulder and one in the heart, causing immediate death.

The murderer fled and his companion attempted to do the same but was apprehended by passers-by as he was climbing into a taxi. They dragged him out, beat him and handed him to police.

The killer is reputed to be a well-known *esmeraldero*.

I pondered the meaning of the article: what was it doing among José's papers? What was his connection to the story? He could have been a witness, a friend of the murderer (or of the victim). Or was the killer José?

I never found the answer although I finally settled on a theory that felt most likely.

The eighty or so books Auguste le Breton is said to have written contain something over five million words but today he is chiefly remembered for one: *'rififi'* – ruckus, trouble, fisticuffs. In his memoir *Ils ont dansé le rififi*, he recalls coining the word with his friend Gégène

Montparnasse at Nantes in 1942 and launching it into the mainstream in his first work of fiction, the 1954 thriller *Du rififi chez les hommes* ('Ruckus among the men'). When the book became a successful film within a year of its publication, the word was made.

As well as providing the plot le Breton worked on the dialogue and co-authored the script – equivocal contributions, since the core of the film is a sequence lasting exactly thirty minutes during which there is no dialogue. For the twenty-three minutes and forty-five seconds of the heist scene there is no music either – just the judicious use of sound effects. The spell is broken only when the gang leader, Tony, opens the bag of loot he and his three colleagues have liberated from the safe of a Paris jeweller. Finding inside jewels and gems of fantastic value, he utters a stupefied '*Merde!*'

None of this, of course, was the author's invention. Rather, it was the work of American filmmaker and actor Jules Dassin, who had once been Alfred Hitchcock's assistant. Dassin had made a series of films in Hollywood in the late 1940s, *Brute Force*, *The Naked City* and *Thieves' Highway*, which have become known as the earliest films noirs. However, blacklisted for his Communist Party membership before the war, Dassin's career stalled. He moved to London, where he made the critically acclaimed *Night and the City*, but work dried up when US distributors refused to handle his films. From London he moved back to the United States, where the film he worked on was never released. Then he returned to Europe. Paris welcomed Dassin and he was offered *Du rififi chez les hommes*. Due to the Algerian crisis the producer had decided that the bad guys in the book, who were North Africans, should be turned into Americans. For this reason he wanted an American to adapt le Breton's novel. For Dassin it was a last-ditch attempt to salvage his career in the movies. Even so, he insisted on making the baddies French. The result, which featured the showgirl Magali Noël and had, in the words of the New York *Daily Mirror*, 'Enough raw sex to elevate every eyebrow', was a great success. It earned Dassin the Best Director prize at Cannes.

In an interview soon after le Breton's death in 1999, Dassin remembered how shocked he had been by much of the book:

I got the screenplay done very quickly, and I remember this marvellous meeting with the author, whose name was Auguste le Breton, and we met, he, the producer and I, and he said, 'I read your screenplay. I would like to know where is my book.' And I said, 'Well, you know what things do when you adapt, and film . . .' And the usual blah blah, and he said, 'That's very interesting, but where is my book?' and I repeated some of the blah blah, and believe it or not, this man who I think patterned his whole behaviour after actors like George Raft in American movies, always wore a hat, and not being satisfied with my answer, I see this man take out a gun and put it on the table, and he said again, 'Where is my book?' I looked at the gun and I looked at his hat and I began to laugh. And because I laughed, because I showed no fear of his hat and his gun, he took me in his arms and we became very good friends. Auguste le Breton, who just died some months ago. Nice man.

François Truffaut's enthusiastic appraisal of the film was scathing about le Breton's literary talent: 'From the worst crime novel I have ever read, Jules Dassin has made the best film noir I have ever seen.' Despite the extent of the adaptation to which Dassin had subjected his book, the film cemented le Breton's reputation.

Le Breton's father had been killed during the Great War. His mother had abandoned him. Repeated attempts to escape from the orphanage led him to be transferred to a secure reformatory on the island of Belle-Île, off the Brittany coast. From reform school he headed to the capital, where he fell in with the lowlife of Saint-Ouen, in northern Paris. The hard man of Saint-Ouen was Milo Jacquot:

Milo barely touched five foot three but everyone who ever crossed him on the basis of his small size regretted it. I've never known a harder man. Small? Yes! But solid, stocky, spiteful. To become a legend at Saint-Ouen, you had to be all that. And more . . . The gun didn't dictate the law there, not yet. It was the fist, the broken bottle, the knife above all. Ah! the shiv, the shank, the Eustache, the rapier, the tool! The interns at the nearby Bichat Hospital must have seen their fill of open bellies and cut throats.

This was the world le Breton celebrated. And when Milo moved on from Saint-Ouen to Montmartre and became 'the king without a crown of the Petit Jardin dance hall on Avenue de Clichy' le Breton went with him, breathing in the life of the streets, its ethic, its language. He was close to Édith Piaf, like him the child of a circus performer, and wrote about her many years later in *La Môme Piaf.*

Le Breton swore that, if he had children, he would write a book about his own childhood to help them understand. In 1947 le Breton's daughter was born and he began his first book, *Les hauts murs* ('The high walls'). The book was a success and led to more biographical writing, much of it excellent, and several long series of crime novels, most of them poor, worked up from stories he had gleaned on the streets and churned out at the rate of three, four or five books a year.

One of le Breton's longtime Montmartre buddies was Didi, the *soigneur* who had accompanied José Beyaert at the 1952 Tour of Colombia. Didi knew Georges Alric – didn't everyone? – and when le Breton followed in Didi's footsteps to Colombia in January 1969 Georges Alric met him at the airport. When Georges took him home le Breton met José Beyaert.

Now more than ever José felt the need for a heroic explanation of his life. Perhaps it was with le Breton that he developed his talent for telling untrue but believable tales to the point where his communications with his friends sometimes contained more fiction than fact. One of his stories was that he had lost a testicle in a bomb blast during the war. Pretending to be not fully a man was one way of being more of a man than ever.

His friends might have exploded his stories by asking a few leading questions but José was too much fun. It was a style of mutual grooming practised at any hour but especially on long nights of smoking and card-playing at Mauricio Brand's or Chez Louisette. In le Breton's case José provided literary material for at least three books: two factual, one a work of crime fiction.

Rouges étaient les émeraudes ('Red emeralds', perhaps even 'Blood emeralds') came out in 1971. Georges Alric ('a gentleman from another era'), José Beyaert ('former champion cyclist and my travelling companion') and another of their circle named Charles Riou ('the vagabond at the end of the world') got a mention in the acknowledgements. More importantly they provided the book's main characters. Their real-life banter over night-time poker sessions echoed through the attitudes, ambitions and fantasies expressed by their fictionalised selves, filtered by le Breton's imagination.

Georges Alric provided the raw material for Honoré Bradiou, an oil worker who dreams of buying a ranch in Argentina: 'From his religious and provincial lyceum . . . he had retained his neatness, his muted gestures and an almost unctuous courtesy . . . His timid, retiring, neutral appearance made him look like a regular Colombian townsman.'

Bradiou's surname seems to derive from that of Charles Riou. Accordingly, Riou's character is called Georges Le Barbu ('Whiskers George'? 'Shaggy George'?). When le Breton met him Riou was white-haired and balding. In the book he is young again, wearing the dark beard he wore into his thirties:

> He wandered Colombia's bewitching extensions searching for Indian tombs. His wearying labours, outside the law and sometimes dangerous, were in reality a game. Unknown tombs, tombs that still contained genuine artefacts, were becoming rare. When fortune smiled he might find a jar, a necklace, a golden mask, but like many adventurers money for its own sake was of no interest to him. It slipped through his fingers. He was amoral, a booming, fighting gambler and womaniser . . .

But the most colourful character in the book is based on José Beyaert. His energy and impulsiveness, his physical strength, but also something in his personality, lent themselves to fictionalisation, and his persona, René le boxeur, demonstrates that he exercised the author's imagination more than any of his friends.

René is the owner of a French bar called 'Trois Couleurs', where the migrants play poker and smoke into the night: Chez Louisette in other words. René is forty: when he took le Breton to the emerald fields José was forty-three. René was never a cyclist but as an ex-boxer his biography echoes José's. He wears 'canvas, para-style trousers covered with pockets', like José. And le Breton adapted José's wartime yarn of losing a testicle and inflicted erectile dysfunction on the miserable bar owner: 'He pulled her against him with the strength he wished had been virile, but which, alas . . . Was he really impotent? He sometimes achieved a little pleasure, a momentary flash of joy that never ended in possession.'

It made René le boxeur a pulp-fiction Jake Barnes, the castrated hero in Hemingway's *The Sun Also Rises*, although he is intended less as a literary reference than as a way of poking fun at José's repertoire of tall tales. Le Breton went further with René's inadequacies as a sportsman:

> [He] had dreamt of world titles, magical rings [an Olympic reference for José?], applause, stomping starlets, femmes fatales.
> In truth, he had never known this type of success except in his own braggadocio. He had been a failure. Like many.

Le Breton's fictional Frenchmen have turned to crime 'to add colour to their lives, to give a sense of adventure to their exile', as if he came to see an émigré's ennui as the driving force behind José's crazy expeditions. And just as José's motives for leaving France and his cycling career were never clear we never learn what has driven his fictional counterpart from his homeland.

In 1969 a 1,759-carat stone, later named Emilia, was unearthed in the Coscuez emerald mine. The *Guinness Book of Records* describes it as 'one of the largest gem-quality emerald crystals in the world, and . . . the largest emerald crystal in the collection of emeralds belonging to the Banco Nacional de la Republica in Bogotá'. In *Rouges étaient les émeraudes*, le Breton turns the find into the centre of his story.

When the largest emerald in history is unearthed at Muzo his Frenchmen set out to steal it. With an undercover operation that sees the suave Honoré (the Alric persona) pose as a government doctor on an official visit to the mines, and a cast of characters from Colombia's underclasses as le Breton saw them – ruthless, noble and soulful – not to mention a few officials on the take, they hijack the helicopter carrying the stone to Bogotá and complete the heist. Then comes the infighting. The stone's beauty and value drives them insane. René gets the emerald by murdering the smuggler Vicente Rodríguez. The killing and betrayal continues until only René and Maxima, a Guahibo Indian girl whom he loves, are left, fleeing eastwards along the river with the emerald towards the Orinoco.

Le Breton, it seems, wanted to write a thriller that was also a *roman-à-clef* for his friends. Its worst flaw is so basic it is surprising a writer as experienced as le Breton would make it. No one would steal the world's largest emerald unless they had been commissioned to do so. Before setting off to Muzo, the problem facing our valiant Frenchmen, and their intrepid author, was this: they needed to find a buyer.

Rouges étaient les émeraudes was successful neither commercially nor structurally. Le Breton opens it with a map showing his own journeys from Bogotá between January and March 1969. The map, at least, is true to life for within days of their encounter José had taken his new friend to Muzo, 'the famous and terrible emerald mine'.

In the rather over-egged account le Breton gives in his memoir *Ils ont dansé le rififi* they were 'the first Europeans ever to spend the night there'. José secured a police escort with a Lieutenant Miguel Barrientos, who was travelling to Muzo on a six-month posting to relieve the previous police commander. He carried an M1 Carbine and a Colt .45 pistol.

The other side of Muzo village, on the road to the mine, José, le Breton, Barrientos and their driver stopped at a roadside stall for food. Le Breton sat outside, alone, his camera on his knee. Suddenly two men appeared. One wore a machete on a belt. The other wore a revolver in a holster. His black eyes, 'sharpened by marijuana', never left the camera. They sat down either side of the writer.

José emerged from the shop.

'Without moving my head,' le Breton wrote, 'I used my eyes to signal the presence of the *pistoleros*. It's the advantage of going around with men of adventure. They don't need it spelling out to them. He didn't even look at them.'

José offered his friend a crust of bread he was holding, then disappeared inside the shop. Seconds later Barrientos emerged, his rifle in one hand, the handle of his pistol in the other. The *pistoleros* rose to their feet. Barrientos took a few steps forwards and stopped. The man with the machete stepped away. Barrientos lowered his eyes to the other man's holster.

'When you carry a gun, hombre, it's because you intend to use it.'

He moved quickly towards his adversary until the brims of their hats met. By now the shop was empty. Even the servant, a Guahibo Indian girl, had come out to watch. Into the silence, José commented: '*Putain!*' ('Shit!')

Barrientos, again: 'What are you waiting for? Shoot. When you carry a gun, it's to use it.'

The gunman, slowly, removed his hand from his gun and stood down. 'As you like.'

José paid the Indian girl and they climbed back into the car. Barrientos didn't take his eye off the gunman. Afterwards le Breton asked him what he would have done if the gunman had drawn.

'I'd have shot him through my holster, without drawing.'

Le Breton fictionalised the adventure in *Rouges étaient les émeraudes*. The gunman acquired the name of Luis Pacheco. Barrientos goaded him: 'You've got no balls, man. Or is that pistol only for scaring women?'

Pacheco broke into a sweat and drew his gun, but Barrientos was quicker. He didn't waste time drawing. He shot the way Brazilian killers shoot. Through the holster.

As Pacheco's partner – it is his brother, Esteban – made his move, Barrientos scowled: 'Wanna die too?'

In the supposedly factual account given in le Breton's memoir he and José make it to Muzo only to be taken by 'a sickly, brown-skinned man with a limp and a moustache' into a den lined with religious images and offered a number of emeralds. 'It's *bella*,' he tells them, in cod Spanish. '*Mucho bella.*' They decide against it. 'Six months later, everyone knows, our limping salesman was wasted in Bogotá's Calle 14, the famous street of the emerald traders. Had he double-crossed a buyer with his sumptuous Bella?'

Regardless of his shortcomings as a novelist, le Breton was a talented dialogue writer and an acute observer. Setting aside its weaknesses, *Rouges étaient les émeraudes* is a valuable expression of what Colombia meant to France – or to a Frenchman like le Breton. We learn early on that René has no papers and that Honoré is on the run from France:

> They all had their dreams and ambitions. They had all come to Colombia to succeed. In what? It didn't matter. They didn't know. But they had felt the attraction of fortunes made and squandered in South America's endless untouched spaces, adventure in its pure state, girls won and lost and great emotions that end in lasting friendship. In short, these were the stories they would tell some other time, when they returned to France, rich and respected, enveloped in an aura of distinction and wealth. Dreams . . . the dreams of children that sometimes come true for adults who had a little luck, some balls in their trousers and a grain of intelligence.

This was le Breton's conclusion: to his new French friends, Colombia was a place you fled to. It was somewhere you went to experience brief romances and overpowering emotions as you despoiled it of its riches before returning home to France to tell the tale. Colombians are 'hard, contemptuous of death, seekers after it'. 'Murders happen every day here. No one raises an eyebrow. We're not in France now . . .'

At one point José's character, René the boxer, standing over Vicente's still warm body, turns to Maxima, the girl he loves but cannot possess, and says: 'You see I've got balls, eh, Maxima? . . . Don't doubt me again. I'm a man. A real man.'

It was caricature but le Breton had caught something central to José's presentation of himself to the world. As a bar owner in Paris after the war, as an emerald trader in the 1960s and later on, working as a logger deep in the Colombian bush, it was something of a survival strategy to be thought capable of violence and perhaps even of murder. But it was more than mere theatre.

José told a story about his father back in the late 1940s. A salesman had left a bag of money in the family bar. José put it behind the bar. His father came across it and asked him what he intended to do with it. José hesitated. His father slapped him hard across the face. José too had come to believe there were occasions when righteous violence was necessary and the inability to administer it was an important personality flaw. For José, le Breton was saying, and in this, at least, he was right, real men could kill.

Le Breton's swashbuckling adventure continued back in Bogotá. While taking photos of the emerald traders he was approached by a distinguished-looking fellow with two bodyguards. The man spoke to him in French, and with a warm smile: 'Monsieur, could you give me your film? I'll have it developed and return it to you tomorrow.'

José, who had observed the scene, told le Breton: 'Give it to him.'

The following day the photographs and negatives arrived, minus the frames with the faces that weren't to be taken.

Rouges étaient les émeraudes was le Breton's fantasy Colombia although the ostensibly factual account in his memoir was also, no doubt, greatly embroidered. After all, even in his books, when there was time to think as the words went down on the page, his Colombians speak comedy Spanish ('*Excusa doctor. Uno momento.*') and swear in Italian ('*Porco Dio!*'). But le Breton was writing in a genre in which these things didn't greatly matter and at a time when Colombia seemed very distant from France and other European countries. Yet one thing is certain: given the limitations of his Spanish, le Breton's memoir contains not so much his own memories of Colombia as José's after-the-event reconstructions. And José was himself a prolific producer of fiction. He just never took the trouble to write it down.

I believe José began to collect newspaper cuttings for his literary friend, with whom he was deeply taken. The piece about the murdered musician was more than likely intended for le Breton, like another gory article among José's papers entitled 'Cadaver found in shark'. The fishermen who had caught and eviscerated the beast had, 'on finding the remains, decided to bury them to avoid problems . . . It was said . . . that the body could be that of Plinio de Jesús Diana, a Police officer who disappeared the previous week while bathing with his wife.'

* * *

AUGUSTE LE BRETON WANTS TO EXPLOIT AN EMERALD MINE IN COLOMBIA

The novelist Auguste LE BRETON (*Du rififi* . . .) has always had a weak spot for precious stones. For his next book, *Rouges étaient les émeraudes*, he went to Colombia, where he organised a full-scale expedition with his chums José BEYAERT, winner of the road race at the London Olympic Games in 1948, and Bernardo [*sic*] MOSER, a former Luftwaffe pilot.

'We explored the Caribbean around Cartagena,' le Breton told me, exhausted by his journey, 'hoping to find the famous treasure of the English pirate MORGAN. We got nothing, apart from sunburn and a bad back! I had to make do with [hunting] the treasure of the Chibchas, an extinct Indian tribe, [which is purported to be] buried somewhere in the Andes! But I'll go back to Colombia because I've been offered a disused emerald mine and, with my friends, I'd like to exploit it. Apart from that, I was received by the Secretary of State for Information of the Colombian government, who promised to provide me with real policemen for the film adaptation of my book. Believe me, sparks will fly . . . !'

Bernhard Moser was one of José's intimates. Born at Cologne in February 1919 to a deeply Catholic family, he served in the German army and was full of war stories. Four missions in a day over Warsaw as the mechanic in a Heinkel He 111 bomber. A serious head wound caused by flak. Seven months of night missions in a Messerschmitt Bf 110, including Dunkirk, a 109 for the Battle of Britain and the Russian front, the Iron Cross, first and second class, another injury. Moser ended the war as an Oberleutnant supervising the production of V-1 and V-2 flying bombs at BMW. Arrested by the Americans on 1 May 1945, he was imprisoned, investigated and released four months later, severely malnourished. The war had destroyed his family: his parents died during a British air raid over Cologne in 1941. One brother died at Stalingrad. Another was captured while serving in the Afrika Korps, transported to the United States and liberated in 1948. Instead of returning home he went to Colombia. After a decade as a Cologne policeman Bernhard joined him.

He explored the sea and the forest for treasure. On a mountain in the department of Tolima, armed with a Geiger counter, he searched for Indian jewels. He found a signal and began to dig. Night drew in, a terrible storm broke out, the rain washed away the path and he found himself stranded. But he carried on digging. Nine metres down he found a handful of tiny golden statuettes.

Bernhard invested his earnings in emeralds and began to work with an *esmeraldero* called Pedro, who had served eight years for murder. One night, leaving a bar, a band of gunmen were waiting for them. Pedro's skill with his revolver saved them. In another book by Auguste le Breton, a series of disparate interviews called *Les bourlingueurs* ('Adventurers' or 'Wayfarers'), Bernhard said, 'He was the best shot I've ever known.'

Having saved Bernhard's life Pedro stole his fortune, a stash of emeralds worth two million pesos. Bernhard was left with nothing. His emotional life went the same way. In 1962 he married Leonor Muñoz, a relative of President Valencia. Six years later cancer killed her.

By the time le Breton met him Bernhard Moser had suffered two serious heart attacks. Le Breton, Moser and José went on a treasure-hunting expedition.

The writer asked José, 'What do we do if Bernhard drops dead?'

'We carry him down.'

Bernhard Moser's story is told in *Les bourlingueurs*. In part it offers a coherent and fascinating portrait of a small French coterie of friends in Bogotá: Alric, José and several of their acquaintances. Le Breton, of course, wanted them to ham up their lives and play the swashbuckler. José needed no encouragement.

– Tell me, the mines they showed us with plans and deeds, do you think we'll be able to work them?

I was referring to a collection of old books and maps deposited with a notary that we had been allowed to study with a view to a possible venture.

José gave me his opinion:

– I think there's a chance we could, because the plans they showed us are inside the emerald area with the government-controlled mines. Five or eight hundred metres from the government mines there's no reason why private miners shouldn't find emeralds . . .

– I think you'll do it, one day. I hope it's with me, although we're destined to go our own ways. In any case, if you hear anything, let me know. If I can, I'll come.

– OK. You bring the guns.

He extemporises on the *esmeraldero*'s code, '*Piedra, plata o plomo.*' Hard to translate such a snappy, alliterative formula: 'The stone, the silver or a slug' or 'The bead, the bread or a bullet.' In short you either returned the stone or you handed over cash. Otherwise there was trouble in store.

'In the emerald milieu your word is worth more than any written contract. Trust is earned. Cross them once – once, not twice – and you won't live to tell the tale.'

Le Breton muses, 'Shame the same principles don't apply to regular businessmen. It'd soon clean them up.'

Even in Bogotá shoot-outs were no rarity. José told le Breton: 'I was near the Furatena café one time. There was an argument. Suddenly there was gunfire. Everyone hit the ground and stayed there until it was over. Seven dead. Dead!'

In Bogotá José never carried a gun. 'I don't like them. You get angry and it's too easy to pull out a tool. Better to avoid it. I've had my problems but my fists have always been enough.'

This contrasted slightly with a comment José gave *El Tiempo* for a page-long profile in 1975: 'I was an emerald trader, but I got out of it because it was too dangerous.'

Even so, he told me, looking back, 'It was the part of my life I most enjoyed because [the *esmeralderos*] are real men. There are no grandstanders. Men! And I'm not just talking about the traders, I'm talking about the *guaqueros*. It was a hard life. From the moment they started work at dawn until they went to sleep at night. Stuck in that shit looking for stones! That black mud stains the skin.

'I was a *guaquero* but then I realised that finding anything was a matter of pure chance. You were much better off buying from the people who find.

'It was a special moment in my life. Very, very, very, very pleasant. Violent but good.'

14

Shortly after the thirty-one years of conflict that began in July 1914 when Austria declared war on Serbia and ended when Japan surrendered four days after Hiroshima, the mayor of the tiny village of Belvès-de-Castillon, close to Bordeaux, assembled his five surviving children and divided his wealth among them. André Julliard's third child, Georges, invested his part of the family fortune in distance between himself and the killing fields of Belgium and northern France, where ten years before he had turned away from his bleeding brother and left him there to die.

At the end of May 1950 the *Mauretania* took him cabin class from Le Havre to New York. Another cabin-class passenger embarked with him in Normandy: a forty-one year old from Bogotá named Francesco De Paula Cadavid. Whether the two men formed any sort of bond, whether the idea of some day visiting Colombia formed in Georges's mind, we do not know. Georges's immediate destination was the Central American Republic of Honduras and the farming centre of Santa Rosa de Copán. He was thirty-one.

Soon afterwards he returned to France, probably to clear up his affairs, possibly also to collect Eugénie J. Lecussan, aged forty-six, and Elizabeth Larmendieu, fourteen, who travelled with him on the *Queen Mary* from Cherbourg to New York in March 1952. Their final destination was once again Honduras.

The Julliards had been a family of warriors. During the First World War André Julliard had spent nearly five years in the trenches. Gas attacks left his lungs with permanent scarring and in later life he accepted a disability pension he had been too proud to claim as a young man. In the 1970s Jean-Roland Julliard, the fifth of André's offspring, published an absorbing memoir of his Resistance years, *Mütti . . . ! (Oh! petite maman . . .)*. In it he notes that his father, throughout his wartime experiences, never saw German soldiers up close: 'He had only ever glimpsed distant, vague shapes: helmets or dismembered corpses in the craters or pitiful cohorts of prisoners who, in any war, bear only a minimal, distant resemblance to real soldiers.'

The occupation came as a profound shock to such men. André Julliard's father had fought in the 1870 war. In the First World War his brothers had fought alongside him and sustained injuries of their own, while his sons included two Second World War reservists and two Resistance leaders. In June 1940 Georges Julliard was fighting in the Belgian Ardennes alongside Denis, the oldest of the brothers, a reserve sergeant in an anti-tank section of the 57th Infantry Regiment. On the ninth of the month, during the Battle of Rethel, Denis suffered a fatal crush wound. As German troops closed in there was barely time for Georges, also seriously wounded, to prop his dying brother against a tree before fleeing. He had little choice and he must have told himself so down the years.

Georges ended the campaign in a prisoner-of-war-camp hospital. His recovery from the physical injuries was full. The facts of his eventual extinction suggest the spiritual wounds remained open for the rest of his days. However, with the assistance of a sympathetic German nurse, he escaped to gain the family home on foot. The thirty-day walk reduced his body-mass by twenty kilograms. He carried with him a revolver that, at Belvès, bolstered the arms cache his younger brothers Jean-Roland and Guy were amassing for their future Resistance campaign.

Years later Georges's gun and brothers took part in the siege of Noyan and La Rochelle, the last French towns to be freed from German occupation. The rollicking anecdotes Jean-Roland narrates in his book are never far from stereotype and caricature and push credibility, not to say taste, to the limits, but they give an idea of the Julliard family brio.

In 1944 Jean-Roland was attached to the Ubangi-Shari Infantry Battalion. 'The officers were mostly reservists, colonists or public officials from Central Africa,' he says, 'but the troops were big blacks, rather primitive but of very good will.' When the Africans took a pillbox manned by very young Nazi marines they found a knot of fanatical adolescents whose hostility and arrogance, even in captivity, nearly earned them a firing squad:

> The Commander stepped forwards: 'I've a better idea!' and he called across to the big blacks.
> 'Do you like human flesh?'
> One of the men threw a glance towards the chaplain in the corner and assumed an expression at once frustrated, contrite, incredulous and sad.
> 'It's forbidden . . .'
> 'Which cut do you prefer?'
> 'Oh, the thigh!' . . .
> The Germans understood little French but they began to raise their hands above their heads. Their faces, fiercely contracted to begin with, had become livid and terrified . . . invaded by a terrible panic at the idea of finishing in a black man's stomach!
> . . . For these young Nazis intoxicated by the myth of a pure Aryanism, it was the worst possible death.

Around the Julliards' Aquitainian home, underground caves and tunnels spread beneath the countryside. They became the children's playground despite their parents' warnings and they inspired colourful wayfaring fantasies in the Julliard boys. Jean-Roland goes on:

> As soon as I was capable of forming an opinion about my future I dreamed of being [an Army] officer . . . I dreamed of adventures in the immense territories of our overseas possessions: deserts with red sand, green oases or great forests in the tropics. I dreamed also of caravans, imagining long rides on the horses of the Spahis, whose officers wore the prestigious light blue kepi.

Georges was five years Jean-Roland's senior. Whatever Georges's childhood dreams, his adult life would be full of tropical adventure.

In 1964 Georges Julliard appeared in Barranquilla, the port on Colombia's Caribbean coast where he met and fell in love with a much younger dark-skinned woman named Cecilia Amador. Between the documented transatlantic voyages and 1964, Georges Julliard's life is a mystery. He had grown coffee and rice in Honduras. He had moved to Venezuela (an unreliable newspaper obituary published many years later dated the move at 1958), where he cultivated and canned mushrooms. In Barranquilla he joined a small group of French investors in a company exporting timber. Cecilia told me, 'He was initially a friend of the French owners. He began working with them only later. They were exporting to France. They even had business dealings with de Gaulle. Georges was the manager and his office was next to mine. I was the secretary and I looked after the contacts with the timber merchants: all the Spanish-language side. When he finished with the Frenchmen he had a sawmill of his own, a modern one called Mejurex, with a partner named Mejía. We married around that time and I went with him.'

According to the same flawed obituary Julliard was investigated and cleared of playing a part in an international spy ring. Cecilia Amador said it did not sound like her late husband. It was in 1968, most likely, that Georges Julliard and José Beyaert met. Julliard's daughter Mireylle told me, 'My father made frequent visits to Bogotá on business. Things were incredibly complicated for foreign nationals so members of the French community always used to meet up in Bogotá.'

Julliard had a new project. He had, it seems, met a businessman with clients in Japan and perhaps elsewhere who were interested in buying balsa wood.

More than thirty years later, José enthused to me about balsa. 'It's light, acoustic, thermal and it doesn't burn. It's the most expensive wood in the world. And five years after you sow the seeds it's ready to cut.'

'It grows that quickly?' I asked.

'You can see it grow!'

As usual he was telling something like the truth. It takes balsa saplings six months to reach a diameter of three centimetres and a height of four metres. At maturity five or six years later they may stand twenty metres high and measure twenty centimetres across. And balsa is more water than wood: five to eight times more by weight. When dried its astonishing weightlessness makes it stronger pound for pound than pine, hickory or oak. It had won the war: the de Havilland Mosquito combat aircraft used balsa in a birchwood ply. And in the 1960s, when José began to work with it, it was a space-age material built into the US spaceships for its insulating properties. No wonder José was so excited.

But harvesting balsa is a fraught affair. Balsa trees are loners, to begin with. They scatter airborne seeds over great distances so that at maturity they are few and far between. In an acre of ideal jungle habitat, with light, ventilation, plenty of rain (1,500 to 3,000 millimetres annually) and good drainage, they may still number just one or two. Felling them is easy. The headache begins with extracting them from the forest. Balsa trees prefer hilly terrain, which means oxen or heavy machinery to drag out the logs. Then there is the seasoning: the sodden wood has to be chemically treated to destroy the parasites, then kiln-dried until the water content reaches 7 per cent. Drying is time-consuming and requires skill. It can take up to two weeks, during which a lot can go wrong. The end product can easily be ruined by cracking or twisting or toasting. Wastage is inevitable.

And if that was not enough, the removal of timber from delicate habitats involves all sorts of politics and permits. In short, balsa is a marvel but a risky investment. Julliard was convinced, though, and José, as ever, was ready for anything.

José had another story for me. Another two stories he had joined into one that was soon one of my favourites. There was no date or context, of course, but as balsa was at the heart of it it needs no finishing to dovetail into the slot and structure of his life in 1969.

He had taken a light aircraft to Mitú, the remote capital of the forest department of Vaupés. His Indian guide pointed out the balsa trees in the forest below and on the ground José made enquiries about extracting the timber.

But there was something else. José had a map. Some Swiss adventurer had crossed the Amazon, made it to Bogotá and met José in Chez Louisette. They had become friends and the Swiss explorer had left José a crumbling parchment showing the confluence of two rivers. An X marked a deep dark pool pounded by the tumble of a waterfall where one of the old rubber barons, fleeing Indians or rivals or madness, had dropped his treasure, planning to go back. He never did.

José and his guide disappeared into the forest to emerge (days, weeks, months later?) beside a gentle cataract at the meeting point of two small rivers, just as the treasure map showed. José stripped and dived into the water, pushing himself down towards the bed of the pool, free-diving away from the light. The Olympian's huge lungs and great strength forced him deeper and deeper. He stretched his arms into the black, willing his fingertips to touch something but there was no bottom. Hurting now, he turned and made for the surface.

The second time, he filled his rucksack with rocks but even weight-assisted, he could not reach the river-bed and surfaced frustrated and gasping for air. If this was where the treasure had been hidden it was, for the moment, out of reach. Anyway, there must have been hundreds of river junctions across the Colombian Amazon that matched the schema given on the map.

Later, urinating from the bank, he glimpsed a movement in the water. He called over to his guide.

'There are piranhas in this river.'

'Yes.'

'You knew?'

'Of course.'

'It didn't occur to you to say anything?'

'You didn't ask.'

'"You didn't ask!" he said.' José repeated the words through the laughter. We were both laughing. José always planned to go back. He never did.

If the Amazon was too remote, too ambitious for small operators like Beyaert and Julliard, the Opón-Carare was more accessible.

There was balsa there too and the timber rights were becoming available. Besides, the virgin rainforest of the Middle Magdalena had all the ingredients for the sorts of adventure José lived for, so he and Julliard acquired the deeds to a parcel of land in the forest and set off for Barrancabermeja on the banks of the River Magdalena.

The explorer Gonzalo Jiménez de Quesada had written that the river flowed between high banks he called 'red ravines', 'Barrancas Bermejas'. The town was built on the eastern bank. But the word Barrancabermeja resonates with something else: the thunder that rarely ceases here. The locals blame the heat, the dust and the petrol fumes that rise from the ground and distort the panorama, or did before the roads were cemented. The humidity too is draining, thanks to the town's position on the Magdalena. Little wonder it became an elsewhere for the defeated, fleeing famine or civil war along the waterways – and Colombia was always riven with conflict – or a prize for capitalists intent on despoiling the wilderness that once surrounded the town.

The river conveys commerce and people from coast to cordillera. It may even have been the artery that seventeen thousand years ago brought the first human settlers inland, people whose name for the river, even before it became Yuma or Arli or Guacahayo, as the final indigenous inhabitants along its banks called it, is long forgotten. The last of its names arrived in March 1501 when the conquistador Rodrigo de Bastidas discovered the mouth of a large river. Henceforth it became the Río Grande de la Magdalena, in the name of the Spanish Empire.

People spend lifetimes inching along it. Families take generations, shifting from settlement to settlement until the sea or the mountains either bring them to a standstill or send them edging back. I met many of them, investigating José's life as a logger in the Middle Magdalena.

Road-builders came in the 1850s, building routes from the trading towns to the east and bringing rubber tappers and workers looking for tagua palm for the wood and nuts and cinchona bark for the quinine. Until then, the area drained by the Carare and Opón tributaries in the Middle Magdalena was the land of the Yareguí, about whom little is known save the date of their extinction. The war between the Yareguí and the traders was really a series of reciprocal massacres over sixty years. It came to a close in 1913. Four years later, according to a telegram sent by the departmental Governor to the capital, forty savages 'desirous of civilisation' walked out of the forest for ever. The genocide was incidental to everyone but the victims, as is often the case with murder: the Indians were an encumbrance to the central task of pillaging the area of its natural resources.

On 7 November 1918 Tropical Oil, a front company for Standard Oil, struck oil. To attract labour Tropical offered twice the national rate and Barrancabermeja was soon bursting with life, much of it low. When the town was incorporated as a municipality with its own district administration in 1922 it was said to have fifty-four brothels. The population was barely three thousand. Depending on their looks and provenance the girls charged either one or two pesos and were taxed accordingly. There were girls from Pereira who said they were from Argentina and Caldas women who said they came from France. But there were also French girls, real French girls, and they charged the highest prices. As early as 1922 Barrancabermeja was described as 'a brothel with a mayor and a priest'. The taxes on prostitution were the town council's principal source of income. Violence too was always part of the town culture. A report addressed in March 1922 to the Departmental Assembly described it as an outpost in the Wild West:

> The men of the town use the heat as a pretext for wearing their shirts outside their trousers to cover the knife they always wear in their waistband, which they are ready to use at any moment to injure or kill for the slightest reason, especially on Tropical Oil's payday, either to take someone else's money, or through drunkenness, or because of some feline killer instinct.

Those old instincts persisted down the years as the town expanded with astonishing speed from 8,300 in 1938 and 35,500 in 1951 to 71,000 in 1964 and 87,000 in 1973. And oil wasn't the only attraction.

In 1968, with West German finance and technical assistance, Colombia's Instituto Nacional de los Recursos Naturales Renovables y del Ambiente (INDERENA), or National Institute for Renewable Natural Resources and the Environment, opened an experimental project in the Opón-Carare. In the tiny settlement of Campo Capote they built a state-of-the-art sawmill that soon employed a workforce of two hundred and fifty in conditions barely less hospitable than Barrancabermeja: average temperature 28 degrees Celsius, average annual rainfall two thousand nine hundred millimetres and minimum relative humidity 60 per cent, despite two to three months of drought at the start of the year.

Alongside the timber extraction a small team conducted experiments in forest regeneration, introducing non-native species to the poor, acidic clay. There were more failures than successes, thanks also to insect attacks, although there was some success with Indian Gamhar, West African Limba and Black Afara. The one unqualified success in the nurseries was Colombian Mahogany or abarco, which reached a height of a metre and a half in its first year in the nursery and three in its second. As the loggers felled the ancient forest the technicians planted replacement trees. But they struggled to keep up.

Campo Capote was the showpiece of a concerted governmental campaign to encourage economic activity in Opón-Carare. Among the thousands attracted by the promise of easy money and adventure were José Beyaert and Georges Julliard.

For the first time in a decade of Colombian life and travel I was apprehensive before exiting my Medellín comfort zone. Barrancabermeja has a reputation. For many years it was a stronghold for irregular armed groups. As long ago as the War of a Thousand Days in 1899, between supporters of the governing Conservatives and the Liberal opposition, the defeated and the deserting fled the battlegrounds by water and swelled the ranks of the Middle Magdalena's disaffected. In the late 1970s the wilderness around Barrancabermeja harboured rebels with the Cuban-inspired Ejército de Liberación Nacional (ELN), or National Liberation Army. By the late 1990s they had moved into the town and entire neighbourhoods had become no-go areas for the legal forces of law and order. Since the legal forces of law and order consisted largely of reluctant teenagers doing their national service; and since these conscripts were poorly trained, badly equipped and under-motivated by comparison with the guerrillas and their principal foes, the privately funded paramilitaries; and since the forces of state shared with the paramilitaries the goal of extirpating the guerrillas, complicity was inevitable. On 16 May 1998 a notorious paramilitary sweep through several of the city's eastern ELN-controlled neighbourhoods killed eleven. Twenty-five more victims were abducted and executed at the paramilitaries' leisure. Murder rates soared. In 2000 the regional Human Rights Ombudsman reported 539 murders in Barrancabermeja – about twenty-five times New York City's murder rate.

However, in the late 1990s Colombia began to modernise its armed forces. Better training and equipment began to reduce the need for cooperation with paramilitary forces and by the time I made my first visit to Barrancabermeja in May 2008 the state was actively hunting paramilitary leaders and disbanding their groups. The town was peaceful, even if peace is relative: only twenty-two murders the previous January. My trip coincided with the 2008 Tour of Colombia, which started there in April. My friends among the riders had friends in the town so I started with an excellent network of contacts. It was the one factor in my favour. That and the stories José had told me in November 2004, which usually shaded towards the darker kind of humour and seemed to change date and biographical context with each telling.

Days wasted in the depleted archives of Barranca and Bucaramanga forced home another truth: INDERENA's documents had been dispersed or destroyed and there was no mechanism for locating any chance survivals. The legal system had been reformed and the files compiled under the old regime had mostly been burnt. The newspapers contained few useful interviews or reports. There was not even a le Breton penny dreadful to dissect.

Whatever I could reconstruct from the debris of José's different adventures was going to be as close to fiction as it was to biography, with all the associated risks of melodrama and sentimentality.

There was a degree of recklessness in my method. I was too tall and bespectacled, too terribly white to be anything other than a stranger. This helped immensely as most of my work consisted of approaching passers-by in the street, especially elderly passers-by, to ask if by any chance, being of a certain age, they had ever known the old Olympic champion José Beyaert ('What? He lived here?!') or could say where I might find any of his old logging crew.

I picked up nicknames and neighbourhoods: a 'Tachuela' who might live in Barrio Nuevo, a 'Ñerito' who always wore a wide-rimmed hat and spent his time fishing in the marshland, a 'Bobo Gil' – 'Daft Gil' – who went to the Torcorama market a couple of mornings a week. Nothing I could look for in the telephone directory. Each new fragment of information sent me back to the draining, sweltering conditions of the street. There was one scrap of comfort. As I pounded the streets, even in quarters I was told it might be better to avoid, I was only ever received with smiles and kindness.

The correspondent in the local office of the newspaper *Vanguardia Liberal* knew nothing of José's life in Barranca but he did give me the names of two of the town's oldest sawmills. A taxi took me to Maderas Abarco in a steaming, airless quarter flatteringly known as Buenos Aires. Olga Cecilia Rangel might have had a presentiment of why I was there as she watched me walk in. Two Frenchmen had done much the same forty years before. I even reminded her of her late common-law husband, José del Carmen Gómez, who everyone called 'Chepe' Gómez. 'He was born in Zapatoca, Santander. There was a detention camp there for Germans' – this must have been during the First World War – 'and they used to brew Klausen beer there. The village was full of people who were tall, white-skinned and clear-eyed.'

Olga had the elegant hands and the slow poise of a woman born beautiful who had acquired a degree of wealth through diligent work and good investments. A wooden bas-relief, a portrait by Chepe that might have been a self-portrait but looked startlingly like José, was fixed to the wall over her right shoulder as she held court at her desk.

'Georges' – although she called him Jorge – 'was a friend of ours.' Julliard had done business with Chepe and Olga when he was still working in Barranquilla. 'So when he brought José to Barranca he brought him to us. José played cards and dice and drank little. He went fishing with a rod,' she said. 'He wore trousers with lots of pockets and carried a big knife. He was a wonderful dancer too. He waltzed.' And the memory came back of those crazy Frenchmen dancing a European dance to European music, with no Afro-Caribbean rhythms or indigenous tonalities at all: the height of the exotic!

'He had many girlfriends in Barrancabermeja.'

Cecilia Amador told me: 'He sang. Women chased after him because he sang very well. He loved playing with children. He was wonderful! He sang boleros. I remember he sang a bolero called "Granada".'

Olga and Chepe would sit with José and Georges in the Isla di Capri, their favourite restaurant, and lose hours to barely believable anecdotes and absorbing conversation.

'They were very good at story-telling,' said Olga. 'Exquisite with words.'

José never named Julliard to me, or Chepe Gómez, or any of his other logging partners and associates, but thanks to Olga I began to compile a list of people and events that eventually shed some light, however murky and inconstant, on his outrageous stories about his life in an isolated sawmill in the Colombian rainforest.

In 1969 José began to travel regularly between Bogotá and Barrancabermeja, playing the celebrity host at Louisette's restaurant and then disappearing into the hinterland. Torrid Barranca, like windy, woebegone Lens, had its dark underground riches. But there the similarities ended. Barrancabermeja felt rather like the last outpost of the civilised world. In any case, once there, José headed for the darkness and danger of the trees. Olga told me, 'He liked it in the forest.'

The logging site was four hours from Barranca. You turned left at a place called Lizama, a kilometre or so from a roadside store called La Fortuna. The sawmill was two kilometres past a stream called La Puttana, near the River Sogamoso. In town José lived with the Julliards, whose son, Pierre, was born there in 1971. Their business base was Maderas Abarco, where Chepe and Olga got involved in the balsa operation and met the businessman with the Japanese contacts: Georges or Jorge Sanguiñan or Sanguignan or Saint-Guignan, depending on your nationality. A small man, Olga said, of Armenian extraction, perhaps in his fifties or early sixties. Beyond that even Olga, whose memory for names and dates made her such an invaluable source for me, knew next to nothing about him.

'The balsa was dried in a kiln here. A worker named Gil Garzón did the rough cuts and Sanguiñan planed it down to four-by-four-by-ninety-centimetre blocks for model-makers. The finished pieces went into boxes made of card. They exported two cargoes of balsa to Japan and one to the United States.'

I was told Gil Roberto Garzón went to drink with friends near the Torcorama market a couple of mornings each week. He had taken to truck driving after his years as a sawmill operator, and his working life ended in a road accident that left him with a serious back injury. He could walk, just, and went by the name of 'El Bobo Gil', *bobo* meaning 'daft'. I asked around. There was a man the right age who walked with a limp and a stick and they called him 'El Bobo'. He might have been an old logger too but he'd been and gone for the day. I went back twice more and hung around. I soon had the entire market looking for him. On my third visit I found him, but he wasn't my daft old man, it turned out; he was somebody else's.

In the meantime Olga made some enquiries and gave me another lead. I should ask around the houses by the railway lines near the road bridge. I braved the heat – I couldn't sleep through the afternoon, I'd lost too much time – and asked directions and recognised him as soon as I saw him, although I'd never seen a photograph. Gil Roberto Garzón wore the neck of his T-shirt too open, showing the skin of a man used to working shirtless in the heat. He moved like a man in his seventies, which he was ('The steering failed. My spine is damaged. I haven't worked in four years'), although he had the complexion of a much younger man, preserved, I wondered, by inhalations of wood dust? He had never married. Even his friends said it was because he was too tightfisted to feed and clothe a wife.

'I came to Barrancabermeja with Georges Julliard. He was buying sawmill machinery I'd been maintaining in Puerto Wilches, portable equipment I knew very well, saws on rails, from a man named Roberto Peláez. Georges had a mechanic called Dima but Dima wasn't any good and Georges looked at me and said, "If he comes with the machines, I'll buy them." I didn't have anyone in Puerto Wilches so I came to Barrancabermeja. This must have been 1967, maybe earlier.'

Gil had been with Georges for about ten months when José Beyaert and Georges Sanguignan arrived. When I asked Gil what it was like working with José, his face lit up: 'José Beyaert was a fine man. Burning with energy, full of strength. Always helpful. Nothing bad to say about him.'

He had, he said, good memories of working with the French. Gil told me, 'I knew José Beyaert, Sanguiñan, another Frenchman named Juan, who was tall and skinny, and another one, also tall and thin, who had a Colombian wife.'

Olga gave me a family name for Juan. He was Juan Muñoz, a Frenchman of Spanish descent then, although according to Gil he could barely make himself understood in Spanish. Sanguignan's Spanish was even worse. One of the drivers told me, 'Juan didn't last long. He came every month looking for money but he didn't do anything so they fired him.' Olga also remembered an Italian she could not give a name to and about fifteen Colombian workers, including the truck drivers.

Gil had no time for the hangers-on: 'There were, what? four of them, and they came to mope around and mess about. We were working hard and Juan was wandering about the place, doing nothing, catching butterflies to take away with him. Tarantulas too. He caught them with a net and put them in a contraption he had so they wouldn't get damaged.'

Both Olga and the driver agreed with Gil that there had been another tall, thin Frenchman, a sharp, shrewd businessman who ate at Louisette's restaurant in Bogotá. José had taken him up to see the sawmill. The driver told me, 'They agreed that the man would get them a contract to sell balsa elsewhere and would look for finance to buy another bulldozer. Instead the two Frenchmen took on a big debt and gave him the money themselves. But rather than buying equipment he disappeared with the money.'

The tall, thin nameless Frenchman was perhaps working with Sanguignan. This would tally with Cecilia Amador's account. She told me, 'I never met [Sanguiñan] because the business was in Barranca and I was still living in Barranquilla, but I know he worked with another man.'

Cecilia told me the balsa deal had left her husband and José with nothing. In 1970, after the shipments, Sanguignan went to Bogotá and never came back. 'There were no more contracts, no more exports, so he left.'

The driver told me the story as he had heard it: 'They were involved with a Japanese company that was either slow paying or ran into difficulties and couldn't pay. José met the company representative in Bogotá to collect the money but the receptionist told José he wasn't in. José went in anyway and found him there. There was a confrontation, José threw a punch, the man went down and that was the end of it.'

Cecilia Amador had heard the same story. It was perfectly believable, although it also had the hallmark of José's compositions at this stage of his life: a confrontation that may or may not have happened in one place spun into a macho tale and told somewhere else. Further away still in time and space, José told me another version. From the vantage point of France in 2004 the collapse of his balsa business became a swaggering affair of threats and murder.

José had entered into a contract to export balsa. He provided the lion's share of the capital and equipment but his partners plotted to swindle him out of the profits. He spread a map of the area on a table, positioned the point of a pair of compasses on the sawmill and drew a circle.

'We are here. This line is fifty kilometres from here. Step inside, ever, and I'll kill you.' Something in his tone, in the size and strength of the hand he raised as he told the tale, conferred a chilling credibility on his threat. Then he told me to switch off my recording device and made a staggering confession. He was working in the rainforest and his partner, variously an Armenian and a Frenchman on the run from the law in his home country in a nation where there were no extradition arrangements, was shuttling between Barranca and Bogotá handling the clients and the money. The next thing José knew, there was no money. His partner had been stealing the profits. For at least the third time in his life José was ruined. He took his partner into the forest.

'When a dog is about to die, it looks at you with pleading eyes. When men are about to die, they look away,' he said. 'It is easier to kill a man than a dog.'

José's tale about the circle on the map left Gil noncommittal: 'I can't say anything. Those were things between them. We didn't get involved.'

So did the suggestion that Sanguignan might have met a violent end.

'I can't say yes or no. When I worked with Georges [Julliard] I worked all day and slept all night. A few minutes for a glass of *guarapo*' – the local lemonade – 'and no time for anything else.'

I brought it up again later. He smiled and shrugged. Minding your own business was the best policy and if Gil had minded his bosses' business any more than he was letting on he wasn't going to tell me.

At Olga's the response was the same. One of her workers was León Velásquez, a Medellín salesman full of words on most subjects who told me a wonderful traveller's tale about how he ended up in Barrancabermeja that involved a voyage to New York when he was eighteen, an odyssey across America from job to job to San Francisco, the draft, a stint in Germany with the Third Armoured Division, the clearing-up after the Palomares incident in Spain, a tour of duty in Vietnam, then the return to Medellín, where he opened a timber store, and a visit to Barrancabermeja in search of a type of wood known as Tolua. But when I asked León about the rumours José spread that he had taken his revenge on Sanguignan, or Sanguignan's sidekick, by murder, he clammed up.

'*Aquí no entraba la ley,*' he told me, nodding – 'The law didn't come into it here.'

Miguel Martínez Rivera owns the La Reforma sawmill in the industrial zone. Twenty years younger than Gil, he was barely a teenager when José came to town but was in his twenties when José left. Born in Maripí in the emerald department of Boyacá, he was an emerald trader before coming to Barrancabermeja and joining the timber trade. Like a true *esmeraldero* he was attracted to José's macho side: 'He knew how to defend himself. At times he fought with his workers. When they first saw him, no one liked him' – perhaps it was the thick glasses and the manner that could come across as over-confident – 'but when they got into conversation with him, everyone grew to love him.'

Martínez Rivera gave me another explanation of the collapse of José's first logging adventure. 'The balsa they were cutting is a white balsa you only find at the river's edge. It's a delicate environment. They went in, cut it down and dragged it out but they never had INDERENA's permission to sell it.'

The old Olympian's contacts in the institutional hierarchy may well have ensured the early shipments made it out of the country. But a clampdown by INDERENA would have cost them their investment in equipment, wages and chemical treatments and left them in dire straits. By 1970 Sanguignan and Juan had gone and José's balsa business was dead.

The fate of Campo Capote suggests INDERENA's practices were not beyond reproach. Look at Campo Capote: by June 1975, after an investment of seven years and 110 million pesos, the plant was in crisis. INDERENA's absurd procedures had brought the sawmill to its knees. The newspaper *Vanguardia Liberal* reported:

> The director is only authorised to process individual sales of no more than fifty thousand pesos. The subdirector is restricted to sales worth ten thousand pesos. So for purchases of two or three hundred thousand pesos, the potential buyer has to travel to Bogotá.

The project had no sales point in Barranca or anywhere else:

> The timber is stored in warehouses, but even to take a look at it the bureaucracy is ridiculous. [You need] a permit from INDERENA, written authorisation from the director in Opón-Carare, a document from the Ministry of Public Works and another from the warehouse itself.

And spare parts were impossible to obtain:

> Recently one of the machines needed a new chain. The purchasing committee was assembled, the paper-pushing began, [and] finally the part to be purchased was designated . . .

Finally, when the order was made for the part, currency fluctuation and a price rise meant the sum allocated for the purchase was no longer enough. The process had to start again from square one. The procedure paralysed the sawmill for several months.

When parts finally reached customs, there was no cash to pay the import duties and release them.

If José's balsa business failed because of this lunatic bureaucracy, or if it failed because the Japanese clients would not or could not pay, he had no reason to murder Georges Sanguignan. But there was no way of proving anything.

José told me more about his balsa adventure. 'I cut down trees but I also planted them. INDERENA once sent two inspectors and we talked. "The only logger we've seen who plants is you." It's wrong to destroy! I planted more than I cut down because one tree has hundreds of seeds. I helped to teach the settlers to sow balsa.'

I wanted to believe him but Olga put José's version of events in doubt. 'Five years ago,' she said, 'they surveyed the Opón-Carare area for balsa. There was none. Not a single tree.'

The balsa disaster did not discourage them. In 1970 the petroleum company Shell Chemicals terminated a prospecting contract in the Barrancabermeja area and auctioned off lots of equipment. José and Georges bought chainsaws and a bulldozer and started again.

One of their new workers was a driver everyone knew as Tachuela.

Olga told me to look for him in the part of town called Pueblo Nuevo. I asked an ageing carpenter, an old woman in the street, several families sitting at the door. The heat was oppressive. I bought an ice cream in a general store and fell into conversation with the shop assistant. She knew Tachuela. She even called him for me.

He invited me in. Tachuela had fixed the fuel pump in Julliard's car and the two men had become friends. When Julliard and José recommenced operations Tachuela went with them.

'We were working in a place that doesn't have a name. It was full of caracolí (wild cashew). Pure virgin forest. Georges took me up to La Fortuna. He said, "I'll pay you forty pesos a day, and if you manage two journeys a day I'll pay you forty more for the extra one," and I said, "OK."' Tachuela left Barranca at three in the morning, and reached the sawmill at seven. By then the chainsaw operators, Gil Garzón, Dima and 'El Mono Luis' – 'Blond Luis' – were out and working, unless there was a rainstorm. 'By ten the truck was loaded and we set off for Barranca. When we got there we unloaded, had lunch, then came back.

'We logged caracolí, ceiba, abarco, a wood called maquímaquí. We brought it to Barranca, cut it and sold it to Chepe Gómez.' Gómez bought everything they could cut for Barrancabermeja's construction industry.

José and Georges took on Tachuela's brother-in-law and another assistant to help with the loading and unloading. They did the eight-hour return journey at least once a day. Everyone else stayed on site.

Georges asked Chepe Gómez if he could borrow one of Chepe's workers, a man known as Ñerito. Ñerito loved fishing and always wore a *voltiao*, the traditional Colombian wide-rimmed hat. This was the description I took to the old railway station in Barrancabermeja. A security guard who overheard my enquiries came over. 'I think the man you're looking for is my uncle.'

Two days later I sat in a café with Ñerito, whose real name was Mario Arroyo Caamaño, and he talked and talked and talked. 'Don Chepe had a bulldozer driver called López, from Bogotá. He asked Chepe if he would let me go to the logging site to help him with the bulldozer and he said OK, but for two weeks only. Then Julliard asked Chepe if he could keep me for another week.' Ñerito ended up staying, fixing the cables around the logs before they were dragged out of the forest.

There were disagreements in the forest, he said. The loggers ate with the oil workers at a refectory in a clearing. Gil Garzón fell in love with one of the cooks. 'The caretaker was known as "Tabla Roja"' – 'Red Plank' – 'a fighting man who carried a revolver. He was in love with the cook as well. Tabla Roja took him into the forest. He was going to shoot him but Georges told him to let him be.'

Gil hid in Barrancabermeja for a few days.

'But mostly,' Ñerito told me, 'we were a group of friends. We were all high-spirited in the forest, the cyclist more than anyone. He was strong too.'

And there was time to have some fun at the logging site. 'There was a stream with clear water and we used to bathe there.'

When Ñerito mimicked Julliard's speech he went into cod Spanish, infinitives with random pronouns and word order and every phrase ending '*O puta!*', a Colombian's understanding of '*Putain!*', evidently Julliard's favourite expression.

'We had a flat-nosed truck for the timber but when it rained the engine used to flood and it would break down. One time we broke down on a bridge and when Jorge arrived he said, "Me get out this." Julliard wore the clutch so hard, Tachuela protested: "You're going to burn it." We had to unload the timber, move the truck, then load it up again. The old man stood there saying, "*O puta!*"'

One day the bulldozer and one of the chainsaws broke down. The mechanic, a man known as Mena, could not get it going and called a friend, Humberto Vallecilla. Humberto told me, 'Mena told me the problem and I went up and met José and Georges and we became friends.'

In fact José had gone to find Vallecilla in person. Vallecilla lived in La Libertad, an industrial part of Barrancabermeja where the companies that served the petroleum industry had their workshops. It was there that Barrancabermeja provided José with the second and last great romance of his life. Vallecilla's daughter Esperanza, a statuesque, flame-haired eighteen year old with an enchanting smile, came to the door.

'My dad isn't in. If you like come back later.'

When I met Esperanza Vallecilla in Bogotá she described the eighteen-year-old girl she had been at the time as 'a clueless little girl on whom his exquisite manners and way of being had quite an impact'.

Her father Humberto went up to La Fortuna and fixed the bulldozer. He began to maintain it regularly and spent time with the other workers. They, of course, were hardened to life in the forest. Humberto was not and he told me, forthrightly, 'Early in the morning the land crabs came out. I'd seen something like them on the beach at Buenaventura, but in the damp forest they were nightmarish. They'd cut off a finger.'

Humberto's son Enrique joined the Frenchmen's logging team while his daughter Esperanza fell in love with José, who fell in love back. Esperanza recalled: 'We were a couple of lunatics. We did crazy things, the things lovers do, everything you can imagine.'

The house stands at the end of a narrow drive stopped by a high metal gate. Behind the gate is an immaculate red Willys Jeep that could have come straight from the showroom but dates to 1952. It used to drive José, Humberto and other workers up to the sawmill. A brick surround protects the base of a towering mango tree and there are birdcages with budgerigars and a mockingbird. Humberto's skin is a deep ebony black and he is sinewy with huge hands that spend their time tinkering with the Jeep in the drive or with engine parts in his room upstairs or in one of the nearby workshops. It is impossible to guess his age. He tells me he was born in Buenaventura, the port on the Pacific coast, seventy-five years ago. Vallecilla was his mother's name. His father didn't recognise him. He started working underage on the railways. The railway brought him to Barrancabermeja, then the railway stopped working and he stayed.

There was little light in the Vallecillas' yard but the industry and generosity of Humberto's wife Flor were luminous. I made many visits. Every time there was a drink, a snack, a meal. Flor was seventy-two but did not show her years. As a young woman she was a beauty. Like her daughter.

'I knew him because he rode past my house in Facatativá [near Bogotá] during the Tour of Colombia in 1952. We all shouted "José Beyaert!" and he waved. And years later he joined my family. He lived here.'

Esperanza told me, 'He arrived at the house and my mother and father said, "Here's the room, you can stay here." It was like starting over. And the business was beginning to go well too.'

The corner room where José and Esperanza slept is dark and dank, not at all the home you imagine for an Olympic champion. José complained about the volume of the television, 'because it's as if they were deaf, the volume on maximum', Esperanza explained.

'And he said, "And that ugly bathroom."

'I said, "You like your double life, don't you? You go back to Bogotá and the bathroom's perfumed. Nothing has changed here. Everything is as it was when you first met me and saw the house. You know how we wash and iron. What you see is what you get."'

'José was frank with Esperanza,' Flor told me. 'He told her he was married.'

Flor tried to mould her daughter into an old-style housewife.

'I told her, "When she takes a man on a woman has to take charge of his clothes and his food." But she was lazy, although she said it wasn't laziness, it was youth. So I had to do everything. I told José to demand food from her, but he wouldn't. He said he liked her like that, so different from Louisette, who was strict and kept everything in its place.

'He used to spend two weeks in Bogotá and two weeks here. He'd go and buy emeralds and sell them in Bogotá or take them to France to sell them. In France he bought canvas trousers with big external pockets. He asked me to see if I could copy them and I said I'd try. He bought the fabric and I made them and he liked them.

'We treated him like a prince.'

They were good days for José and Georges. Olga told me, 'They were making good money, selling blocks of wood to clients here and in Bucaramanga, shipping them out on trucks.' The rusting hulks of two gigantic blue Chevrolets still stand in Olga's yard. Their consecutive registration numbers, INJ 456 and INJ 457, indicate they were bought new and as a pair.

José started making a little extra from a new hobby. The exhaust fumes from the vehicles attracted beautiful blue butterflies from the woodland. José copied Juan Muñoz and began to catch and mount them. Esperanza recalls, 'I helped him catch them and he taught me to kill them without damaging them. He cut the frame and the glass and arranged the specimens and he sold them to the same people who bought his emeralds.'

The tarantulas received the same treatment. 'He caught them and put them in a jar. One day he didn't close the jar properly and he arrived with his backpack and the spider got out. He didn't say a word. At night, I was sleeping when I felt something walking on me. I swept it away and woke him up.

'"There was an animal."

'"The tarantula."

'He switched on the light and there was his poor tarantula, flattened against the wall.'

One day he asked Humberto to wrap a spider he had caught in his shirt to carry it into town. The next time Humberto wore the shirt, the poisonous hairs brought him out in a fever. José even captured a beautiful native squirrel that he brought down from the forest and took to Bogotá. Colombia's forest was a store of riches that José caged or tore down.

Still, he was happy and doing well and by April 1973 Esperanza was pregnant. On 3 January 1974 Esperanza gave birth to a daughter. They called her Mayerly Carolina Beyaert Vallecilla.

But according to Tachuela, José and Julliard had bought their equipment with a bank loan and the next parcel they logged, Aguablanca, by the La Colorada river, wasn't productive. The partners were suddenly over-extended and their situation was made worse by the dishonesty of some of their associates.

Up at La Fortuna José and Georges employed two hands called Julio Pinta and Aurelio. One Christmas Eve, most likely in 1973,

Georges Julliard was travelling in one of the trucks with Tachuela and Aurelio when there was an incredible downpour.

'Georges said, "We'll have to go on foot for a new fan belt," but he left the cashbox in the cabin so the banknotes wouldn't get soaked. When we got back, Georges said, "We can't do anything with the timber so let's go and buy a bottle of aguardiente to celebrate Christmas."

'At four in the morning we got back to the truck. Georges looked in the glove compartment but there was no cashbox.'

Suspicion fell on Aurelio when the owner of a local store told Georges that Aurelio had bought a huge amount of supplies before absenting himself from work for a couple of weeks. But Georges and José didn't threaten him. 'Georges went to the police but the police refused to go up to La Fortuna. They said it was too dangerous. They'd only go in a tank. It wasn't true. It had a reputation but there was no danger. There were bandits and guerillas elsewhere but not there.'

As ever, José kept up appearances. As well as his many-pocketed trousers, his hats he brought from France. And when Louisette visited Barrancabermeja she always stayed at the best hotel, the Pipatón. Cecilia remembered, 'José had a little dog he took everywhere. During the holidays he took it to the Hotel Pipatón and the dog swam in the pool.'

Before Louisette's visits José took his backpack up to the logging station and set up his camp bed there. Then he moved into the Pipatón with his wife. Esperanza told me, 'If Louisette was in Barranca, I didn't so much as leave the house. I had no reason to humiliate her.

'José would say, "*Mon amour*."

'"What is it?"

'"Louise's coming."

'And I said, "It's not a problem. Go and take care of her."

'I didn't want any fuss. The number one is the number one. Number two comes afterwards.'

Georges's taste for aguardiente was not restricted to Christmas. During 1974 he began to drink heavily. Several of the loggers told me he would drink a litre of liquor while driving up to the site in the morning. He was chain-smoking too. When Georges Julliard was worried, he paced. In December 1974 he took to pacing from the street entrance to Maderas Abarco to the end of the lot and back, time and time again, with his hands behind his back and his head bowed. Tachuela told me, 'I said to the helpers, "He must have something big on his mind to be pacing like that." That was Georges. A heck of a pacer.'

His employees had been working for nothing. 'He hadn't been able to pay us,' said Tachuela, although Julliard had assured him that better times were coming. 'He said, "Next month I'm going to sort things out. I'm going to pay you a bit more. I've settled a debt."' The creditor was the owner of a parcel of land Julliard had been logging. If this was Aguas Blancas, where the timber had not been good, the debt may have been because the return had not matched the value of the logging rights.

Louisette went to Barrancabermeja for the first weekend of 1975 so José and Esperanza celebrated their daughter's first birthday during the week, a couple of days early. On Wednesday 1 January 1975 they went out for a drive. On the Bucaramanga road, Julliard came the other way in his truck.

'We looked at him. José said: "Julliard."

'"Yes. Don Jorge Julliard."

'"The expression on his face."

'"He looks like a corpse."'

In Barrancabermeja Julliard sat down with an old timber merchant named Vicente Wuiza and his sons. They started drinking at ten in the morning. Wuiza was crying when he told Tachuela, 'At five in the evening I said, "Don Jorge, let's go home and sleep. I can't drink another drop."

'Don Jorge said, "The last one. You never know if you'll be dead in the morning."'

The following morning in his workshop in Barrancabermeja, Georges put a shotgun to his gut and pulled the trigger.

The death certificate reads:

In the Municipio of Barrancabermeja, Dpt of Santander, Republic of Colombia on ten (10) of the month of January nineteen hundred and seventy-five, Tobias Oliveres stated that at blank on 2 January 1975 Señor Jorge Pierre Julliard Peyrat sex Male age 55 natural of blank, Republic of France marital status married, last profession businessman, legitimate son of André Julliard and Maria Peyrat, died at Hospital San Rafael and that the principal cause of death was wound, firearm as certified by Doctor Hugo Rey.

Hospital notes say 'firearm wound perforating abdomen'.

Julliard's suicide was a scandal in Barrancabermeja. Every sort of rumour went round. Some said he had begged to be saved but was turned away from the hospital because he had bad debts. Tachuela told me what he had heard. 'He was alive when he reached the hospital, but he said, "I don't want to go on living. Give me an injection to kill me quickly."'

Tachuela was convinced Julliard's financial problems drove him to suicide. Miguel Martínez Rivera agreed: 'Julliard had provided the capital. He was the worst affected.'

But Tachuela heard that Julliard had told the doctors, 'I'm suffering a miserable illness.' This is the version that made the newspaper: 'A well-known French businessman suffering depression as a result of incurable illness turned his rifle on himself and took his own life.' The newspaper was wrong about most aspects of his life: it said he was from Rheims when he was from the Bordeaux region; it said he had three children when he had two; it said he reached Santa Marta, Colombia, in 1949, when he was in fact taking his first steps in Honduras. It was probably wrong about his death, although if Julliard was suffering a fatal illness, it was most likely due to his heavy drinking and smoking: cirrhosis or lung cancer.

Another of Julliard's workers, Ñerito, attributed his suicide to romantic disappointment: 'He had money, a wife, two kids, but he was in love with a woman who rejected him and that's why he killed himself.' His widow Cecilia Amador doubted he was having any sort of affair: 'Everything was fine between us. When I was in Barranquilla and he was in Barrancabermeja we saw each other every weekend. When he saw that the timber business was easier in Barranca we moved there.' More likely, she said, financial worry drove him to end his days. 'Business was bad, the guerrillas, other difficulties. And because of the deal with the Japanese he lost a great deal of money.'

However, the workers who went to the logging sites denied there was any guerrilla activity much before 1977. Ñerito was surely right when he told me, wistfully, 'No one is in anyone else's head. You think one thing, they think something else.' Yet I found it impossible to avoid another scenario. After some otherwise insignificant personal event – not the spectre of fast-approaching financial ruin, perhaps, but a silhouette seen in the twilight or some sort of minor accident up in the trees (a worker sits by a tree with bleeding legs . . .) – there comes back the memory of his elder brother Denis in the same position in the Ardennes, thirty-five years before, and, just for a moment, death seems to offer some comfort.

The funeral was a dismal affair. Long after nightfall dozens of poor workers manhandled the coffin chaotically into an unconsecrated grave.

The workers had no inkling that the Frenchmen's business had slipped out of their hands and was effectively owned by a small group of Barrancabermeja-based creditors, including Chepe Gómez's brother Héctor, three brothers named Quiroga from a family of timber merchants, and a money-lender named Gerardo Bueno.

But the fact was, logging had always been more of a lifestyle than a hardheaded business operation for the Frenchmen. Logging was for people with no option but to perform dangerous tasks at all hours for the minimum wage. The businessmen who made the money did not work in the forest: they stayed in town, running the sawmills, cultivating their clients, taking care of business. While José and Georges had been swashbuckling in the forest like a couple of frontiersmen their financiers had been taking care of themselves.

Tachuela, who saw more of the goings-on in Barrancabermeja than the Frenchmen, told me, 'Timber was being stolen. And they were cutting it to sell in Medellín when they needed wood that was commercially viable here if they were to pay off the debt. That's why Georges Julliard killed himself. I said, "José, I'm going to Barranca. I'm leaving. Things are turning ugly here."'

Vicente Wuiza wanted out too.

After Julliard's death, the creditors moved in. The big sawmill was taken over by Gerardo Bueno. The Quirogas disappeared. A few of the workers were given redundancy payments but others owed wages went without.

Cecilia Amador could only watch. 'It was a robbery. I kept the small sawmill but a launch was stolen with motors and spare parts. José took the bulldozer. He made me sign a document because he said he was going to trade it in. I signed and that was the last I heard.'

Excessive ambition and financial mismanagement destroyed the business and ruined Julliard and Beyaert. José, at least, had the resilience to outlive the catastrophe. Esperanza told me he went to Bogotá, sold a batch of emeralds and brought the money back to Barrancabermeja. He bought a parcel of land he called La Rochela. (The French town of his eventual death was already on his mind.) However, José's new venture was delayed by a mysterious court case that nearly cost him a spell in prison.

On 11 June 1975 *El Tiempo* published the following report:

> José Beyaert, the winner of the second Tour of Colombia bicycle race, has recently been found guilty by the Superior Customs Tribunal and handed a six-month prison sentence for contraband.
>
> The former sportsman, who is at present engaged in a range of industrial and commercial ventures, has no criminal record and his good conduct means the sentence has been suspended
> . . .
> Some time ago the authorities discovered in Beyaert's Barrancabermeja works two machines valued at forty thousand pesos, which were considered to have been introduced into the country illegally.

The old independent customs service and its tribunal had been dismantled and absorbed into the National Revenue and Customs Division (DIAN) in the early 1990s. I spent a few days following up the suggestions of some of the old customs men in Bucaramanga but the archives seemed to have disappeared into thin air. The local press did not mention the case and none of the loggers could give me any specific information. Olga guessed that Shell had imported the bulldozers with a customs exemption and that José may have been required to make a customs payment before using the machine. Either way it seems José had remained uncharacteristically quiet about his conviction.

Within seven months of Julliard's death Esperanza gave birth to a son they named José Luis Beyaert. José Senior was ready to start again on his new plot. 'It was pure forest,' he told me.

'I had sixty hectares with exploitation rights from INDERENA. I had the right to do what I wanted there. And after two or three years it became my property, although I never claimed it. What do I need a parcel of land there for? No one needs it.'

I wanted to go up and take a look at La Rochela but Esperanza discouraged me. 'It's a guerrilla zone now. You can't go in. The ELN has it.'

Cecilia Amador and José stayed in the timber business but worked apart. Gil Roberto Garzón worked with Cecilia for two more years. 'Then we sold the machines and I started driving buses and trucks.'

José had been ruined for the third time in his life and the strain came out in more stories of deceit. José had bought machinery for a French businessman, 'to help [him] work at the same level as me. It wasn't a robbery,' he told me. 'It was a swindle. I'd given him the money to pay Shell and he bought a building with it.' It sounded like a fictionalised version of Julliard, or of Julliard conflated with someone else. The building may have been Julliard's townhouse in Barrancabermeja: 'I'd given him the money to pay Shell and he'd bought a beautiful building instead.'

By chance José came across a letter demanding payment and confronted the man he had been trying to help. 'If I hadn't found the letter the thing would still be being paid for there. He was spending more than he was earning and he was swindling me.'

I asked if he recovered the money.

'No: his wife had the house in her name. He'd pawned a truck we'd bought in his own name without saying anything to me.'

This partner, whoever he was, was involved in an accident and died.

'I realised the truck was mortgaged because they came to claim the truck and he had legal papers that I knew nothing about. Another swindle.'

José took on new workers. One was a bulldozer driver known as 'Cochise' or 'Cantagallo' ('Cockcrow'). I had heard the old loggers met opposite a petrol station to play cards and reminisce. Each group I asked pointed me towards another group along the road. Eventually I was told to look in one of the houses opposite the square with the statue of the Indian Cacique. I went from house to house, asking for Cochise or Cantagallo, the bulldozer driver. Eventually I found his son. Cochise was in the forest working for Ecopetrol. There was no way of contacting him. He had been due back days before. He could arrive any day. I left my mobile number.

I was fast asleep when he called, close to midnight. He had just arrived home and found my message. He was leaving at 4.30 a.m. for another job. Could I come now? Dark-skinned but with remarkable eyes, light blue, backlit, penetrating, he had little time but he was keen to talk about José. Thirty years on Gabriel Chávez Veleño was still under the old man's spell.

He had met José a decade before he started working for him. It was 1966 and José was in Bucaramanga to give coaching tips to young cyclists. Gabriel Chávez Veleño was one of them. He was seventeen, he told me. 'I'd won a race that finished outside the Hotel Bristol. I was famous! José told us he was the Olympic champion. He told us his story.'

But cycling did not pay the bills and Cochise became a bulldozer operator with Jorge Álvarez, the man who administered Julliard's money. Humberto Vallecilla maintained Álvarez's machinery and it was Vallecilla who brought José Beyaert back into Cochise's life.

To gain access to the land José and his workers had to open the first road through the trees. Vallecilla told him Cochise could help them. Cochise agreed. 'But,' he said, 'you'll have to find work for my family.' Soon Cochise's parents and brother were all working for José.

Cochise's mother, Dulce María, had the same dark skin and watery blue eyes. 'My father wasn't from here; my father was Spanish. I was born by the Magdalena, at El Banco. I moved to Tamarameque and married. They called my husband "Meque". He died, so they call me Meque now.'

Dulce María's husband operated the winch, dragging the logs up the steep incline to where they could be cut and loaded. Humberto told me, 'The slope was very steep. The only way of getting back up was to pull yourself up using the branches. The winch was used to get the wood out. It was work for men.'

There was an Alfredo, whose wife Alicia cooked and washed for the workers and whose two sons were also employed there.

José's road, forced through the woodland by Cochise, allowed settlers into virgin territory. Dulce María told me, 'They built a settlement the other side of José's land, that they called La Punta, and another group of houses this side, thanks to the road Cochise built. Buses began to use it.'

'José was the founder of a village?' I asked.

'Yes.'

Dulce María cooked for her family and for the soldiers who lived in a nearby barracks. She remembered, 'They had a liquid that scared off the snakes, they used to spray it around. There were big, many-coloured tarantulas, blue and other colours. Pretty, hairy things. José sent a big chest full of them off to France.'

'Butterflies too?'

'Butterflies too.'

José had his eyes open for other opportunities too. He convinced Dulce María that he had found emeralds in the rivers.

'He gave me five tiny stones. There's a river up there, the other side of La Colorada, and there's a lake where you can swim and that's where he said he found them. He said, "Look what I've found," pleased as punch. "Some stones." He said they were good ones. He gave them to me and told me not to throw them away. I took them and I didn't even mention it to Gabriel. The people who lived beside the lake weren't rich because they didn't know about the emeralds.'

Up in one of the villages near La Rochela I met Fanny Tolosa, who had worked as a cook, providing the oil and timber workers with meals during the working day. Fanny had more stories of José's eye for hidden riches.

'Below La Punta there's a stream that runs down the hillside. The oil men sank a well there and said they found emeralds. I used to break the *panela* and crush the bananas by the stream. One day I found a heavy rock there. It was jet black and round. I wanted to open it with a machete but José said he'd buy it from me. I gave it to him. I think it ended up in a museum.'

Fanny remembers José as a straightforward, kind-hearted man.

'He sometimes saw I was working hard and helped me cook and serve. He said we were all equal. Once a winch-axle broke and blocked the road and we arrived late. When we finally reached the refectory José had made the meal. Everyone ate the same food. There was no favouritism.'

Logging appealed to José's sense of adventure. He told Dulce María he wanted to make a film about it. 'He said, "When I leave here I'm going to make a film about this place and all of you will be in it."'

José enjoyed teaching his workers new tasks and his workers respected him for it. I met Humberto Uribe, one of José's drivers, standing beside the same 1946 Ford F6 truck he used to collect the timber at kilometer 23, Yarima. 'They were taking out sapan, a hard wood, and guayacan. José was a hard worker. No one could follow him when he walked in the forest. And he was paying off his debts with sweat.'

José loved playing with his children too. There are photographs of them playing at La Rochela, and of Mayerly caressing her father at Barrancabermeja airport before one of his departures. Flor considered him a good father and husband: 'For two years he cooked, made

French bread, changed nappies and looked after Esperanza and his children.'

But not everyone was so charmed by him. According to Esperanza, 'José became increasingly jealous. He wouldn't let me go out, I had to use a long dress, no make-up, and if I went out, I went out with him and I couldn't say hello to anyone. And I was well known in Barranca.

'One day I ran away and went dancing in the Club Miramar. José stormed past the doormen looking for me. My friends sneaked me out and home. When José got back, he said, "Where have you been?" I said, "I was dancing until you came in, creating a scandal." We argued.'

Flor told me, 'When they went out people believed he was her father and called him *suegro* (meaning 'father-in-law').'

Humberto and Flor mostly saw things from José's point of view, although on one point they agreed with their daughter.

'José was very hard on Mayerly when she was small,' Flor told me. 'She must have been eighteen months old and he was going to smack her with his hat, which was full of stitches. He made her kneel down in the laundry. I said, "How can it occur to a man your age to make a little girl kneel down? It's no way to punish a child." I told him, "Just so I don't have to see how you treat her, get yourself a house and go and live there." He was shouting at her, "Kneel down, kneel down." Humberto didn't like it either.'

In the end Esperanza threw him out. José left the Vallecillas and took a room at El Cruce with a widow, but he was in a kind of madness over Esperanza.

'He always knew where I was and he kept watch to see who I was going out with and at what time. I'd take a taxi to the hairdresser's and José would be across the street, parked up for hours.'

He visited Flor and Humberto from time to time. Flor received him well. However, as José's relationship with Esperanza ended, the woodland around Barrancabermeja became increasingly violent. It had always been a perilous world. Flor said, 'The forest was very dangerous but [José and his men] didn't get involved. They didn't have any enemies.'

Humberto told me, 'You made sure you were courteous to everyone and you kept your mouth shut. If someone wanted a drink or a lift you gave it to them, no questions asked. We never had any problems.'

But by the late 1970s the ELN was taking over the forest and threatening the town and Barrancabermeja's timber industry began to close down. Cecilia Amador closed the sawmill she was running with Gil Garzón because of the ELN. Miguel Martínez told me, 'It was the start of the hard years.'

The coming of the guerrillas gave José Beyaert more opportunities for exuberant storytelling. He told me he was forced out of the rainforest by a guerrilla band who appeared before the sawmill one afternoon. One of José's workers went out to speak to them. The guerrilla leader put a pistol to his head and shot him dead.

Esperanza and Cecilia believed the story to be true. The workers who shared José's wilderness experiences do not recognise it. José was describing the scenario every logger feared. The fear, not the fact, was what drove them out of the rainforest and back into Barranca. José brought back what he could but left a winch and other heavy equipment in the woods.

He told Flor that the equipment he had left in the forest was hers. She should sell it and keep the proceeds for the children. But there was no way of recovering it. In 1977 José left Barrancabermeja, never to return.

In Bucaramanga I met Mayerly. She was old enough to have a few vague first-hand memories of her father.

'He wore Brut and Brillantina, he smoked Marlboros and he wore a hat that he never took off. He always kept a clean, perfect handkerchief and a comb. I used to take off his hat and comb his hair. I remember his voice, his French pronunciation. He called Esperanza "*Ma chérie*" and I didn't understand and I thought it was something to do with the sheriff in Westerns. There was a badly taken photograph of him that cut off his head. He told me he could take his head off and I believed it was true. And he used to walk on his hands.'

Mayerly's brother José Luis Beyaert has no childhood memories of his father. His physical similarity to his father is arresting. Esperanza always says, 'All he needs is his father's glasses.'

Esperanza's brother Enrique had also joined the Frenchmen's logging team. He was cursed by bad luck. First he was bitten by a rabid cat on the way to La Punta. It sank its teeth and claws into his leg and he had to have forty injections through his navel. Then the handle of a machine smashed his teeth. Flor told me, 'José was useless. He wouldn't even buy him antibiotics.' With Esperanza, too, José was becoming tightfisted. Flor again: 'He conducted his business but we didn't see any of the money. He said he gave the money to his wife when he went to Bogotá. He didn't give any to Esperanza. If she needed clothes he went with her to the boutique and paid for them, but he didn't give her money. He didn't pay rent or electricity or water here.'

Chez Louisette's tiny restaurant, with its excellent food and low prices, may not have been making money. A 1974 English-language restaurant review noted, in its excruciating faux-anglais, 'Prices ping-pong so sweetly around the sixty-peso mark, another asset.'

Chez Louisette closed temporarily in 1977 as José and Louisette relocated. The reason was a falling out with Georges Alric that also left the Beyaerts homeless. Louisette's assistant in the restaurant, Lola, sometimes took her children to work, where Louisette welcomed them. José once took her son to Barrancabermeja, with his own son. Lola's teenaged daughter Elizabeth confided to her mother she was pregnant: 'She was seven months, and I didn't know. She hadn't said anything.' The father was José's son. 'I had to find a solution because she was my youngest daughter. Louisette asked how I knew it was him. She said I kept my daughter more in the street than at home. She said I was blaming him to get money out of them. There was an argument between Alric and them because of Elizabeth's pregnancy. Georges Alric told him to recognise the child, not to leave me like that, but he refused. When the child was born, I left. But it was because of the pregnancy and the argument that followed that José and Louisette left.'

José may have been nursing a broken heart but he was quite able to keep things to himself. José's emerald suppliers shared his secrets. Guillermo Robayo told me, 'I knew he had children there.' But he kept his Barrancabermeja family secret so tightly that when I mentioned it to Lola she was deeply shocked. She assured me Louisette can have had no idea of the extent of José's double life.

In all our conversations José never mentioned Esperanza or his two children in Barrancabermeja. The only mention of another woman was a pretty girl named Blanca he had met in Barranquilla in the 1950s. I wondered. By now I was convinced José had not murdered Sanguignan, in spite of what he had told me, but had confessed to that crime as a way of expiating another killing that he never mentioned. I wondered if his confession about Blanca bore the same relation to his infidelities in Barrancabermeja.

Robayo went on, 'Almost everything he got involved in made a loss. He was built that way: an adventurer, a risk-taker.'

Even so, Louisette had always kept her husband's finances within the limits of reasonable recklessness. But now there was no sawmill, no restaurant and no home.

15

Salvation came in the unlikely form of an escaped convict who had made his way to Bogotá and wandered into Chez Louisette sometime in 1975.

By the time he walked into the Beyaerts' restaurant Charles Laurent Baptiste Fiocconi, or 'Charlot', was a celebrity. Born in 1941 at Perpignan in south-west France, Charlot Fiocconi travelled young to Corsica and grew up in the tiny hillside village of Pietralba. His uncle Jean-Thomas Giudicelli, known as 'U Caputu' – the boss – was a player in the criminal underworld and on Giudicelli's death in 1960 Fiocconi is said to have inherited his network of bars. As a thirteen year old he was arrested – robbing food to feed his starving family, he claims – and sent to Belle-Île, the island reformatory that had held Auguste le Breton. Released at eighteen, Charlot made for Paris and found work waiting in a Pigalle restaurant, again unknowingly following in le Breton's steps. There he moved in with a prostitute named Colette, living on the money she earned on the street, and entered the Paris underworld.

An unlikely encounter in the bar of a Paris hotel introduced him to the heroin trade. The visitor was an Italian-American with a contract to take home six kilograms of heroin. Through his reform school contacts in Marseille Fiocconi found the goods. He later told the Colombian newspaper *El Tiempo*, 'I'll never forget the feeling when I got back to my flat and laid the twenty-four thousand dollars I'd just earned on the floor like carpet.' He was eighteen and he had discovered the activity that would both make him his fortune and cost him many years of freedom. The early shipments were taped to their couriers' bodies, six or seven kilograms at a time, two or three times a month. Then there were false-bottomed cases carrying twenty-kilo cargos and finally luxury cars, their innermost recesses packed with seventy or eighty kilograms, inspired by reports of the French nightclub host and TV presenter Jacques Angelvin, who had been arrested in January 1962 after bringing 51.1 kilograms of heroin into Canada and across the border to New York, concealed in the bodywork of a tan 1960 Buick Invicta.

Receiving these shipments in New York was a sidekick of Fiocconi's named Jean-Claude Kella. He would be instrumental in the chain of events that led to the encounter between Fiocconi and José. Kella thought of crime as primarily political. As an adolescent he had joined the Communist Party and in *L'Affranchi*, the book he wrote as an adult, he rails against white-collar crime while defending proper proletarian armed robbery of the type that had brought him, by the time he was twenty, tailored suits, silk socks, Italian shoes, a brasserie in his native Toulon and two medium-sized brothels in Florence.

Shortly after Kella's release on a technicality from detention at the Paris prison La Santé, where he had been awaiting trial for the armed robbery of the offices of the Gaumont Film Company, he met Fiocconi. 'Charlot was waiting for me with a number of guys. I shook hands at each presentation. The atmosphere was heavy. I was in foreign territory with people who were doing nothing to hide their hostility towards me.'

Fiocconi had summoned him after a complaint from an associate, now in jail, involving Kella and the jailbird's girlfriend. Kella defended himself robustly all the same.

'Charlot,' he wrote, 'liked my frankness and my audacity.' The two men became firm friends and, as Kella's trial approached, they skipped the border to commit 'some nice, quiet hold-ups' in Spain and enjoy the company of an entire community of expat fugitives.

One of their cross-border encounters was with a certain Felix, whose uncle, Auguste Joseph Ricord, had helped lay the very foundations of the post-war heroin trade. After the Liberation Ricord had been condemned to death *in absentia* for his membership of the notorious

Bonny–Lafont gang, otherwise known as the French Gestapo. Henri Lafont had been a petty criminal before the war. In 1941 he had taken German nationality and joined the Gestapo. With a former policeman called Bonny and a vicious goon squad he founded one of the most hated gangs in Paris, informing to the Gestapo and growing rich on racketeering. At the trial of the gang's twelve principal members after the war the charge list took three hours to read. Ricord had made away, taking with him, according to some, the gang's remaining loot, estimated at over a million dollars.

Ricord invested in Marseille's first heroin laboratories, which supplied Lucky Luciano and his Mafia allies, then headed for South America, taking refuge in Uruguay and Venezuela before settling in Paraguay. He disguised his criminal activities behind a series of false identities and a restaurant chain he named Paris-Niza, like the bicycle race. Thanks to his efforts France led the world in drug trafficking. In the 1960s and early 1970s it was estimated that 80 per cent of the heroin consumed in the United States arrived in Marseille as morphine base to be processed in laboratories in and around the city before crossing the Atlantic. According to Richard Berdin, Fiocconi's former control man in New York who was later turned by US customs and became the star witness against him, anyone attempting to leave the US with large sums in cash was suspected of drug dealing. 'If you were French as well, the equation was automatic.'

This identification was reinforced by the publication in 1969 of Robin Moore's brilliant *The French Connection*, describing the NYPD investigation that dismantled the smuggling ring that surrounded Jacques Angelvin, the TV host. In 1971, when the book became a film that won five Oscars, the 'French Connection' label was extended to cover every France-based criminal organisation smuggling to the United States, from Ricord's post-war activities to Fiocconi and Kella, who controlled much of the French heroin trade by the end of the 1960s.

Richard Berdin's 1974 book *Code Name Richard*, the cover blurb of which styles him 'the man whose testimony broke the French Connection', describes the moment he first heard talk of 'Charlie' Fiocconi:

I was curious to meet the man who, still no more than twenty-seven or twenty-eight, had managed to seize control of a good portion of the French end of the drug trade . . . Of medium height, his light brown hair already thinning despite his age, Charlie was dressed sportily but not loudly in a brown turtle-neck sweater, beige slacks and an obviously expensive sports coat. He could just as easily have passed for a junior executive in some business or a bank manager's assistant.

Berdin bought his way into the organisation by bringing a potential driver, a distinguished-looking businessman named André Labay, a financier, mercenary, spy and smuggler who had made and lost any number of ill-gotten fortunes since the war, thanks to a bewildering assortment of bad jobs and good contacts which had sunk him deeper and deeper into the criminal underworld. Labay had worked for a US import–export company in Morocco, founded an air-taxi firm in Dakar, laundered money in the Tunisian property market and fought as a mercenary in the Congo, where he later headed the government information service. At one stage he planned to collect blood in Africa and sell it to US hospitals. He was said to have provided the intelligence services with information on French-colonial extremists in Algeria, although the branch he worked for, the SDECE, was notoriously pro-OAS and anti-FLN. Labay is also said to have hosted the former chief of the FLN commandos Yacef Saadi in Paris at a time when Saadi was officially barred from entering mainland France.

By the mid-1960s Labay had shifted operations from Africa to the Caribbean, smuggling goods between the free ports and becoming the lover of Papa Doc Duvalier's daughter Marie-Denise. He was station chief for French intelligence at Port-au-Prince while buying and selling Caribbean islands and providing a front for drug-smuggling. A report for the US Department of Commerce on Mafia bank accounts in Switzerland mentioned his name. A showman as well as a criminal, he provided seven hundred thousand francs to finance Jean-Pierre Melville's 1966 heist film *Le deuxième souffle*.

While Labay minded a drug-crammed Bentley on its transatlantic journey Berdin took a circuitous route to New York to meet him.

There he encountered Kella, who had been living under false identities for more than a year.

Kella and Berdin took an instant dislike to each other. Berdin put it down to the fact that he was the only Parisian in a network of Corsicans and Marseillais. Kella suggests, with too much hindsight, that he always sensed Berdin would betray him. Their enmity was only exacerbated when the Bentley was unpacked and two kilograms of heroin were missing.

Berdin later confessed to operating as Fiocconi's control man. He met Labay after each voyage to New York and in the course of three operations involving the Bentley, a Lancia and a Mercedes he recovered 179 kilograms of heroin. Fiocconi's client – the Italian-American in that hotel bar in Paris? – was Louie Cirillo, the principal buyer for the New York Mafia. US customs estimated that during 1970 and 1971 Cirillo had paid out over twelve million dollars in cash for heroin. Cirillo was arrested in Miami on 12 October 1971. He said they had the wrong man: he was a baker with the Midtown Bagel Bakery in Manhattan on two hundred dollars a week. He stuck to his story even after five million dollars' cash was found in hermetically sealed boxes in the garden of his home in Queens.

US Customs had been aware of Fiocconi and Kella as early as November 1969, when one of their couriers had been stopped in Boston. In August 1970 Interpol traced them to the Tuscan coast. A massive operation by police helicopters and launches ended in their arrest, which was filmed by invited television crews. A month later the United States Embassy in Rome requested their extradition. Despite the assistance of some of Italy's best and most expensive lawyers, including Giovanni Leone, who would be appointed president of Italy within a year and a half, Fiocconi and Kella were flown to the United States in October 1971. Cameras filmed them leaving Rome's Fiumicino airport, arriving at Boston's Logan and shuttling between the Charles Street Jail and the courtroom. The half-million-dollar certified cheque drawn on a Swiss bank with which they posted bail made the papers. So did their re-arrest moments after being released, in a bar opposite the court, where they were on the point of tasting their first cold beer in two years.

From Boston they were removed to Brooklyn. There before the District Court for the Southern District of New York they were charged with receiving, concealing, and selling thirty-seven kilograms of heroin in the Southern District of New York. Bail was fixed at a hundred thousand dollars each. This time they couldn't post it.

In America as in Italy Fiocconi engaged the best lawyers money could buy. Raymond B. Grunewald, formerly one of the most feared district attorneys in New York State, led the team. In the evolving charge sheet Grunewald detected a breach of the extradition ruling. The court in Florence, Italy, had surrendered the two men to US justice 'so that they can be subjected to judgment according to the writ of indictment against them formulated by the Grand Jury of the District Court of Appeals of Massachusetts [*sic*] dated 20 November 1969, and according to the consequent order for arrest on the same date'. Grunewald filed for his clients' release on the grounds that they were being detained on charges other than those for which they had been extradited. While his petition was being considered a second indictment replaced the first, accusing Fiocconi, Kella and twenty-one others of importing thirty-seven kilograms of heroin on 27 May 1970 and selling them two days later, with a further count of conspiracy to import and sell illegal substances between January 1970 and January 1972.

Grunewald filed another petition for release. It was turned down and the trial was underway before there was time for the appeals court to publish its reasoning.

Grunewald's next ruse was to claim that Berdin had never met Fiocconi or Kella and that the US Marshals had had to engineer a close encounter between them in the corridor outside the courtroom to allow him to recognise them. As Grunewald made the point Fiocconi broke into a broad grin as if the whole trial had just been blown open, although the jury wasn't fooled.

After Berdin's set-piece testimony the highlight of the seven-day hearing was the appearance of a Hollywood cop who had been called to a movie set where Labay's old Bentley, which had been sold on after the smuggling operation, was being used as a prop. A firearms specialist had supervised a scene in which the car was riddled with bullets. When technicians removed the two front seats, which had been damaged in the shooting, they found four plastic packets containing white powder. The two missing kilograms had been found. The car's history was traced back to France and Fiocconi and Kella were found guilty as charged. They were each sentenced to twenty years' imprisonment for conspiracy and five years for each of the offences committed at the end of May 1970, the two five-year terms to run concurrently with each other but consecutively to the twenty years.

The Appeals Court then published its response to Grunewald's petitions for release: it agreed that the receiving country should not try an extradited person for an offence for which the surrendering country would not have granted extradition. However, considering whether the surrendering state would regard the prosecution at issue as a breach, the court concluded 'we do not believe that the [Italian] Government would regard the prosecution of Fiocconi and Kella for subsequent offenses of the same character as the crime for which they were extradited as a breach of faith by the United States', especially 'in the absence of any affirmative protest from Italy'. It was a landmark ruling, regularly cited in decisions involving extradition, although for Fiocconi and Kella, at twenty-five years apiece, making legal history came at a price.

They were then flown back to Boston to face further conspiracy charges that earned them two concurrent nineteen-year terms each. In April 1972 at Atlanta Federal Penitentiary the gates closed behind them. With no prospect of their opening again for a decade or more the two friends donated their Italian suits to a charity for newly released prisoners. They'd be out of fashion by the time they next saw the streets.

Late in 1972 Fiocconi and Kella's names came up again. Marcel Boucan, the captain of a sixty-ton fishing boat called *Caprice des Temps* out of Pointe-à-Pitre, Guadeloupe, had already made two successful crossings from Marseille to Miami. He was starting his third when French customs officers intercepted him, escorted him back to port and took his boat apart. Hidden in the rebuilt keel they found the biggest heroin cache yet seized in France: 425 kilograms.

During his interrogation in Marseille he named his suppliers as Fiocconi and Kella.

The magistrate in charge of the investigation made a request to the United States. Fiocconi and Kella were brought to the West Street Jail in New York to be interviewed, despite the fact that they had never discussed their activities with the police or taken the stand in either of their own trials. Predictably enough they exercised the right to remain silent. It was, it turned out, inconsequential: Boucan got fifteen years anyway. However, for Charlot Fiocconi, the New York transfer was providential. In West Street Kella made contact with an associate of the bagel chef Louie Cirillo who had bribed a prison guard for access to the keys to the seven doors that stood between the cells and freedom. Everything was in place. On the day of the escape the CCTV would be out of order, a driver would be waiting at the exit of the prison car park and a Mexican who was part of the escape team would get them to South America with false passports and money.

Before the plan could be put into operation, Kella was taken back to Atlanta, where he would serve out his sentence and put in for parole when the time came. Fiocconi, meanwhile, put the metalwork skills he had learnt at reform school to good use. In the fanciful version of events he later gave the Colombian newspaper *El Tiempo* he took impressions of the keys in a paste of breadcrumbs mixed with saliva, then spent six months carving replicas from cutlery he had lifted out of the prison refectory.

On 22 September 1974 he and six others walked out of jail. It could hardly have been easier. The street outside was empty. Even the guard post of the police station opposite the garage entrance was unmanned. There are several versions of Fiocconi's voyage to freedom. He told *El Tiempo* in Colombia he had boarded a US fishing vessel bound for Cartagena. Kella writes that he flew into Bogotá. When I met Fiocconi at his home in Pietralba, Corsica, he told me another story. He had boarded a light aircraft and headed for Mexico. Mid-flight, for reasons Fiocconi couldn't satisfactorily explain, there was a change of plan. The pilot changed bearings and turned the plane towards Cartagena.

* * *

José would have liked Corsica: brush and peaks, difficult access, a few empty roads in-between. Smuggling and rebellion, and more than a hint of danger: the National Liberation Front of Corsica and other Corsican terrorist groups were responsible for ten thousand terrorist attacks between the mid-1970s and 2000. There had once been a Tour of Corsica, although José never rode it.

Pietralba is a small white brush-stroke on a hillside where the walls are made of stone and the doors and windows stand open despite the autumn chill. In an excited confusion of Spanish, French and Corsican dialect, Charlot Fiocconi was telling me about his wrongful arrest on 20 January 2004 following the discovery of 323 kilograms of Colombian cocaine in a Nice warehouse. Set up by vengeful police he spent twenty-five months in jail before his innocence was accepted. He laughed his way through the tale and then we went out for lunch.

Like José, the Corsican enjoys a striking emotional resilience. Remembering Fiumicino on the day of their extradition, Kella wrote, 'At the Police office I found Charlot guffawing with a group of armed carabinieri.' He described Charlot joking with US Marshals and enjoying a sunny relationship with his lawyers. Fiocconi's mood was impervious to the collapse of his criminal universe and his approaching long-term imprisonment. The old *L'Équipe* descriptions of José ('gaiety personified', 'permanently joyful', 'remarkably well-balanced') described Fiocconi perfectly, although the stun gun he was wearing on his belt served as a reminder he had enemies as well as friends.

Fiocconi arrived in Colombia carrying a false passport, reportedly in the name of Victor Engwall. According to Fiocconi the true Victor Engwall was a multimillionaire coffee importer who died in 1972 in Europe, leaving no heir. In the account Fiocconi gave *El Tiempo* a French conman had adopted Engwall's identity to perpetrate a massive fraud:

> At the time of his death, Engwall was owed forty-five million pesos by the Colombian Coffee Federation. The conman used a passport in Engwall's name and attempted to extort this money but he was foiled by an attentive employee. When the

extortion failed, the conman dumped his passport, which fell into the hands of the people who sold it to me when I escaped from prison in New York. This was five years after the extortion attempt, which took place when I was in prison.

In fact Victor Theodore Engwall was a Swedish coffee entrepreneur who founded a coffee company in 1853. In 1920 his grandson Sven Engwall created the coffee brand Gevalia. Sven's son Jacob Engwall, the head of the coffee company from 1963 to 1972, sold it to Kraft Foods in 1971. Jacob Engwall died in 1986. The passport was perhaps in the name of Jacob Engwall and the extortion may have centred on the Engwall family's recent sale of Gevalia. But Charlot was exaggerating: five years hadn't passed. Two, perhaps less.

On 10 July 1975 a warrant for Fiocconi's arrest was issued. Soon afterwards he was detained at Bogotá's Modelo prison. On 13 September Interpol cabled a summary of Fiocconi's criminal record to Bogotá. Three days later a charge list was drawn up for attempted extortion and possession of false documents. And then he was gone. On the evening of 22 October 1975, while everyone was watching Colombia play Peru in the Copa América, Fiocconi climbed a wall. He told *El Tiempo*, 'I've always preferred tennis.'

Fiocconi was not the only Corsican in Bogotá. His cousins Dominique Giudicelli, the son of 'U Caputu', Jean-Thomas Giudicelli, whose bars Fiocconi had inherited, and Tony Mathieu were also in town, perhaps looking after Fiocconi's business interests. Giudicelli and Mathieu had eaten at Bogotá's premier French restaurant and encountered José. Soon after his escape Fiocconi, whom Giudicelli and Mathieu called 'Napoleon', walked into Louisette's restaurant. He had heard about José and he'd come with his men to see for himself. They ate and drank before falling into a game of dice with José. Liar's poker. According to a single source – not Fiocconi, who was tight-lipped about details – one of the Corsicans was cheating. José wasn't fooled. He watched for a while then made his move.

'I think it might be best if you left. You don't need to pay for your meal.'

Fiocconi and José talked privately. Fiocconi liked José's robust style. It was reminiscent of Fiocconi's first encounter with Kella.

Fiocconi told *El Tiempo* he had gone into hiding, although hiding didn't keep him from regular appearances at Chez Louisette. 'I asked Louisette for couscous,' he told me. 'She had it imported. Delicious!' He frequently dined beside diplomats from the French Embassy. They didn't speak to him but they knew who he was. They also knew he was on the run.

Fiocconi and José may have had more in common than a taste for Louisette's cooking. I had a well-positioned source who said so and much more. An event that meant nothing to her at the time and as little when I interviewed her at her Bogotá home in December 2008, lodged in the memory of his lover Esperanza Vallecilla. Someone had come looking for José. He had made the journey from Bogotá and found his way to the Vallecillas in Barrancabermeja. The visit had a date too. Esperanza and José's son José Luis, born in July 1975, was a babe in arms, months old, no more, placing the visit late that year. It was the only time anything of the sort ever happened.

'I told him, "He should be here at six. If you want to wait, feel free." When José saw him, when he arrived, I said, "Heck, what if Louisette sent him?" I said to him, "Don José, a man is waiting for you," like that.

'The gentleman came to Barranca and spoke to him in his language, and José was saying, "No, no, I can't at the moment," and pointing at me and the two children. The man's name was Tony.'

The only Tony I could find at this period of Beyaert's life was Fiocconi's cousin Tony Mathieu. If it was the same man, this much is clear. Late in 1975 Fiocconi had some sort of a proposition for José. Something important enough to justify Mathieu's trip to Barrancabermeja. Something José was unwilling or unable to do. Something he uncharacteristically used Esperanza and the children to get out of. Was it possible that two years later, at a time when José desperately needed money, the proposition had resurfaced, and that this time, in these circumstances, it offered José a lifeline?

José's passport suggests as much. The entry and exit stamps promise more than they reveal, and the absence of a number of stamps make it impossible to reconstruct the precise itineraries, but there were repeated comings and goings between Venezuela, Peru and France from September 1977 to September the following year. These journeys never quite cohere and in following them I was frequently disorientated in a maze of trajectories.

However, before José's relationships with the Corsicans could become professional another valediction had to be made. As José turned his back on Esperanza and their children in Barrancabermeja he also jettisoned a friendship.

The subject came up in France in November 2004 when José was telling me about Frenchmen on the run in Colombia.

'There were lots of them. I had many friends who were in that situation.'

He turned and reached for something: a Manila envelope, from which he pulled a ream of handwritten pages, pinched in one corner by a rusty staple.

'I have here . . .' he said, and then repeated the words, with punctilious humour: 'I HAVE HERE . . . ! What's it called?'

'A manuscript.'

'A MANUSCRIPT! Written by one of them. You've heard of the book *Papillon*?'

'Yes. Henri Charrière.'

'Henri Charrière. The story of Papillon, I have the manuscript of *Papillon* – the original Papillon, the real Papillon. Because Charrière was Maturette. The queer of the group but the most intelligent. He took advantage of this by passing himself off as Papillon because he thought Papillon was dead or dying. Because Charrière had a hotel in Maracaibo. I knew him.'

'You knew him?'

'I knew him. I keep telling you, I met people! So my friend the writer Auguste le Breton was at my place, talking to Papillon . . . Émile was his name. The book *Papillon* had already been published and Émile was telling him, "He stole my story and told it as best he could but I've got the true story here, in my words."

'Le Breton put him down. "It's already out there. Publishing something similar just wouldn't be worth it."

'So Émile said, "Never mind."

'Sometime later, Émile died. On his next visit le Breton asked me, "Do you know what he did with the manuscript?"

'"I have it."

'"I thought so. Give it to me."

'And I said, "No. You didn't want to do it when he was alive. You're not going to do it now he's dead, full stop."'

I wanted, of course, to see the manuscript. I thought there would be plenty of opportunities. I was wrong.

According to José the episode poisoned his opinion of le Breton. 'He was a strange man. A layabout, really, although he had a special intelligence when it came to writing. He had a superiority complex. The money had gone to his head. I said, "You're not the man I thought you were. Do me a favour and don't come back."'

More than that, José said, 'We, a certain group of us, eliminated him from our circle.'

Henri Charrière's memoir *Papillon* was the publishing sensation of 1969, although it was immediately greeted with scepticism from historians and former inmates of the penal colonies in French Guiana, who said there had been a prisoner called Papillon but he was not Henri Charrière. Investigation threw up a rabble of Papillons: one with the word tattooed across his chest, another from Alsace who laboured on the railway lines between the camps, another afflicted with leprosy who earned his living by catching the same blue butterflies Charles Hut described and who hanged himself in 1959, and a Georges Papillon who escaped to Trinidad in November 1922.

Many of Charrière's supposedly first-hand experiences did not add up. The solitary confinement Charrière describes was an anachronism. In 1926, following Albert Londres's reports for *Le Petit Parisien*, the penal colonies had been reformed. The ball and chain – that cartoon artist's favourite – had been outlawed, diet and medical inspections humanised and solitary-confinement prisoners were allowed out of their cells for an hour every morning. After three months they were required to work in groups, observing the strictest silence, outside the solitary confinement quarters and sometimes even outside the prison itself. Charrière had arrived at the penal colony in 1933 but he describes the old, pre-1926 regime.

He ransacked the oral and written stock of escape stories and claimed them as his own. One of his most shocking anecdotes was the subject of such a claim by Charles Hut, the former cyclist. Six escapees are washed ashore in Dutch Guiana. They split up into pairs and set off into the virgin forest. For two weeks they eat nothing but a few roots and young plants. After thirteen days four of the six meet. They are close to starvation. Then the fifth member of the group arrives. He claims his companion, weak and unable to walk, told him to go on without him. But the new arrival is wearing the other man's shoes. The truth emerges: he has killed the sixth member of the group and eaten his flesh. Among his things they find more pieces of human flesh. They light a fire, cook the remaining meat and dine on the dead man's flesh. Then, recognising the hopelessness of their situation, they hand themselves in to face charges for escape aggravated by anthropophagy.

Charrière says a safe-breaker called Marius de La Ciotat told him the story. Charles Hut said Charrière had adapted the tale from the more extensive treatment given in chapter eleven of his own memoir.

The French media took up the story and began to investigate. There were interviews with the author in *Le Nouvel Observateur* and *L'Express*. *Paris-Match* invested heavily in the story, taking Henri Charrière back to the Salvation Isles, Trinidad, Venezuela and Colombia with a couple of reporters. Another *Paris-Match* contributor, Georges Ménager, gained access to the police files and wrote a book, *Les quatres vérités de Papillon* ('Home truths about Papillon'), asserting that Charrière had been rightly convicted of murder and that his claim that he had been framed was unfounded.

Yet another writer with a *Paris-Match* connection, a photojournalist named Gérard de Villiers, went to such lengths to debunk Charrière that his book *Papillon épinglé* ('Papillon punctured') played much the same macho game as Henri Charrière. 'I covered about thirty thousand kilometers in aircraft, cars, ships and canoes ... I journeyed up the Maroni River in a canoe, all day and all night, as Papillon claims to have done in his book.'

De Villiers drew the line at re-enacting the most famous of Charrière's escapes, from Devil's Island across shark-infested seas on a raft made of two sacks full of coconuts. It is the final scene of the Hollywood film. As he disappears into the distance, Steve McQueen, playing the death-defying Papillon, bellows 'I'm still here!'

De Villiers says the escape could not have taken place. Charrière was never sent to Devil's Island, and anyway it would have been impossible to cross the shark-infested waters on a bag of coconuts.

In reality Charrière had stolen the tale of a detainee known only as 'S', who worked as a nurse among mentally ill prisoners at Saint-Joseph, one of the Salvation Isles. 'S' built a raft using a wardrobe door, the boards from his bed and two sacks of coconuts. He floated for fifteen hours before the current washed him up on the mainland and he was arrested by waiting gendarmes. Or, going further back, Charrière may have known of one of the earliest escapes in the 1880s by one Bouyer Blaizy, who escaped from the Salvation Isles on jute sacks filled with coconuts.

Auguste le Breton was another sometime *Paris-Match* contributor. His 1972 book *Les bourlingueurs* belongs to the post-*Papillon* wave of books that seek both to debunk *Papillon* and imitate it. In it, Georges Alric talks extensively about a penal colony escapee named Émile Renard.

According to Georges Alric, Émile escaped more than ten times from the penal colony. On one of his escapes he reached a Venezuelan village where he found work in a small shop. There, for the first time in a life spent mostly behind bars, he fell in love. The object of his desire was the cashier, who reciprocated. Her father agreed that they could marry. Émile of course had no papers and, as an escaped convict, no prospect of getting any. One day he left the village, telling his love he was going to Caracas to legalise his situation. He told Alric, 'I knew I'd never see her again.'

Another of Émile's stories took place in a Venezuelan prison in the 1930s. His cellmate was a Venezuelan general imprisoned for political reasons and Émile, still young and tremendously strong, carried the general's ball and chain – another anachronism, here? – allowing him to move more freely. When the government fell the general was released. But he did not forget Émile.

Some time later France's Algerian-born war hero Marshal Franchet d'Esperey paid an official visit to Venezuela. On learning that there were French citizens detained in the country's prisons, he arranged to meet them. D'Esperey appeared before Émile with his chaperone, Émile's former cellmate. There and then Émile was pardoned and granted a wish. He asked for a small boat to continue the journey he had begun in Cayenne.

Alric tells le Breton, 'It's a shame you couldn't speak to Émile about Papillon. He'd have told you the truth. Émile was famous over there. The king of the escape.' 'Émile,' he goes on, 'died three years ago of cancer.' The author is vague about dates: he tells us that when he flew into Bogotá in January 1969 Georges Alric met him at the airport, and he closes the book with the inscription: 'St Paul les Dax 1970–1. South America'. These dates place Émile's death between January 1966 and the end of 1968.

José did not meet Auguste le Breton until January 1969, therefore the conversation he reports could not have taken place. Or, rather, it could not have taken place if it had involved José. But José may have done to Alric what Émile accuses Henri Charrière of doing to him: he reported an event that took place in Alric's life, that is, the falling out with le Breton, as if José had been the protagonist. It seems likely. There was, once, a manuscript. Alric mentions it to le Breton in *Les bourlingueurs*: 'Émile Renard, whose manuscript I arranged for you to get from our mutual friend Didi, and which you haven't been able to publish.'

Didi was José's old *soigneur*.

After José's death his son and I searched his papers for the manuscript. We found a document that turned out to be a Spanish translation of one of le Breton's novels but nothing by Émile Renard. What, then, were the papers José had waved in front of me? I never got close enough to see. José's son said he believed his father may have burnt them.

Polarities reverse, of course. Friendships sometimes turn. But if José's account of the falling out with le Breton was fictional, what, then, is the truth?

Le Breton enjoyed Colombia for the same reason he enjoyed José's company: there was always a good story to pick up. He kept his eyes and ears open and his pen poised. If José was contemplating something illegal, if he was thinking about doing exactly the sort of thing le Breton was interested in, an author with a notebook and a sharp eye would have been a danger. I wondered whether the circle of friends who had rejected le Breton included Fiocconi.

Whatever the truth, José soon started a long series of journeys. He travelled to the Colombian border-town of Cúcuta, where on 20 September 1977 he crossed into Venezuela by land before taking an internal flight to the capital. It is plausible that he decided against an international flight from Bogotá to Caracas to conceal his movements. The border at Cúcuta was notoriously porous. To pass unchecked was, under normal circumstances, child's play. The entry stamp may have been down to bad luck. A random control, an unexpected surfeit of border guards.

The following day he flew out of the Caracas airport at Maiquetía, gaining Lima. After ten days in Peru he boarded a flight back to the Venezuelan capital. Then, for two weeks from 30 September, nothing. A return trip to Bogotá via one of the porous terrestrial borders?

On 15 November he was in Caracas again, for another flight to the Peruvian capital. The trip lasted nearly three weeks. On 3 December he flew back to Caracas. Then five more weeks of silence.

On 9 January 1978 he yet again exited Caracas airport. This time the absence of an entry stamp at the other end of the journey is easy to explain: he had landed in Paris, where, three weeks later, the French police stamped his passport on his way out of the country bound for Caracas. He arrived on 31 January. Once more the passport contains no record of José's whereabouts for a period of five weeks. Then, on 4 March, a stamp showing entry into Peru at Lima international airport. Where had he been? Where did he start his journey? No way of knowing.

Six weeks later, in mid-April, José flew out of Lima. There is no entry stamp: it is possible his destination was France, either the mainland or one of France's Caribbean possessions. Most likely he returned to Caracas and the stamp was simply forgotten. On 3 May he was at Caracas Maiquetía again, leaving, presumably, for France. He returned to Caracas on 19 August. Confusingly, a month later, there is a French police stamp in his passport dated 19 September 1978. The following day he entered Venezuela at Caracas Maiquetía.

José disapproved of drug use: he surely disapproved of the drugs trade, too, although perhaps not of the opportunities for adventure it offered. And for money. After all, since Esperanza's rejection and his departure from Barrancabermeja and the argument with Alric that had led to Chez Louisette's closure, he had had virtually no income. He had been depleting Louisette's savings and he had most probably had to borrow money from his emerald-trader colleagues. He was no doubt fed up with living like that. As he warmed to the task of covering up his consciousness of the abominable moral choice he was about to take, it may have further occurred to him that he was a family man whose wife and child had basic needs that he ought to be able to meet.

According to a single source José began to work with Fiocconi. He made snaking, difficult-to-follow trips to France via Peru and Venezuela as Fiocconi's eyes and ears. Airport security staff were bribed to allow a pretty girl with hand luggage only to pass into the departure lounge. On the plane her case would go into overhead storage. At a stopover on one of France's Caribbean islands, Martinique, even Curaçao, the girl would leave the plane and another mule would board. I was told of two black mules. At Paris the second mule would disembark with the hand luggage, which, of course, contained women's clothing that would allow the courier to deny all knowledge with some plausibility ('I've picked up the wrong case'). José simply sat on the plane and kept an eye on the merchandise. Never physically approaching the case, he made sure it didn't go astray. In Paris he would note down the registration number of the taxi taken by the mule, make the briefest of telephone calls, then head for the factory of the Lejeune brothers, with whom he had ridden in the 1940s, to buy a shipment of bicycle frames before returning to Bogotá. He was, I learnt, well rewarded for his work.

Fiocconi himself denied this out of hand. 'He may have been inspired by me. He never worked for me.' This much is true: anyone could have taken a shipment of cocaine to France or paid others to do the same. José didn't need Fiocconi to do that. But once there the problem that had to be resolved was this: they needed to find a buyer. This is where José needed Fiocconi. Fiocconi said no: it simply didn't happen. But would he have admitted it if it had? It would have run counter to everything he believed in.

And there was another rumour, another vague story, this one impossible to investigate because devoid of all concrete detail. José had taken a man into the forest. He had bound him hand and foot and suspended some sort of shelter, a tarpaulin, overhead. Then he had strangled the man, dug a pit and buried him.

For this too I had one source, a different one. He believed the victim might have been a police informer. The killing might have taken place in France.

If true it certainly wasn't a story José would have disseminated: it wasn't one of his inventions about wartime heroism or snakebites. The scarcity of sources added to its plausibility. I mentioned the story to Fiocconi. He recognised it. That made two sources, and Fiocconi could add a country: 'It was in Peru.' Fiocconi, of course, denied all involvement. But I wondered. Fiocconi had enemies and money but he lacked freedom of movement. Could José Beyaert, at his lowest ebb, have carried out a contract killing in Peru for him? Is it so unthinkable? It would presumably have solved not just his immediate difficulties but also his longer-term financial circumstances.

Fiocconi was arrested in northern Bogotá after eight months on the run. He was returned to the Modelo prison until the US Embassy asked that he be moved to the high-security La Picota prison. 'José visited me in prison,' Fiocconi told me. 'And he sometimes took food to my wife.'

In La Picota Fiocconi made friends with Humberto 'El Ganso' ('the Goose') Ariza, the old emerald bandolero from the 1960s.

The extradition proceedings continued during his confinement. Fiocconi's case was so preposterous only a lawyer or a confidence trickster could sustain it. His legal team, as usual, included the best: to whit, an ex-magistrate in Colombia's Supreme Court of Justice named Humberto Barrera Domínguez.

According to the story Fiocconi spun in Colombia his father had abandoned his mother two months before the birth of their son. Agathe remembered nothing but his name and nationality: Hernando Rojas Gooding, Colombian. That was why Fiocconi had fled to Colombia: to look for his long-lost father.

In Cartagena Fiocconi had met a girl named Ligia Helena Durango Bedoya. In August 1975 they married. They moved along the Caribbean coast to Barranquilla and opened a hotel. Meanwhile Fiocconi located Rojas Gooding in a bar in central Bogotá.

'I asked him if he'd been in France during the war and if he had had relations with a French girl . . . He was staggered. He told me that everything I'd told him was true. "Then I'm your son," I said.'

Rojas Gooding travelled to France to meet Agathe. On 9 March 1976 the Prefecture in Paris issued a document in which Rojas Gooding recognised Fiocconi as his son. Five months later the document was registered by a Bogotá notary. Charles Laurent Baptiste Fiocconi became Charles Laurent Rojas Fiocconi, the son of a Colombian, therefore Colombian himself. As such he couldn't be extradited under existing agreements.

While the courts were digesting Fiocconi's fairy story he told it to *El Tiempo*, which turned his life story into a sentimental thriller in five parts and emblazoned it on the front page every day for a week from 1 to 5 November 1977. For cooperating with justice Berdin is characterised as unprincipled, ungenerous: he was guilty of betrayal, a crime of which the honourable Fiocconi was quite incapable. In 1952 José's series of articles in *El Siglo* after the Tour of Colombia gave the nation's cyclists the considerable gift of cycling expertise from France, the sport's homeland. But there was a time when France had led the world in drug trafficking too and through *El Tiempo* Fiocconi was allowed to publish a masterclass in the logic and ethics of the Corsican–Marseillais drug trade. Colombia's drug traffickers took note.

El Tiempo published the articles under the title 'A Colombian in the French Connection', although his organisation wasn't the French Connection and Fiocconi wasn't Colombian. In fact, as he told me quite openly, his father was a Corsican from Pietralba. He had been arrested during the war, deported to Germany and never heard of again.

On 1 September 1978 the front page of *El Tiempo* included the following brief paragraph: 'Laurent Fioconi [*sic*], French criminal, whose extradition to his country of origin was authorised yesterday by the Supreme Court, is accused of being a member of one of the most notorious bands of drugs traffickers of all time.'

The revelation made up Fiocconi's mind. Early in the morning of Monday 18 September 1978 he extended an improvised bridge made of electricity cables and bed linen from the roof of the prison building to the external wall of La Picota. Then, it would appear, rather than shinning across the cable, which would have been close to physically impossible, he left it to distract investigators and walked out of prison through the main entrance, having bribed the prison staff.

Nine others went with him.

According to my source, waiting for him on the outside was José Beyaert in his car. He took Fiocconi to the restaurant, where he stayed for several weeks before skipping the capital with his wife and sons and fleeing deep into the Amazon to the village settlement of Carurú. José and Fiocconi would never meet again. But their involvement didn't end there. Fiocconi had arrived in Colombia with another document: a formula, provided by a friendly chemist, for the manufacture of cocaine. The recipe was in French. He took it to José, who translated it into Spanish. Fiocconi had his copy but, some years later, he found evidence that José had kept one for himself. At a forest settlement called Juruparí, members of the Fuerzas Armadas Revolucionarias de Colombia (FARC), or Revolutionary Armed Forces of Colombia, showed Fiocconi their cocaine recipe. He recognised it immediately as the Beyaert translation. Had José sold them the formula? There is no way of knowing.

In 1982 Fiocconi fled Colombia and moved across the border to Brazil. Six years later he was arrested and extradited to the United

States. He served twelve years at the US Federal prison in Terra Haute, Indiana, getting out in 2000. Today he lives in Pietralba with his wife and their two sons.

Auguste Ricord's end was worse. On 15 March 1971 he was indicted in the US District Court for the Southern District of New York. Over the next two months the State Department sought his provisional arrest. Ricord was extradited to the United States in September 1972 and in January 1973 he was sentenced to twenty years in prison for conspiracy to smuggle narcotics into America.

Italian president Giovanni Leone was forced out of office in June 1978 following his involvement in a bribery scandal involving the aerospace firm Lockheed, who, it was revealed, had paid twenty-two million dollars in bribes to members of friendly governments to guarantee contracts for military aircraft.

Jean-Claude Kella walked out of Atlanta Federal Penitentiary in April 1979. Soon afterwards, he told me when we met in Nice, he was contacted by Auguste le Breton. The author wanted to write his story.

One source, a passport showing a few unexplained journeys, a couple of rumours and perhaps a little over-interpretation. Not much with which to convict a man of murder. But if it was true, and the fee was paid, José might have had some financial stability for the first time in years. I thought again of Sanguignan, the Armenian José claimed to have killed in the forest above Barrancabermeja. The crime was surely imagined. If he had killed he would never have spread rumours about it unless he had become unhinged, and José was too emotionally resilient for that. But could he have committed a real murder and then invented Sanguignan's death to expiate his guilt, admitting a fictitious crime because to admit to one that was very real would have been self-destructive? There is no way of knowing. The trail goes cold before it has even begun.

16

In 1980 *Paris-Match* published a nine-page feature article about the Colombian emerald fields. The strapline missed no opportunity for overstatement:

> 'Green Fever' has Colombia in an emerald rush. For the first time, a journalist – *Paris-Match* correspondent Roger Holeindre – has been allowed to enter the mines at Muzo, the legendary 'El Dorado' that the Spanish conquistadors never found. He lived with the *'guaqueros'*, adventurers who have abandoned everything to sift through mountains of mud – the slag rejected by the mine – with a shovel, searching for *'esmeraldas'*.

Holeindre's claim to have 'lived many days among these men' as 'no other journalist before me has ever been able to' echoed Auguste le Breton's assertion more than a decade earlier. It almost certainly came from the man who guided both men, 'a son of Pantin who still speaks in the Parisian argot of the Liberation years' and who 'in 1948 at the London Olympics, was consecrated road-race champion, one of the few French medals'.

As the article opens José 'Bayert', as Beyaert is spelt throughout, is driving Holeindre through a rainstorm along treacherous, unmetalled mountain roads. The concentration required to keep the car from sliding off the track and into the two-thousand-foot ravine that flanks it silences the normally verbose José. Even so, at one moment he loses control and the wing slams violently into the rock face opposite the fall. A truck careers past, missing them by a hair's breadth. The rain has washed away a bridge. Local kids charge them to slip the end of a rubber tube over the exhaust pipe. A boy wades beside the car holding the tube aloft to let the fumes escape. Another guides them along the ford to the exit point.

In Muzo Holeindre meets the police chief. There have been until recently six murders a day. The murder rate means that the police chief is also the mayor and, when news of a killing reaches town, he invites Holeindre to attend the scene. On the way the policeman indicates 'a colossus, defiantly wearing a huge straw hat . . . a true killer suspected, but only suspected, of having killed thirteen men these past years'. He is, Holeindre comments, 'an accurate caricature of the "baddies" in the spaghetti westerns'. He has, it seems, struck again: a young man, black with mud and grime, his skull shattered by a slug from a Colt .45, is lying in the gutter. The police ask for witnesses: 'No one knows anything, no one saw anything, no one heard anything.'

The rest of the piece is devoted to the emerald mines. An old man with one arm ('the outcome of a machete fight over an emerald the size of a walnut') tells him about stones, dates and places in the same salacious tones in which other men speak of women. Muzo is a place of tales and legends that attract dreamers and romantics from all over Colombia. This José well knew, for he was one of them.

Holeindre's version of the mines, like le Breton's, was clearly heavily filtered through José Beyaert. Holeindre's erroneous transcriptions from the Spanish show he could not have conducted interviews in the language. But insight into other cultures was not at the heart of his life's project. Corsican by birth, Roger Holeindre had fought in Indochina and Algeria before founding the Front for French Algeria and later joining the OAS, which led to a prison sentence. In 1972 he became a founding member of the political bureau of the extreme nationalist organisation the National Front, created in 1972, becoming Jean-Marie Le Pen's vice president.

Not surprisingly, Holeindre's Colombia illustrates the strength and projection of French cultural images. In the cinema attached to the parish chapel the French actor Alain Delon is all the rage:

'His sombre, virile looks have earned him the billing of "the French macho".' Even the prostitutes listen to tangos 'interpreted by Carlos Gardel, the French champion of the genre, now long dead'.

He wants, or so he says, to see the real Colombia, 'to get to know this immense country in the details of daily life, in contact with the common people, honest workers, poor peasant farmers, smugglers or pimps at the sinister mines, well-to-do bourgeois and prosperous farmers'.

However, he informs us with no irony or apology that his guide is not a French-speaking Colombian but a Spanish-speaking Frenchman.

Holeindre's language has a great deal in common with that of Henri Charrière, Auguste le Breton and, indeed, the virtuoso storyteller José Beyaert. Charrière had the Arab janitors he referred to with racist expressions like '*bicques*' and '*crouilles*', lubricious Indian girls who gave themselves readily to him, and an extensive cast of saintly nuns, wise mother superiors and compassionate lepers. Le Breton had his macho policeman and ruthless killers, as well as a nymphomaniac Guahibo Indian girl.

In Holeindre's piece the killer glimpsed on the way to the murder scene is not the only caricature. Colombian drivers are 'macho' without exception. The men are all armed; the women are all prostitutes. Three times he compares Muzo to the Wild West, without counting the man from the spaghetti western.

If this cast of mind united them, profound political differences separated them. Holeindre was a far-right-wing nationalist and disciplinarian. To him and the other *Papillon* debunkers on *Paris-Match*, including the author of *Papillon épinglé*, Gérard de Villiers, who was also an Algeria veteran and a National Front supporter, the sheer popularity of Henri Charrière's anarchic and anti-authoritarian *Papillon* posed a serious ideological threat.

Holeindre no doubt recognised in José many of the attributes that had made Charrière's composite, partly fictional Papillon so attractive: humour and energy, exceptional emotional resilience, the refusal to live on other people's terms, that irresistible urge to go out and pursue his fortune in life. But Charrière was a counterfeit: José had stood on the Olympic podium in London and become a French national hero. He was a genuine swashbuckler with great physical strength, as anyone who arm-wrestled with him knew. Although profoundly disengaged from politics and certainly no right-winger, he hated Communists.

Holeindre felt his magnetism. He tells us he spent a month with José. Whatever else he did in Bogotá, and there were plenty of former OAS colleagues he may have met up with to reminisce about the past and perhaps even make plans for the future, he became fascinated by José, so much so that he asked him for permission to write his biography. The book would have been the perfect complement to the attacks on Henri Charrière published by Holeindre's *Paris-Match* colleagues: after the demolition of a questionable and rather threatening romantic adventurer, the elevation of a malleable Olympian into a proxy-*Papillon* sympathetic to the Right.

However, José fell foul of the National Front's ideology on several counts. First because his father was a Flemish labourer who had migrated to the mines of the Pas-de-Calais in 1920. Second because he had turned his back on his homeland in 1951. And third, because his children were as Colombian as they were French.

All this could have been overlooked. But the book was never written. José refused to have anything to do with it.

The only trace of the far Right's post-*Papillon* flirtation with José is Roger Holeindre's *Paris-Match* feature. The piece is illustrated with Holeindre's own photographs, posed rather than observed and as trite as the text. One image, however, requires comment. It shows a group of men perched on a pile of slag in front of a bulldozer. The caption focuses on José, who is standing at the centre of the group in a dirty T-shirt and jeans, his hat pushed back to reveal a white expanse of forehead above the thick black frames of his glasses: 'Beside the mine owner, José Bayert [*sic*] (glasses), a child of Pantin, Olympic champion in 1948, emerald trader for the last ten years.'

To José's right is Menardo Rojas, mentioned in the text as the mine administrator. To José's left, a man with a paunch and an immaculate short-sleeved shirt and hat holds a prospector's hammer in one hand and a can of drink in the other. José's hands grip a bottle of something: clearly they were drinking, perhaps chatting together, before the photographer asked them to pose.

José's drinking companion is the gangster and murderer José Gonzalo Rodríguez Gacha. Born in the village of Pacho, Cundinamarca, on 18 May 1947, Rodríguez Gacha had first gone to Muzo as a lieutenant and protégé of Gilberto Molina, known at the time as the Emerald King, for whom he is reported to have worked as a *guaquero* and hired killer, gaining a fearful reputation. His appearance there coincided with the failure of Fiocconi's jailmate Humberto 'El Ganso' Ariza, the successor of the bandolero Efraín González, to monopolise power over the emerald fields. A bloody factional war endured from the 1960s until 1973. In the middle of it all, the Bank of the Republic, formerly the administrator of the mines, withdrew from the region. The violence ended in 1973 when the army moved in and forcibly removed the seventeen thousand miners and *guaqueros*.

Already active in emerald smuggling, in 1976 Rodríguez Gacha visited the isolated department of La Guajira, in Colombia's far north-east, and joined its flourishing marijuana trade. By 1980 he had returned to his birthplace and with Molina consolidated his control over the black market in emeralds. He kept control over the mine through the murder of many who opposed him. This was the story awaiting Holeindre, if he had cared to look.

Like many in the emerald community José admired Rodríguez Gacha. 'He was a good man,' he emphasised when we spoke. It was an opinion based on his encounters with him in the 1970s. He gave it to me in full knowledge of the remainder of Rodríguez Gacha's life.

At the start of the 1980s Rodríguez Gacha transferred the Mafia structures of the emerald traffickers and their culture of extreme violence into the cocaine trade. In the vast expanses of land he had bought in the south of the country he opened a number of cocaine laboratories. Initially Rodríguez Gacha paid the FARC guerrillas a fee to protect them but when they began stealing cocaine shipments he declared war on them and created Colombia's first paramilitary group. When demobilised guerrillas formed a political party, the

Patriotic Union, Rodríguez Gacha's men began to assassinate them. Members of the FARC murdered associates of Rodríguez Gacha in the town of Villavicencio in 1986. Rodríguez Gacha's anti-Communism became entrenched. His great wealth allowed him to construct a network of infiltrators in the army and police force.

From Gilberto Molina, Rodríguez Gacha acquired land in the Middle Magdalena, where he set up still more cocaine labs. He quickly became the principal financier of paramilitary groups there.

Rodríguez Gacha was close to Pablo Escobar. *Fortune* magazine listed them annually with the richest men in the world but Rodríguez Gacha was thought to be the wealthiest and most vicious of all the Colombian cocaine barons. *Fortune* put Rodríguez Gacha on its cover, estimating his worth at five billion dollars. US intelligence agencies believed it was Rodríguez Gacha, not Escobar, who had ordered the assassinations of the director of the newspaper *El Espectador* in December 1986, the founder and chairman of the left-leaning Patriotic Union party in October 1987 and the presidential candidate Luis Carlos Galán on 18 August 1989 as well as the bus bomb that exploded outside the headquarters of the DAS, the police intelligence service, in Bogotá, killing sixty-three, in December 1989.

Escobar eventually came to see that Rodríguez Gacha's connections with the paramilitary movement and his insistence on opening new fronts in the war on the guerrillas placed their business in danger. Fighting for control of the corridor connecting Pacho with the Middle Magdalena Rodríguez Gacha allied himself with the controllers of the mine at Coscuez and declared war on the group led by his old protector Gilberto Molina, which controlled the mine at Borbur. In 1989 on a farm in Sasaima an assassin sprayed Molina with bullets. He and sixteen others were killed, on Rodríguez Gacha's orders.

Nine days after the DAS bus bomb Rodríguez Gacha met his own demise. In late 1989 his son Fredy was released from the Modelo prison in Bogotá. Fredy was followed to Cartagena, where he met his father, who was accompanied by no fewer than thirty bodyguards. With the roads blocked by police Rodríguez Gacha, his son and five of his best men made a night-time voyage in a powerful motor launch along the coast to the village of Tolú, south-west of Cartagena. They were spotted by a Colombian Navy patrol, which contacted the national police. At Tolú Rodríguez Gacha and his men boarded two 4x4s and sped off. In the car chase that followed there were three shoot-outs. Rodríguez Gacha, his son and five bodyguards sped off-road through a wooded area. They abandoned the vehicle and made away on foot. Fire from police AH-6 Little Bird assault helicopters killed Fredy and four of the bodyguards. Rodríguez Gacha boarded a truck and sped off. Seeing it was useless with the helicopters giving chase, he climbed out holding a Galil assault rifle and two hand grenades and fled into the trees. At 1.45 p.m. on 15 December 1989 the helicopter opened fire and killed him. According to Mark Bowden's book *Killing Pablo* the United States had a task force of Delta Force operators and SEALs on the USS *America* just off the Colombian coast.

The bodies were placed on display afterwards. The lower half of Rodríguez Gacha's face had been shot away.

17

José had left Colombia's cycling milieu early in the 1970s after two decisive episodes. One was victory in the 1969 Tour of Colombia by a rider under José's direction named Pablo Hernández. The other was a doping incident towards the end of another Colombian race in 1972. Climbing La Línea, one of the steepest and highest ascents in world cycling, the race leader had terrible breathing difficulties. José gave him a pill containing ether (probably polyethylene glycol). The rider won the race but returned a positive dope test for the use of stimulants and the title was taken away from him.

According to the version I was told by a cycling insider the doping incident was caused by an exchange of water bottles. The race leader received a water bottle from another rider. The water contained amphetamine. The race leader, who had been clean, drank and tested positive. The rider who had passed him the bottle won the race. But cycling has its own law of silence and the truth never came to light. Someone had to be blamed and José was chosen. He walked away from the sport.

José had certainly been no stranger to doping as a rider. He told a story of the 1948 Olympic road race that sounds like a straightforward macho tale but may also be true. There was a crash, José said. He swerved to avoid it. When he did so he lost one of his water bottles, the one containing amphetamines, which meant no pick-me-up for the final sprint. José simply told himself, 'I don't need any help. I can do this on my own.' I imagined it was a tale he told the riders he trained. If true it demonstrated two things.

One was that he knew all about amphetamines, like any rider in the post-war period. The other was that he crossed the line in London clean.

In 1982 José returned to the cycling milieu as the director and strategist of a team sponsored by a champagne brand called Champagne Madame Colette.

Exhibiting rice products, wine and champagne in the pavilion of the association of small and medium industries, the Inverca Group was a noteworthy success at the recent International Fair, noted *El Tiempo* in July 1981. Inverca – Carrillo Investments – comprised nine companies operating in two construction companies, rice, wines and aperitifs, cattle and horses, an importer of heavy plant, automobile imports, financial advice and commercialisation of food and drink.

The item says nothing about sport, although the group's owner, Fernando Carrillo, described elsewhere as an emerald entrepreneur 'involved in other, unknown business activities' had paid off the debts of the Bogotá football team Independiente Santa Fe in 1980 on becoming club chairman. Nor does it mention cocaine, although Carrillo had been connected to a Miami-based cocaine operation in November 1978 and Colombian police reports identified him as the owner of a chain of pharmacies through which he distributed chemical precursors necessary for cocaine production. Shortly before the start of the Tour of Colombia in June 1981 Carrillo was indicted in the United States for cocaine trafficking to Florida. The following year Inverca offered to bankroll the Colombian cycling team at the Tour de l'Avenir in September. In July 1982 the offer was withdrawn 'because of issues arising at the last minute'.

For the Colombian press Inverca remained a legitimate industry newsworthy only because it was examining the beefalo, a domestic cattle–bison hybrid developed in the US, and was looking to expand its wine imports. In 1981, to promote his Los Frailes wine range, Carrillo took on a cycling team with some success: four stage wins, two apiece for the nineteen year olds Francisco 'Pacho' Rodríguez and Israel Corredor, who also attained a top-ten placing in the final classification.

The following year Carrillo changed the sponsoring brand from Los Frailes to Champagne Madame Colette. And to direct the team he turned to the experience of José Beyaert.

Champagne Madame Colette–Hotel Barlovento, to give the team its full name, was built around two fine riders and potential winners. One was Julio Rubiano, who had twice finished second in the Tour of Colombia. The other was a local legend: Alfonso Flórez, the Tour of Colombia champion in 1979 and the winner, in France the following year, of the Tour de l'Avenir, sometimes called the amateur version of the Tour de France. Supporting them were the previous year's successes, Corredor and Rodríguez, and two more youngsters with international futures: Martín Ramírez and Argemiro Bohorquez.

From the start José's team rode an intrepid tour. The race started with a long solo attack by Pacho Rodríguez, who was beaten on the line by a counter-attacker named Edgar Corredor (no relation to Rodríguez's team-mate Israel). There were stage wins for Martín Ramírez on stage six, and back-to-back victories for Israel Corredor on stages eight and nine, which helped him to the King of the Mountains title and third place in the final classification, two minutes behind the winner but just one second away from second place. Israel Corredor's Champagne Madame Colette team-mate Julio Rubiano finished sixth overall.

I asked Pacho Rodríguez if José was a good director. He told me, 'It's as if I wanted to be a *directeur sportif* now, when I'm very out of date and things have changed a lot. They [that is, cyclists of José's generation] saw things as they were in their day. Things had changed. And he wasn't a young man: he must have been sixty-ish.' In 1982 José was fifty-seven.

From the cyclists' point of view the drug money now slopping around cycling was a good thing. Pacho Rodríguez said, 'My sponsor had a drugstore. I supposed it was legal. They sponsor me: great. I go to the race as a sportsman and I don't give a damn where the money comes from. Drug money was in the sport but what were we supposed to do? Ninety-eight per cent of us came from very poor families, which is strange because it's an expensive sport. Bikes, cycling shoes . . . Everything costs money. We didn't care where the money came from as long as it meant we could take part in the Tour of Colombia as athletes. We didn't know who these people were.'

Drug money had been in Colombian cycling since 1979, when three members of a team sponsored by a chain of pharmacies called Droguería Yaneth finished in the first ten of the Tour of Colombia. In 1980 the drugstore's sweet-smelling twin, Perfumería Yaneth, was up and running. As their riders concentrated on their racing Droguería and Perfumería Yaneth were laundering the money of José Beyaert's friend José Gilberto Rodríguez Gacha, the emerald and drug Mafioso. The team was organised and led by a rider named Carlos Julio Siachoque. Years later Bogotá anti-narcotics police found a ton of 95 per cent pure cocaine in Siachoque's apartment. The line separating the riders and the shady world that paid their wages was not entirely impermeable.

In 1981 Bicicletas Ositto – 'Bear's Bikes' – joined the Colombian peloton. The Bear in question was Roberto Escobar, whose younger brother Pablo had already made many millions of dollars from the cocaine trade and would soon be one of the wealthiest men alive. Between 1964 and 1968 Roberto had ridden three Tours of Colombia and four RCN Classics. At the Bolivarian Games in Guayaquil in 1965 he won a gold medal. 'I won thirty-six races one season – more than anyone else in the region. It's still a record.'

After his cycling career Roberto took a job repairing radios and televisions for Mora Brothers but cycling exerted an irresistible pull and he began to coach. In 1975 he went to live and work in Manizales, the capital of the department of Caldas. There, he opened a small factory producing bicycle frames. He had added a 't' to his nickname ('"Ositto" looked more Italian') and Bicicletas Ositto – Bear's Bikes – was born.

Even today Roberto claims his team was self-financed. This is certainly false: factory visitors noted a huge disparity between their expectations and what they found. Efraím Forero drove one of his protégés to Manizales to meet Roberto. 'When we got there all we found was a tiny bike workshop. It didn't add up.'

'No one knew at the time,' adds Samuel Cabrera, in 1981 the best young rider in the Tour of Colombia. 'Not directly. You wondered how a little company like that could sustain a team at all, let alone one as strong as that, because Bicicletas Ositto was a monster.'

The team leader, Manuel Ignacio Gutiérrez, had won the 1975 under-23 Tour of Colombia and finished runner-up in the 1980 Tour of Táchira. He proved his abilities in the 1981 RCN Classic. On the final stage Alfonso Flórez accelerated away from the peloton, dragging Gutiérrez, Fabio Parra and Patrocinio Jiménez along in his wake. Flórez won the stage: on his wheel, Gutiérrez gained two minutes on the previous leader and won the race overall. It was Bicicletas Ositto's finest hour.

During the race a staff member of the Bicicletas Ositto team was witnessed handing out marijuana to other members of the caravan. The race organisers investigated the accusations but found no proof. The affair was forgotten until the morning of stage thirteen in April's Tour of Colombia, when in the coffee-producing town of Pereira one of the team's mascots handed out free marijuana to the crowd. This time he was caught and thrown off the Tour. Roberto pleaded lese-majesty: 'I had dressed two actors up in theatrical bear costumes to hand out miniature teddy bears for publicity purposes. They gave a teddy bear and a Bicicletas Ositto shirt to the owner of RCN during a television interview – great publicity for us but it created a lot of jealousy. So all sorts of stories were invented to discredit us.' But a masseur working at both races told me, 'Roberto, Pablo and their entourage followed the RCN Classic and the Tour from a small *chiva*, a customised jeep that was enveloped in a cloud of marijuana smoke. They made a welcome show of largesse by handing out fifty-thousand-peso notes to the *soigneurs* and team auxiliaries.'

In 1981 Bicicletas Ositto sponsored the Colombian national team at the Tour of Cuba. 'Although it may appear differently from today's perspective,' argues Héctor Urrego, a respected sports journalist who joined the team to cover the Tour of Cuba for RCN radio, 'at the time Pablo and Roberto Escobar were perfectly respectable figures in social and sporting circles. Pablo was a distinguished Colombian industrialist sponsoring the national team in good faith. He came to enjoy the racing, support his riders and nothing more. He was just one more member of the team.' This was the official line. But another member of the entourage on that trip told me, 'Pablo was looking for new routes to get coke into the US. The purpose of the trip was for Roberto to explore the viability of using Cuba as a possible slingshot stopover, and that's what he did.'

The chairman of the Colombian Cycling Federation, Miguel Ángel Bermúdez, took a principled stand against cocaine money entering Colombian cycling. The hostility between Bermúdez and Roberto Escobar peaked during a race in 1982. Bermúdez left his car at the roadside near La Pintada. Quickly, during his absence, a bomb was installed and the car destroyed. Soon afterwards the Bicicletas Ositto cycling team disappeared.

José's return to the cycling milieu led to a late career as a cycling commentator. In 1983 the Tour de France had broken with tradition by opening the event to amateurs as well as professionals. Invitations were extended to teams from beyond cycling's European pale, including Russia, East Germany and the USA. The only nation that accepted was Colombia. It had been their ambition from the 1950s and since the victory by Alfonso Flórez in the amateur counterpart of the Tour de France the Colombians had been spoiling for the opportunity to measure themselves against the best professionals.

The Colombian media prepared for a feeding frenzy. No less than twenty-three Colombian journalists covered the whole event and the Colombian radio stations invested heavily in their Tour coverage. Radio Caracol prepared to broadcast every racing moment for the first time in Tour history. As late as 24 June 1983, perhaps realising at the last moment that a French speaker with a deep knowledge of cycling might be useful, Caracol's national sales director asked José along as a commentator and translator. He was given his ticket and a thousand US dollars to cover his wages and expenses.

Three Colombian radio stations sent crews to France. The rivalry between them was so intense it soon erupted into violence. On 6 July *El Tiempo*'s special correspondent José Clopatovsky reported from Le Mans:

The only news story from the excitable Tour de France radio tribune, the second storey of which is occupied exclusively by Colombians, are the dark glasses sported by Rubén Darío Arcila, the Todelar commentator, who yesterday took a thundering blow from [Radio Caracol's principal commentator] Edgar Perea.

Some light is shed on the argument by the scheme temporarily adopted by the team from Radio Caracol to protect the channel's investment. Like a dictionary that includes non-existent words or false definitions as booby traps, thus allowing plagiarists to be identified, they began broadcasting fictional attacks:

One of these was ... an attack by Alfonso Flórez, to see if other channels listening in Bogotá called their commentary teams in France to tell them to mention the attack. Whether Caracol's trap took any victims, you will know in Colombia. Here in France, no one is saying anything.

Twenty-four hours later, making no mention of fisticuffs or false commentary, Radio Caracol made a public apology for 'incidents in France that have affected the radio broadcasts' and counter-attacked by accusing their rivals RCN of failing to respect the exclusivity of Caracol's live radio rights to the event.

Something similar took place within the team. Two of Colombia's great riders of the past, Rubén Darío Gómez and Martín Emilio Rodríguez, were hired to direct the team. Rodríguez, also known by the nickname 'Cochise', was, and perhaps remains, the greatest Colombian cyclist to date. He had been the first Colombian to ride the Tour of Italy, where he had won three stages as a member of the Italian team Bianchi, and in 1975 he had become the first Colombian to ride the Tour de France.

He had put the Colombian Cycling Federation in touch with one of the great European riders of his era, the 1973 Tour de France winner Luis Ocaña. Ocaña was hired to give technical advice. However, the relationship between the Spanish Ocaña and the Colombians broke down midway through the Tour and Ocaña said so to the French newspaper *Le Figaro*:

They have another mentality. My role was to advise them during the race and to help them in their daily affairs. But I realised early on that they are self-centred and I have no dealings now with Cochise or Gómez. They have poisoned the atmosphere . . . They won't become proper professionals with the attitude they are showing. They have everything to learn but they have to want to learn it. They can be moulded but they'll have to come and join a European team.

Ocaña had not recognised that the Colombian racing style of launching frantic attacks at the slightest increase in gradient was not only determined by the Andean landscape, it was also so deeply ingrained in the riders' characters that it was virtually a matter of cultural identity. If it was unlike the European style, then this was because the Colombians defined themselves, in part, by difference.

By the time the peloton reached the mountains, ten days of interminable flat stages, long even by Tour standards – 299 kilometres one day, 257 the next, 222 a few days later – had drained and demoralised the team. Two individual time trials penalised them one at a time and the team time trial on stage three punished them collectively. The team leader, Alfonso Flórez, in particular, suffered with the pace and the cobblestones. Much had been expected of him but by the morning of the first mountain stage, ten days and 1,600 kilometres into the race, he had had enough.

By then, as well as internal squabbles, Clopatovsky's reports suggest that the exchange between the radio and press staff, who were in some sense representing Colombia, and their French counterparts was causing a degree of cross-cultural anxiety that placed José Beyaert in a rather uncomfortable position:

BORDEAUX, 9 [July 1983] – Last night, French television dedicated half an hour to Colombia. Thirty minutes during which one Colombian, a Spaniard and another Colombian who has lived in France for twenty-five years spoke, saying good things and bad.

There was no need to personalise the comment by adding 'about us and our country'. It went without saying. The article continued: 'Summarising, they let the time slip away without using it to talk [meaningfully] about our country, which is such a difficult thing to achieve.'

After the programme, which left those of the Colombians who could understand it perplexed, Clopatovsky approached three French race commentators (José's old team-mate Robert Chapatte, who was also writing for the *Midi Libre*; Pierre Salviar, who also penned a column for *Le Point*; and the great former rider Raphaël Géminiani) who were staying in the same Nantes hotel.

Clopatovsky admits, 'It was not easy to start the conversation.' This is unsurprising. It had no doubt been a long, draining day, the commentators were extremely well-known national figures enjoying a rare private moment, and there was a significant language barrier to overcome. There was something else, too: the elaborate prescribed greetings and introductions with which Colombians start such social interactions can seem long-winded, even annoying, to Europeans, who tend to view deference and formality with suspicion.

'I told them we [Colombians] had enjoyed the notes [about the Colombian team] prepared for the European television stations, which largely consisted of a story in which José Beyaert taught our cyclists to shave their legs.'

The point Clopatovsky was eager to make took the opposite tack: José Beyaert was a Frenchman, not a Colombian, and Colombia had its own reality, which they might be interested in hearing about. The version of the conversation that made the press emphasised this with the subheading 'With or without Beyaert' above a passage in which Clopatovsky tries and, he claims, convinces his French colleagues that:

> with or without shaving their legs, that is, whether or not Beyaert had gone to Colombia, our cyclists would be here, because the sport is innate to the people. It sprang from local necessities and has been promoted by the vast system of radio communication and has its origins, like in France, in the support of a newspaper

(*El Tiempo* in Colombia, *L'Équipe* in France) that created what the French call 'le Tour de la Colombie'.

The French parties to this conversation, whom the Colombians very probably considered, and who almost certainly considered themselves, to be economically, technologically, culturally, historically, educationally, perhaps even morally, superior, not to say physically bigger and distinctly whiter-skinned than their exotic first-time visitors, restrained themselves. They did not point out that it was a simple matter of historical record that racing bicycles on the public roads, and then doing so in stages and in the format of a national stage race, were French ideas and that the Tour de France pre-dated and certainly inspired every other national Tour, and that there had been thirty-seven Tours de France before anyone ever thought of launching a Tour of Colombia, and that in any case the Colombians were absolute newcomers to this venerable French national institution, were still amateurs, and had achieved nothing there. If they had seen *El Tiempo*'s reports to come, informing its readership, for example, that after crossing the towering Col du Tourmalet, 'the Nobel Prize of mountains', in first place ahead of 'the Frenchman Millar', who was of course Scottish, Patrocinio Jiménez had proven himself not just a fine climber but also 'the best climber in the world' they might have said more. Instead, out of high-minded generosity or, more likely, practical diplomacy, they let it pass.

Mistaking Robert Millar's nationality, by the way, was unforgivable. He had ridden in Colombia twice with his Peugeot team. There he was a pushover. In this environment the tables were turned. Near the brow of the Peyresourde, the final climb of the day, Jiménez was pushing a much bigger gear than the Europeans and Millar dropped him. On the descent into the town of Luchon Jiménez faded into fourth place. Nevertheless he had won enough mountain points to end the day leading the King of the Mountains competition. It was a moment of enormous significance to the Colombians: never before had a Colombian, and a Colombian amateur at that, worn the Tour de France mountain leader's polka-dot jersey. Three days later he was ready to attack again. While he was sharing the stage lead with France's Gilbert Duclos-Lassalle it emerged that the previous day's stage winner had failed a dope test. The peloton announced a go-slow in protest and Duclos-Lassalle persuaded the Colombian to relent, thereby sacrificing his efforts. Nonetheless Jiménez spent five days in the polka-dot jersey, finished third on the classic climb up the volcanic Puy-de-Dôme and sounded Colombia's intentions for the future.

Nonetheless, if one thing emerged from this unequal encounter – not just between the Colombian riders and the international opposition but between all the other Colombians, journalists and technicians, who were far from home and on the defensive and therefore greatly overstating their case, and the Frenchmen in the middle of their most characteristic and admired national celebration, and who could hardly have been more certain and confident of their identity – it was that the dream José Beyaert had entertained of developing Colombian cycling and integrating it into the international system and the Tour de France had betrayed him at the very moment it came true. Just when he might have felt prouder than ever of his part in their success story Colombia took its distance from him.

The day had more discomfort in store for José. He was taken to hospital in Nantes to receive treatment for acute neck pain. It kept him away from the Tour for eight days, after which he rejoined the Caracol team at Saint-Étienne only to be thrown out of the radio tribune the following day at the Alpe d'Huez ski station because he did not have the right accreditation.

El Tiempo commented, 'He is the only member of the entire Caracol crew with an in-depth knowledge of cycling. He has spent most of the time ill and the rest of the time he has not been able to get to a microphone.'

The 1983 Tour de France was gruelling for the South American amateurs. Five of the ten Colombian starters had abandoned by the time the race reached the Alps. One evening five European riders, convinced that Jiménez, the Colombian team's best rider and a fine climber, could reach the podium, offered him their services – for a price. Cochise Rodríguez's reaction was necessarily realistic: 'It would have been a waste of money. Pride would never have allowed the professional European riders to let an amateur South American win the Tour de France.'

The race finished with an incident that summed up Luis Ocaña's relationship with the Colombians. Edgar Corredor finished third on Alpe d'Huez. The following day, during the final long mountain stage that finished at Morzine in the Alps, Corredor was again on the attack. Behind him, the Colombian's best classified rider, Jiménez, was fighting for a high position in the general classification.

'It was a tangle with Van Impe and the lug where the brake levers are mounted snapped off. I timed the wait and seven minutes went by . . . There was no one with me,' Jiménez said.

His spare bike was on the roof of Ocaña's car but Ocaña had gone ahead to support Edgar Corredor. Jiménez crossed the finish line in tears and told Clopatovsky: 'Corredor was playing an occasional role that I don't want to devalue, but this was the key stage for me to climb into the top five riders in the Tour, and they left me abandoned . . .'

That evening Cochise Rodríguez explained that there had been philosophical differences between the Colombians and Ocaña. 'It's better to be tenth in a race of heroes than the winner on a single day. Ocaña wanted Corredor to win a stage' – he ended up finishing third at Morzine – 'and abandoned the leader.' Cochise called Ocaña 'voluble and ostentatious. He broke up the team, and we Colombians helped him with our lack of character.'

Corredor overtook Jiménez as the highest-ranked Colombian. They were sixteenth and seventeenth overall. The Great Adventure had been a qualified success. But the breakdown of relations with Ocaña underlines the insecurities felt by the Colombians during their first European experiences. It also proved to José that although he no longer belonged in France he would never fully belong anywhere else either.

In 1984 a slender twenty-three year old named Luis Alberto Herrera took Colombia's first stage win in the Tour de France on the celebrated climb ending at the Alpe d'Huez ski station. The following year Herrera and Fabio Parra took a stage win each. In 1988 Parra finished the race third overall and stood on the final podium in Paris. José, who had laid the foundations for these remarkable achievements, was now travelling regularly between Bogotá and Paris either to work for Radio Caracol or collect consignments of bicycle frames from the factory owned by the Lejeune brothers, with whom he had ridden as an amateur at JPS in the 1940s. In Bogotá he built the frames into bicycles and sold them into the vibrant cycling milieu.

In 1985 José visited a bicycle workshop in Bogotá's Calle 68 belonging to José Duarte, who had ridden under him for Avianca at the end of the 1950s. Duarte told me, 'He had a Vitus frame with him. Vitus didn't weld their frames; they glued them with epoxy resin. He asked me if I could take it apart, which I did. He left with the tubes. Soon afterwards he brought them back. They were the same tubes but they weighed a little more. I put the frame back together again and José left.'

Weeks later José reappeared. He had been in France, he said. 'He told me, "It went well with those emeralds."'

Fortune did not always smile on José. Late in 1985 he found himself locked up. In the 1980s, on a state visit to France, the Soviet leader (the source for this anecdote could not remember which one: he guessed at Brezhnev) arrived at the Soviet Embassy. My informant had a brother who was staying in a small apartment in Paris opposite the embassy. He went into the street to watch and struck up a conversation with a French policeman in the security cordon.

The policeman asked him, 'Where are you from?' and they began to chat.

'I'm Colombian.'

The policeman said, 'Ah, we've got a Colombian in the cells.'

'What's his name?'

'José Beyaert.'

'What? That old bandit? He's not Colombian! He's French!'

The Soviet leader was not Brezhnev, who died in 1982, but Mikhail Gorbachev, who went to France on his first trip abroad as General Secretary of the Communist Party of the Soviet Union on 2 October 1985.

There was no trace of José's arrest in the Colombian newspapers and there is no passport for this period: on 11 March 1987 at El Dorado airport José reported lost the passport that covered December 1981 to early 1987. If the bike frame packed with emeralds had been intercepted, or if José had been carrying anything else, he would have been charged and the news would surely have leaked. If it had been related to smuggling he would have been dealt with at the airport. In any case José entered the United States at Miami in 1997. This rules out any question of an arrest for drug trafficking in October 1985. More likely José had got into some sort of scrape in Paris and was locked up overnight to cool down. José seems to have wriggled out of his prison cell with his reputation intact.

18

José turned sixty in 1985. He was still vigorous and powerful. There was also a wanderlust about him: it may have been a reaction to the disappearance of some old friends.

Edmund Bougaud had died in September 1975, when José was in Barrancabermeja. Hearing cats fighting on the doorstep Bougaud opened the door and made to kick them away but missed and kicked nothing but air. That evening he felt pain in his groin. A blood clot had formed. It travelled to his heart, entered the pulmonary artery and killed him.

Georges Alric passed away in 1982. Another of Bogotá's French hairdressers, Jean-Jacques Bettent, had collected him in his Alfa Romeo to take him to a medical check-up. He had the check-up – the doctor told him he was fine – and then the two men went to lunch. Jean-Jacques parked the car, turned to Georges Alric and found that the old man had silently passed away.

José kept his sights on new adventures. A French source we will call Big Blond told me, 'He arm-wrestled everyone to show he still could.' Big Blond, in his late thirties, was one of the rare challengers who could match him. The impulse driving José on brought him to the brink of disaster.

The story involves yet another Frenchman living in Colombia. His name was Jean Gay. Like Roger Holeindre, Gay had joined the OAS in the early 1960s, for which, like Holeindre, he served a custodial sentence. There is no way of knowing when he reached Colombia but by the mid-1980s he owned two or three thousand hectares of farmland around Bogotá. He was a major exporter of strawberries, tomatoes and orchids and owned a large restaurant in Bogotá.

Gay's restaurant interests and his nationality would naturally have led him to cross paths with José Beyaert. When they met we do not know. Roger Holeindre may have been the conduit: he might easily have brought together his emerald guide and his former OAS colleague during his visit in 1980.

Alongside his legitimate business interests Gay was also a major cocaine trafficker and a pioneer in a sector new to Colombia: the manufacture and export of Colombian heroin. In the mid-1990s cocaine bosses would bring in experts from the heroin production areas in China and south-east and south-west Asia to boost production, creating a genuine industry. US intelligence sources didn't recognise poppy farming for heroin production in Colombia until 1990. Jean Gay was already looking for distributors in the late 1980s. Just as Fiocconi pioneered cocaine manufacture in Colombia Gay was among the forerunners of Colombia's heroin manufacture.

By the time I had heard about him Jean Gay was dead. But I learnt more about him from another former OAS colleague named Michel Paret, who had a fleeting acquaintance with José.

Paret was a fortune-hunter. In 1958 obligatory military service – twenty-nine months of it, in those years – had taken him to Algeria with the Tenth Parachute Division that had seized Algiers on 13 May 1958.

The OAS was where Michel Paret headed after demobilisation. After the OAS he went to prison: Toul, Rouen, Fresnes. A 'Tour de France des prisons', he calls it, echoing Charles Hut. Paret, Holeindre and Gay all served time at the detention centre in the town of Toul, a few miles west of Nancy. Paret and Holeindre remain close. By 1969 Paret was working as a professional offshore diver. A family friend, a white Russian resident in Paris named Henry Gorganov, began to talk about Spanish galleons and the lost gold of the conquistadors. They hatched a plan to make their fortunes salvaging treasure from the shipwrecks of the Caribbean.

'I spent three months planning the expedition but Gorganov was always looking for more investment so I gave up and went back to work. One day he told me he was 5 per cent short. I had a friend who was a wine exporter in Algeria. I was down there one time when he asked, "How's the project going?" I said, "We're still a bit short." "I'll pay all of it."'

Paret and his French-Algerian financier decided to go it alone. Paret began to study palaeography and with the help of a university historian he began to research the shipwrecks of the Spanish Main. After a year they set out on their first expedition.

For Paret it signalled the start of many years of wandering the Caribbean in search of salvage and sunken treasure. Over the years he has accumulated a vast library of shipwreck data. Today he is an indefatigable gravel-voiced raconteur simmering with stories of pirates and Indians and cursed hauls of gold. With a number of financiers and partners he has located and dived two hundred and sixty wrecks.

At the start of the 1970s Paret moved to Guadeloupe. He spent four years there, running a small construction company and transporting goods and people in a small boat he also used for wreck dives. A television crew visited him on the island and the channel France 3 showed three fifty-minute documentaries about Paret's dives.

Paret was living in Guadeloupe when Marcel Boucan's Pointe-à-Pitre-registered *Caprice des Temps* was intercepted off Marseille and those 425 kilograms of heroin were found. 'It was quite a scandal,' Peret told me. 'It was the first time we'd read stories of boats full of heroin. He used the same port we used and he told them he searched for wrecks to salvage, the same as us, so life became a little uncomfortable for a while. One time we failed to declare an airlift. Customs were on our backs immediately because of the *Caprice des Temps* scandal.'

In the late 1970s Paret island-hopped to Saint-Barthe. 'While I was there the documentary-maker for the France 3 project came to find me again. The stories of sunken galleons and Indian gold had got to him and he was determined to do something. I didn't believe in it but he said he had the money and he was ready to go. He found a boat, although it was in such poor shape it took us a year to make it seaworthy, and that's how he started.

'We found things but the boat wasn't strong enough to bring up anything heavy or bulky so we covered our expenses and simply enjoyed the adventure.'

The film-maker, the Frenchman we are calling Big Blond, now lives in Miami. His stock of tales gives an inkling of the conversation he must have shared with Paret as they pursued their buccaneering fantasies.

'There is a story,' he told me, 'that, as Bolívar was approaching Lima, the Spanish rented a ship from an English broker, and the wealthiest of the city's Spanish loyalists bought their passage out. The space that remained was loaded with as much Peruvian gold as the stevedores could cram in. A few days into the voyage the crew, driven mad by the presence of so much treasure, murdered the passengers, dumped the bodies overboard and anchored off Colombia's west coast, where they stashed the treasure.

'Every few years an Indian comes out of the forest with a piece of that Peruvian gold. It must be hidden in a grotto somewhere. But every man who finds gold goes insane. The Indians blame the treasure: they call it "Madman's Gold". More likely there are bats in the cave and they infect all who enter with rabies.'

Paret had friends in Bogotá. One was a French interior decorator married to a politician's daughter. He had worked on the Tequendama hotel. 'Every time I went to Bogotá on my way back to France I spent a week there.' This, despite Bogotá lying far from the flight path between the French islands of Guadeloupe and Saint-Barth and mainland France. And Paret had another French friend in Bogotá, another old OAS colleague: Jean Gay. Through Jean Gay, Paret met another former OAS man who had become even more notorious than Charles Laurent Fiocconi.

'I was in a hotel in Bogotá. Jean called up to my room and said, "Walter's here and he'd like to meet you."

'I said, "Walter? Who's Walter?"

'"Come down and you'll see."

'I went down and there was a guy getting out of the car and I recognised him immediately: Spaggiari.

'I said, "Hello, Albert."

'He said, "You recognised me."

"'Yes, why?"

"'I've been operated on three or four times."

"'You should sue them!"

Albert Spaggiari was a former wedding photographer and right-wing fanatic who had reached Colombia while on the run after an audacious bank robbery known popularly as the heist of the century. He had fought in Indochina alongside Roger Holeindre with the Third Parachute Battalion. Holeindre has described Spaggiari as 'a good combat companion you could trust on the battle ground'. After a number of prison sentences Spaggiari had become a photographer in Nice. Between soft-porn shoots in the studio and weddings at the town hall he fantasised about fame and wealth. His daydreams were fed by an interest in crime fiction. Robert Pollock's 1974 crime thriller *Loophole, or How to Rob a Bank*, in which a group of safe-breakers enter a bank vault via the sewers, stuck in his mind. In his copy of the book, beneath the French title, *Tous á l'égout* ('Into the sewers'), he wrote 'and make for the Société Générale'.

The Société Générale was Nice's most prestigious bank. The town's wealthiest families stored their valuables in its safe-deposit boxes. From a town councillor who worked at the bank Spaggiari learnt that the walls of the bank's main vault were considered so thick and the door so heavy that there was no need for an alarm. He tested this by putting an alarm clock in a safe box in the vault and set it to go off overnight. The noise and vibration went undetected.

At night Spaggiari began to wander the sewage ducts beneath the city. Eventually he identified the tunnel wall closest to the vault of the Société Générale. All he needed now was a team of professionals to execute his plan. He assembled twenty-three former OAS colleagues and Marseille crooks and they set off into the sewers with perhaps a ton of equipment. They had eight metres of stone to get through and after each night of digging they had to hide their work and equipment behind a temporary cover so that council workers would not find it. The first tunnelling team simply gave up. A new group of excavators had to be found. Late on Friday 16 July, after months of preparation and many nights of tunnelling (Spaggiari later bragged, 'It took ten days to cut through one rock'), he and his men entered the vault. The tunnel was a professional job with timber joists in the roof and carpet on the floor. Spaggiari had even hired a cook to prepare meals inside the vault so that the work of breaking open the safe-deposit boxes could continue through the weekend. In the small hours of Sunday 18 July the water level began to rise in the sewers outside. Running no risks they retreated with spoils worth fifty million francs. Behind him Spaggiari left a note that read 'No arms, no violence, and without hatred'. The press published the slogan and the unknown robbers became Robin Hood figures. The left-wing *Libération* wrote:

> The men who spent two days and two nights tunnelling no doubt sweated more that the people who come to deposit their valuables in the secret of a vault. The story of this bank job is at root a deeply moral one.

Albert Spaggiari had become a folk hero. In truth he was a neo-Nazi fantasist in whose Nice home police found a veritable arsenal together with a collection of images of Hitler. Spaggiari had renamed the house 'Oies Sauvages' ('Wild Geese') and on the sign attached to the letterbox he had redrawn the final 's' of each word in the style of the Nazi SS logo. He told investigators he had carried out the heist to raise funds for a neo-fascist organisation called 'Catena'.

His role in the OAS had been minor yet he told friends he had once been dispatched to assassinate de Gaulle. He had taken up position along the route of a presidential drive-past, armed with a rifle and telescopic sight, only to receive a telephone call suspending the operation. Moments later de Gaulle passed within feet of him. Spaggiari said letting him pass alive was the greatest regret of his life.

On 10 March 1977 he cut short an interview with an investigating magistrate by leaping out of the window and mounting a waiting motorbike. Window bars were inserted after the incident. Spaggiari's whereabouts during the following twelve years remain a mystery: the book he published in 1978 describing the heist, *Les égouts du paradis* (translated into English as *The Sewers of Gold*) gives the author's location as 'the dark side of the moon'. It was *in absentia* that Spaggiari was sentenced to life imprisonment on 23 October 1979.

He was said to have fled to Brazil on 4 May 1977 using papers belonging to his half-sister. He visited Argentina and Paraguay. The CIA learnt he had at one time been in the pay of Pinochet's intelligence service in Chile. René Louis Maurice's book *Cinq milliards au bout de l'égout* (published in Britain as *The Heist of the Century*) places him briefly in Guatemala.

In Colombia Spaggiari seems to have reached the isolated desert peninsula of La Guajira, for that was where he sent Michel Paret: 'I was looking for lobsters because I had clients with some very big boats to fill. Spaggiari sent me to see some Indians in La Guajira.'

Spaggiari was not free to go with him but Paret had recently been accompanying a wealthy client on a sailing trip across the Caribbean: 'Thierry Roussel, the guy who married Christina Onassis. We were talking on the boat and I mentioned lobsters in Colombia and he said, "Let's go and have a look." So I took him with me. It was a curious trip. When we got to the first hotel in Riohacha [the capital of La Guajira department] there was barbed wire everywhere. It had been attacked five times by the guerrillas. Afterwards we were with the son of the governor, who was an Indian, and we were stopped by smugglers who knew him. They were armed to the teeth with Colts, shotguns, everything you can think of. We were obliged to drink hot whisky with them in the desert.

'It was a very dangerous place. Every night I slept with one of the governor's daughters. He had nine of them. I hung the hammock on a branch in the hut, which shook as we slept with these Indian girls. I said, "Gently, or we'll bring the place down!"

'I toured the La Guajira and I couldn't find a single Indian who wanted to transport lobsters because they said, "In one night carrying packages, I earn more than you're offering for a month's work." I couldn't find a single Indian and that's how it finished. One time I bought four tonnes and we went to store them in a freezer at Riohacha. In the night they stole two. Two tonnes from the freezer.'

Despite one disastrous enterprise together Paret enlisted Spaggiari's assistance in another oddball adventure. 'One time I was carrying a cargo of strawberries for Jean Gay on a twin-engined launch. I'd bought a batch of emeralds with Spaggiari's help. I put an emerald in each strawberry to get them out of the country.'

The emeralds went to a girlfriend of Paret's in Guadeloupe.

'They were beautiful and everything and I lent them to a girlfriend who had a beauty salon where all the ladies of Pointe-à-Pitre went for their massages. They saw the emeralds around her neck and said "Ooh la la! Are those real emeralds?"

'"I've got more if you want to buy some."'

The emerald dealer who had sold him the stones was not José Beyaert: 'Whoever it was, he made a big profit from the deal. I paid five times the value of the stones.'

In Bogotá Spaggiari talked about the famous bank job with Paret, who told me, 'He said, "What do you do?"

'I said, "I work at sea, this and that," and at one point we talked about thermal lances. I told him I know how to build them.

'He said, "If I'd only known you in the old days. I could have opened the three thousand safe-deposit boxes."

'But if you used a thermal lance in a bank vault you'd suffocate.'

Sometime in the mid-1980s Paret took Big Blond on one of these trips to Bogotá. In a bar Paret introduced him to Jean Gay. Gay made quite an impression on Big Blond: 'Jean was on the run from the police when I met him. He'd been condemned to twelve years. And he was an incorrigible womaniser. He could sit down with any girl, sixteen or sixty, and he would end up taking her to bed.'

Big Blond was so impressed he dubbed him 'the Artist', although Gay's seduction technique, whatever it was, undoubtedly rested primarily on picking the right woman and then impressing on her the mystique afforded by his nationality, not to mention his money and power.

When Gay met Paret and Big Blond he took the Olympic champion with him. As well as the truth about his Olympic win José spun him fantastic tales: he claimed he was a Resistance hero. He told him his well-rehearsed tale about losing a testicle in the war. He also said he had received the *Légion d'honneur*. These were the first of many hours of conversation and laughter Big Blond shared with José.

Big Blond recalls, 'Jean Gay and José were friends but they were very different. José was a nice person. He said cocaine was recreational but heroin destroyed lives. But Jean was the boss.'

When Paret left Bogotá Big Blond stayed on. José began to teach him about emeralds.

'He taught me to drop the stones in water the better to gauge their colour and to suck them for traces of the sweetness left by the acids and oils used by counterfeiters to create a false "garden" [mimicking the natural insertions that add value to an emerald].

'The mines at Muzo were producing fewer and fewer emeralds and prices were on the up, so I started to smuggle small caches of stones to Paris. I was living in the Marais and I sold them to jewellers in Paris. There were never big sums of money concerned. The emeralds paid for my trips to Colombia, little more.'

It was pocket-money crime. But Big Blond was about to get mixed up in something more serious.

Gay and José welcomed him into their activities and between 1986 and 1988 the three men made several trips to Europe, in part seeking buyers for Gay's heroin but also coordinating and safeguarding Gay's cocaine operations.

By this time Spaggiari was in perhaps the least obvious and most surprising place on earth: Paris. His heist millions long gone, he seems to have been surviving by ripping off other criminal gangs. On one occasion Gay's cocaine mules reached Paris as planned then disappeared. Big Blond and José were dispatched to Paris to investigate and report back. They learnt that Spaggiari had been receiving information about Gay's activities from people with knowledge of Gay's organisation.

Gay identified the traitors and, in Big Blond's account, invited one of the men most implicated in the rip-off on another journey. He went with José, whom he knew he could trust, but kept the newcomer Big Blond at a distance.

In Big Blond's words, 'José didn't stay to the end of the trip but he told me one of the men wouldn't be coming back. I never saw him so angry.'

Why the rage? Big Blond told me to be very careful with the story.

The implication was that José had become Gay's executioner. It was the fourth time suspicion of murder had been laid at José's door and this time I had someone close to him who believed in his guilt.

José had always been an adventurer. Not content with the reputation that was his due he had enveloped himself in a myth and by the late 1980s he may have become its prisoner. He had killed so many times in fantasy that when he was called to do so in reality there may have been no way out. Lying about his existence had become second nature to him. It may finally have taken its toll.

Big Blond described another trip with José and Jean Gay. This time they were headed for Spain. José's passport entries support Big Blond's account: he flew out of Bogotá on 15 October 1987. The absence of an entry stamp suggests his destination was France. There, says Big Blond, 'Jean met us in his car, and we drove to Spain. He didn't want to fly there: flying meant too many controls.'

However successful the trip was, and Big Blond was reticent on this, it revealed an unexpected side of José's character.

'He had the ability, wherever he was, to bring out the worst in people. We were in a bar once and someone said something in Spanish. Suddenly José stood up and grabbed him. He attracted aggression.'

José left Madrid Barajas for Bogotá on 8 December 1987.

Months later Big Blond accompanied Jean Gay on a trip to Amsterdam for a meeting with an established dealer. It was his undoing.

'Interpol had the dealer under surveillance. When we got back to France Gay and me were being watched. His lawyer told me and José it was time to keep Jean at a distance. I heard the police had photographs of me and José with him, although nothing ever happened to us. Jean Gay was arrested soon afterwards and went to prison for many years.'

Gay spent the final years of his life there. He was, it would seem, given his freedom to die at home. He died on 19 July 2004, his last address a leafy hillside in Mandelieu-la-Napoule on France's opulent Mediterranean coast, close to Cannes. There was clearly money to the end.

19

José never heard anything from Interpol but the loss of his freedom must have felt chillingly close. Perhaps in answer to an impulse to distance himself from Jean Gay's associates and the activities that had so nearly landed him in jail, José took an interest in Saint-Martin, a stunning Caribbean island, divided, he told me, 'in two, half French, half Dutch. How can that be? I went to take a look. And it was true: there was no frontier or anything, just a line on the ground: France here, Holland there.'

Between September 1987 and March 1989 José made four visits to the island. The longest was a two-week vacation, the shortest an overnight stopover, breaking the journey from Paris to Bogotá. Saint-Martin was known as a stopover point for drug mules. Its banks were favoured by money-launderers. Neither came up in our conversations, although José clearly had money to invest.

'I liked it! I liked it so I went to an estate agency and there were parcels of land on sale. I chose a place, I went to see it, there was drinking water and a well. My imagination began to work.'

José's idea was to build a holiday chalet to rent to wealthy French visitors. He returned to Bogotá, found a company that manufactured timber chalets at half their French price and flew back to the island with Louisette.

'The first thing we did was go and look at the plot. She loved it: the white beach, the palm trees, the delicious shade. I outlined my idea. She liked it so we went to sign the deeds.

'"It's no longer the same price."

"'What do you mean?"

"'Monsieur Beyaert, you have to understand . . .'"

'They'd just passed a law in France that every company that invested in the island, the money they spent there was tax deductible. Companies were buying up everything in sight. A piece of land worth a thousand pesos was suddenly worth ten times that.'

The fiscal package José was referring to was known as the Pons Law after Bernard Pons, the minister for overseas departments and territories. It had been passed fourteen months before José's first visit to the island and led to sharp price rises that scuppered his plans.

'I had just about enough to buy the land but why buy land when you can't afford to build on it?'

José and Louisette went home disappointed.

However, in Bogotá José met a friend who was selling a house in Colombia's island outpost of San Andrés, 480 miles north-west of the Colombian mainland and 140 miles from the Nicaraguan coast. 'I went with my wife, we liked the house so we bought it and we went to live for a few years in San Andrés.'

Seven and a half miles by two, San Andrés was mostly peopled by a mixture of Spanish-speaking Colombians from the mainland and the English-speaking descendants of slaves transported there by the British, who long ruled over the island. In 1670 buccaneers commanded by the Welsh privateer who became Admiral Sir Henry Morgan had taken over the island until Morgan's death in 1688. There is a Morgan's Cave that may be more than a tourist attraction: Morgan is rumoured to have cached his treasure in the vicinity.

José's first San Andrés visa was issued on 5 October 1989. He was given a residency visa on 22 November 1990. He had other motives for moving away from the mainland. He was perhaps thinking of his 1970 voyage with le Breton, looking for Captain Morgan's treasure. In the altitude of the Bogotá plateau Louisette had been experiencing breathing difficulties. The move down to sea level was partly for her health. José may have made the move with a lacerating guilt and a panicky sense that he would be lost without her. Marcel Plazz-

Lartigau told me, 'He wanted to compensate her for his absences and infidelities.'

José and Louisette moved to the urbanised northern tip of the island, where, still inspired by their abortive Saint-Martin project, they ran a guest house. They soon found a stunning cottage halfway down the island, looking westwards out to sea. A taxi took me along the coastal road. At The Cove I found José's second house on the island, a beautiful brick construction finished in weatherboard. Perhaps four hundred yards back towards the capital, I found 'Las Olas del Mar' ('Sea Waves'), a tiny roadside stall where Plácido Rojas Morales makes a meagre living. Plácido had been a close friend. He told me, 'José came here looking for peace.

'He bought a launch he named *Doña Luisa*. I was the captain. Every Monday we went to Cayos de Albuquerque [an atoll south-west of San Andrés] to fish.'

One day the motor broke down. There was no money to fix it so José helped ensure his captain didn't starve.

'He helped me find this piece of land and buy timber to start building. He was a kind man. He always wanted to help people. He always had a lot of friends.'

José told me he had learnt something special about San Andrés: 'There is no water. All the houses have wells and septic tanks. The water isn't drinkable. So everyone has to buy water.'

From Plácido's store José watched the hill in the centre of the island. José told me, 'I could see it was dripping with water although it hadn't rained for days.'

José had already spoken to a man who was selling water on the island, an old man who had spent time in the United States. He went back to find him.

'"Yes, there are always drops of water on the hill."

'"Where does the water go?"

'"I don't know. I suppose it filters through and goes to the sea."

'"That could take ten thousand years! There's water!"'

José told the old man to find something to collect it with.

'In no time at all I had a glass of water,' he told me. 'I tried it. It was good.'

'"Have you had this water analysed?"

'"I didn't know there was water here to analyse."

'"You've got to make a hole, cement it, and in the meantime put some tubes in like this, cut with . . . so the cement dries around them, and you're going to collect water."

'The cement dried very quickly in the heat,' José recalled, 'and in a couple of weeks we had three hundred litres of water there, permanently, day and night.'

The government sent an inspector: '"Where does this water come from. It's very pure!"

'So we made larger boreholes, we acquired water filters, and that was my job, selling water. I bought forty or fifty ten-litre containers. They eventually gave us a certificate so that our water could be used in babies' bottles. The others couldn't do this because they took the water from wells and it had to be treated and filtered. Not ours. We filtered it but only as a precaution. It wasn't enough to serve the entire island's needs but for a business . . .'

José painted a vivid picture of the way he transformed life on San Andrés. He added, 'When I left the island, the old man said, "I'm not carrying on with this." He had a very good pension from the US and he didn't want to work. He wanted to sit and smoke. He's probably still there.'

The old man was Willhem Alfonso Peterson. He was no longer on the island but his brother, Walwin Godfrey Peterson, was, and the story he told me was rather different.

Walwin is the island's historian. He and his brother were the sons of a Danish father and a Scottish mother. He told me water had been discovered on San Andrés by Scandinavians, not the French. 'The president of Colombia in the 1930s, Alfonso López Pumarejo, had studied in Denmark and married a Dane. Their son, Pedro López Michelson, became governor of the island. They encouraged Scandinavians to come to the island.'

The Petersons' water was the best on the island. Walwin, a geologist, told me, 'The island is a sponge with swamps that drain into underground caves.'

Walwin owned the wells. His brother Willhem owned the

extraction plant and had the technical training to monitor the water quality.

'We used to help José. I was in Barranquilla when he won the Tour of Colombia. He was in all the newspapers so everyone knew him. When he came up to see me about the water I realised who he was and told him he was welcome here. He bought five-gallon bottles and we filled them up with filtered water. When we began producing water in plastic cups and water bags he distributed those too.'

José made water deliveries along the west side of the island. This was how he earned his living on the island. José was right when he said that the end of the water business had an American connection, but it wasn't Willhem Peterson's pension. Walwin told me, 'We were put out of business by Coca-Cola, Pepsi-Cola and Postobón. They began shipping in water at prices we couldn't match.'

One of Walwin Peterson's stories suggested the murky world José was moving into when he bought his motor launch. Peterson had a son who was murdered in 1991, when José was on the island. The boy had bought a small boat he sailed down the Nicaraguan coast, sometimes as far as the Bocas del Toro in Panama. He met with Indian traders and exchanged crayfish for cigarettes there. It was illegal, Walwin admitted, but it wasn't drugs. He invested the profits in a bigger boat of wood and fibreglass. In November 1991 the new vessel was one of three that left the East-South-East Quay in San Andrés. Walwin's son never returned from that voyage.

San Andrés had not turned out to be the paradise José had hoped. His stay was beset by financial and health worries. The climate was extreme: severe tropical storms interrupted spells of beautiful Caribbean sunshine and rainfall was followed by intense humidity. The success of José's business activities was not unqualified. He was experienced but older, and continuing the fight was a demanding business made more so by doubts whether his skills were adequate and whether they even represented the right approach.

Marcel Plazz-Lartigau told me, 'Soon after reaching San Andrés, José bought a fishing boat and a powerful engine. He hired local fisherman but they bartered their catch for consumer goods with the Nicaraguans and charged José for their fuel and salary. When José found out, he was so angry he had a heart attack.'

Guillermo Robayo, his old emerald supplier, told me José suffered not a heart attack but prodromal symptoms, or a pre-heart attack, and returned to Bogotá for treatment. Marcel Plazz-Lartigau had renewed his friendship with José on the island. 'I'd lost touch with him. I'd heard he was dead. There had been a report on the radio saying so. I went to San Andrés to look for him and I found him. He was living in a beautiful house but he had no money. I offered to buy the house for a good price and charge him no rent to stay there but he turned down the offer.'

Instead José and Louisette sold the house for less than Marcel's offer and moved into a bungalow near a hog-shaped rock called La Rocosa, or Brook Rock. The rock had been thrown up by the sea during a tremendous storm in the 1940s. There one of José's neighbours, Elizabeth Martínez Martínez, remembered them warmly. She told me a Spaniard named Juanito had lived in the house to the rear, looking out at the runway of San Andrés airport. Juanito was Juan Antonio Luna, a Basque who was fanatical about cycling. He had been José's closest friend on the island. I met his daughter, María del Carmen. She was terribly moved when I told her José had died, although her questions led me to believe she was confusing José with someone else.

José's final passport was issued on 26 January 1993. It gives his address as San Andrés, Carrera 9A, No. 11-A-07 'La Rocosa'. It was soon after this that José and Louisette returned to the mainland.

Marcel Plazz-Lartigau told me, 'Louisette couldn't breathe in Bogotá so I bought them a house at Mesitas del Colegio,' in a valley at an altitude of 4,265 feet, less than half that of Bogotá. José, sixty-eight that year, and Louisette, four months his junior, lived there for two years. Both were in failing health. José did a little coaching for local cyclists. The local sports centre bears his name. They later moved a little closer to Bogotá. After decades of frantic adventures the years began to catch up with them. Robayo told me, 'The last time he called me he had a two-carat stone so I went to see him. Louisette was ill, close to death, and José wasn't well either. His health was starting to fail. He liked to drink and smoke. He smoked a lot. But he was still great fun.'

Robayo linked this to his parlous financial state. 'He'd earned money all his life but he hadn't invested any of it. He had never wanted anything. Everyone else was working to buy a house or a flat. Not him. He wasn't attached to anything.'

José and Louisette talked about returning to France. In February 1998 they opened a bank account at Royan, where José's brother Georges lived with his father, near José's dreamed-of La Rochelle. Before they could act on their plans, on 5 October 1999, Louisette died.

Marcel Plazz-Lartigau attended the funeral. 'No one went. José, his son, me. It must have made José feel dreadfully isolated.'

1999 was also the year of José's father's death, aged ninety-nine.

José told me, 'He was nearly a hundred. Deaf but otherwise fine. His health was remarkable. He had never visited a doctor. My brother took him to see a doctor and they both had a check-up. He took their social security cards and they reimbursed my brother's expenses but not the old man's.

'Georges took him back to see them.

'"Why didn't you reimburse the old man?"

'"He isn't registered. He's certainly dead."

'"He's standing in front of you."

'He was nearly a hundred and they'd removed him from the records because they believed he didn't exist. But to re-enter him they had lots of problems. They'd wiped him out! Never, never, never ill. He was a phenomenon: a man who worked all his life.

'He wore wooden clogs all his life. We were shoemakers and we made shoes and he walked around in clogs. He had shoes for cycling but he made each pair last fifteen years.

'On Boxing Day 1999 there was a terrible storm along the west coast of France. It pulled down pylons and the electricity went off all over the region. The chimney collapsed. My father was deaf but he must have realised something had happened because he got up. He couldn't see a thing. He tripped over the chimney, cracked his skull and died. They only found him the following morning.'

In the space of twelve weeks José had lost his wife and his father. He would soon lose his adopted country too.

* * *

As José grieved two kidnappings took place that redefined the almost mystical relationship between Colombia and its cyclists. On 21 January 2000 a recently retired cyclist named Oliverio Rincón, a Tour de France stage winner and top-five finisher in the Tours of Spain and Italy, was seized by the ELN guerrilla force. On 4 March Luis Alberto 'Lucho' Herrera, who had been perhaps the finest climber in world cycling in the 1980s, was abducted, probably by the 42nd Front of the FARC. Neither man was kept long: Rincón, six days; Herrera, less than twenty hours. But the message was clear: international sport was making wealthy men of Colombia's best cyclists. As such, the delinquents considered them fair game.

There were demonstrations against the kidnappers: José took part in them. But, he told me, 'they were waiting to take me, too. The Olympic champion! They figured there had to be plenty of money. I'd bought a little house in Mesita but I abandoned it when my wife died. I went to Chía to live with my son. My neighbours there alerted me. There was a car here and a car over there. It might not even have been the guerrillas, it could have been common criminals. But someone was looking for me.

'I'd already agreed with my son that if I was ever kidnapped they should forget me. Leave me to my destiny. And if it was him the same thing applied, because if they'd failed with me they might have taken him.

'I went out into the street to smoke a cigarette, to show them I was still there. Then I went out of the back door and climbed over the garden wall. My things were in a plastic bag. A suitcase would have been too obvious. I called a friend at Air France and made a reservation.

'I said, "Don't put my name on the passenger list. Add it at the last minute. Because if they have access to the list and they see I'm leaving, it could be dangerous."'

He left Colombia on 22 July 2000. *El Tiempo* covered his departure, although it made no mention of any kidnap threat:

José Beyaert's patience has run out. The first overseas rider to win the Tour of Colombia waited forty-eight years for Colombian nationality. It never arrived. Twenty days ago he packed his bags, left his home in Chía (north of Bogotá) and returned to France, his country of birth.

The adventure of his life was over.

FIVE

FRANCE

20

Do not learn the language of this land. Nor even listen to it, for I tell you that if you do, one of two ends will befall you, for it will either drive you mad or you will wander restlessly for the rest of your life.

Coloquios de la verdad
Pedro de Quiroga (1555)

When I met José in November 2004 his hair was white and scant and his face had a ravaged look. His memory was spotty and he was addicted to fantastic statements yet for those few days he beat back his disabilities and his furies in the therapeutic recall of his old adventures. He regretted not having been felled in battle nor in any other physical test of strength and courage, rarely did he relax the curtain of self-promotion that concealed the man, but his vitality and his enormous spirit of fun shone through and his stories revealed the restlessness and gusto with which he had pursued his adventures, ceaselessly affirming the possibility of life in this tough world.

Death-haunted, he told me, 'I love Colombia.' It was another of his leitmotivs.

'I can't say exactly why. The climate. People are very kind, people in general; I'm not taking about the guerrillas. Even very poor people would give me gifts, feed me, offer me something to drink and refuse to take my money. Not the day after I won the Tour of Colombia: twenty-five years later! I'd have liked to have died in Colombia.'

To him it represented a vital outpost of the imagination.

All his life he had been incapable of depression but in France melancholy took possession of him. Experience had embittered his heart against the world and his voice seemed winnowed of vigour.

As Paris campaigned to host the 2008 and then the 2012 Olympic Games, as a gold medallist José was asked to sign petitions and attend official functions, which he hated. All his life he despised the blather and bullshit of politicians and elected officials, the people who wanted to shake his hand for a photograph. If he had won his Olympic title in 1960 or later, he reflected, he would have qualified for a special annuity. Instead he drew a small state pension, which paid for cigarettes and little else.

However, his sense of humour was intact and when he was talking, dredging up the old stories in no particular order, he felt less weary of life, less vanquished.

Louisette had been dead for many years when we met, six months before his death at the age of seventy-nine. But José was still fighting with himself over her. In the stories he told me an aching for her could be felt in every word.

'She understood me. She understood how I worked. When I had to go somewhere else and do something different, when I was going to head off on some adventure somewhere, she could feel it. At times my behaviour wasn't up to scratch but you don't always do what you want, you do what you can.

'She was an exceptional woman. Cooking, she was cordon-bleu. When she made sauce she said my mood could turn it. She was formidable. Formidable. She had the bad luck to find a guy like me but I had the good fortune to find a woman like her.

'I've only met two honest people in my life,' he told me. 'My father and my wife. They never did anything to anyone.'

In 2003 José returned to Colombia to take part in the Tour of Remembrance, an event for past Tour of Colombia winners. In Barrancabermeja, Flor and Humberto Vallecilla saw him on the news. Flor asked José Luis, whom she had raised as her son, 'Did you see your father on television last night?'

He hadn't.

José did not go out in a blaze of light but with his body worn out and old and his illusions shattered, dispossessed by age and illness and no longer able to live up to the image he had created for himself.

Death came in a La Rochelle hospital on 9 June 2005. There were several versions of his death. In one he had been prescribed blood-thinning treatments for high blood pressure, which had caused a stomach ulcer to haemorrhage. In hospital he had contracted an untreatable hospital virus.

Georges saw things differently.

'He may have caught microbes when he was in the jungle. No one knows. He'd had enough. He'd had to leave everything there. He'd lost everything. He'd had enough.'

It was in any case amazing that he survived anywhere near as long as he did. He told me he never expected to live into old age. It is possible he deceived his doctors. He had after all been deceiving people all his life.

There was a great deal about José's life I never fully understood.

Why he had abandoned his cycling career in Europe, for instance. There was the nationality slight, of course, and the clash with René Vietto, yet in three professional seasons, despite suffering grotesque over-training and then exposure early in 1950, and then failing to recover for the 1951 season, he won five races in a buccaneering style that made him extremely popular. In a ten- or twelve-year career those early problems would have been forgotten. He might have become a formidable classics rider. He would surely have won stages in the Tour de France. Instead he turned his back both on his celebrity, which perhaps felt bogus to him, and on the rigid hierarchies of professional cycling in the 1950s and took off somewhere where he could live life on his own terms. The more I thought about it the more laudable his decision seemed.

In any case there was much in José's life that he too failed to comprehend. He loved the forest. He'd let tarantulas crawl up his arms. The insects and arachnids he killed and framed. The mammals were caged and shipped. Dead or alive, he found a market for them. He loved the forest but he tore it down to trade in balsa, sapan, caracolí, abarco, garrapato. He loved the forest although he lost everything there. He told me one day, 'Once upon a time I was in the Amazon, alone in the forest, just me and my machete. There was no noise, nothing. I remember I asked myself, "What are you doing here, José?", and I couldn't find an answer. "Why have you come here?" I was all alone, lost in the jungle, and I had no idea why. I think it's simply that I've always been restless. I've always had this need to be able to move on.'

His 'once upon a time' was from a fairy story. 'Alone in the forest . . . lost in the jungle' sounded like the title of a bestseller by Germán Castro Caycedo, one of Colombia's finest investigative journalists, published in 1998, when José was still in Colombia: *Perdido en el Amazonas* ('Lost in the Amazon'), the true story of a soldier who makes first contact with an Indian tribe, then disappears. Or a front-page newspaper headline in 1965 after a Catalina flying boat had come down in the Amazon:

FOUR LOST IN THE JUNGLE SURVIVORS OF THE 'TAO' AIRCRAFT

One group of survivors remained with the wreckage and were saved; another group set off into the forest to look for help and they were never heard of again. José, as artful a constructor of narratives as the newspaper men or the author, used many of the same techniques: the curt phrase, the striking image, dialogue that drives the story on. The difference was, José's stories were mostly about himself. I suspect he mostly told them to himself too. Without them, life would have been unbearable. Take this one, about his favourite spot, the emerald mines:

'One day an old man arrived in the morning bus. He'd taken two or three days to arrive from Cúcuta. He was seventy-five or seventy-six.

'"*Buenos días.*"

'"*Buenos días.*"

'"Tell me something. Where can I find emeralds here?"

'I said, "Where have you come from?"

'"I come from Cúcuta."

'"When did you arrive?"

'"This morning?"

'He had a case with enough space for a toothbrush and a change of underwear.

'"What are you doing here?"

'"I've come to look for emeralds."

'He had probably been going on and on about them at home and they'd finally thrown him out. The old fool.

'I said, "You have to go to the river."

'"And where's the river?"

'"Down there, a few miles away."

'I was late for some reason, so I said, "I'm going down there now. If you like, I'll take you."

'I had someone's truck. Someone had lent it to me.

'I took him down there and when we got there, he took a good look at all those thousands of people.

'I said, "Let me get you a coffee."

'I took him into a shack. I knew everyone, so I said, "Do you have a shovel he can hire?"

'"Of course, José."

'So we drank our coffee but the old boy was in a hurry.

'"Where do I go?"

'I took him to the river, not far away. Somewhere there was plenty of mud.

'"Why here?"

'I looked at him.

'"Why not there?"

'I said, "If I knew where there were emeralds, I'd be there myself. They're everywhere. And nowhere."

'Half an hour later (or let's say an hour so we don't exaggerate) the old man comes up to me.

'"Is this an emerald?"

'I had a look.

'I said quietly, "Hide it."

'He hid it.

'"Don't talk about it."

'It was pretty. I couldn't buy it. I could have cheated him but that's not part of my life.

'"Come with me. We're going to sit and drink coffee until the dealers arrive."

'I knew one of them better than the others and I called him over.

'"Take a look."

'It was a nice emerald!

'He gave him two hundred thousand pesos. A lot of money. In cash. And the old man had found it in half an hour. He kissed my hands.

'"You knew it was there."

'"I didn't know anything."

'The following day he went back to Cúcuta.'

José's attitude to the old man contains everything he aspired to: worldliness, magnanimity, a sort of prophetic instinct. But, even if it is largely true, doesn't the old man also represent José, who kept to the margins and sifted the detritus of the world because of an inarticulate feeling that it was there among the rags and the dirt that the jewel called life, which he had always felt compelled to pursue, shone brightest? And then this man, whose insatiable appetite for life led him to live several of them and invent many more, died. I was left with a few stained, fading, slightly scratched photographs and his voice in my recordings, full of conviction early in the day, growing tired as the afternoon wore on, but never, ever short of a story.

There was, in the lives of José and Georges Beyaert, something of the fable of two brothers, one who sets out to pursue his fortune, the other who stays at home and lets life come to him. Georges, who stayed at home, ran a successful business and lived well. José, the adventurer, left France a relatively young man; he returned to Europe when he was nearing seventy-five and died five years later in the west of France. It seemed to me pertinent to ask to what extent he ceased, during his life, to be French and to see the world as a Frenchman. Working in one of Bogotá's few French restaurants in the 1970s José can hardly have failed to be acutely aware of the difference and strangeness, to him as a Frenchman, of the Colombian way of life and of the French way of life to his Colombian friends.

He was a professional cyclist and a fine one. What could be more French? Isn't cycling and all its vocabulary French? Yet Colombia too is a nation of cyclists. He was a wonderful dancer as well. Isn't dance and all *its* vocabulary French? Yet Colombia is a country of music and dance to a greater degree even than France. He made his living, at different times, as a Frenchman peddling hairdressing and beauty products: how clichéd! And from selling precious stones and finished jewellery – to the French! And if there is evidence to suggest he may on occasion have trafficked illegal drugs, don't the stories of Auguste Joseph Ricord, Charles Laurent Fiocconi and Jean Gay show that this too was a very French pursuit?

José told me a comic anecdote about two clients who walked into Louisette's restaurant.

'One asked for steak tartare, the other asked for a chateaubriand.

'The chateaubriand said, "*Bien cuit.*"

'I said, "To eat a steak *bien cuit*, you don't want a chateaubriand. A chateaubriand is a thick steak."

'He told me to slice it through.

'"If I cut it in two, it isn't a chateaubriand any more."

'No, he wanted it *bien cuit*, and his friend, the one who'd asked for steak tartare said, "Me, too. *Bien cuit!*"

'Steak tartare, *bien cuit!* It's the punchline to a joke!'

But José wasn't poking fun at his clients' ignorance, as Colombians, of French cuisine. He was laughing at their boastfulness: in trying to show sophistication they were making fools of themselves. José was no snob. He was always telling me, 'You mustn't judge people who have no education': he said it of the Colombians he brought to Paris in 1953, he said it of his parents, he said it of people he saw around him in the tiny village in western France where he had gone to die.

By the end he belonged neither to France nor to Colombia but acted out a constant interaction between the two. It is impossible to imagine him without his fifty years in a Colombia he made to suit his own fantasies, his daring, his pride. His younger brother Georges outlived him, if the word can be used in the chronological sense alone. He still lives in Pantin, just beyond the north-eastern city limits. We met at the bar that had been his local for fifty-five years. He walked me to the house of his childhood at Rue Jean Nicol 2. It is a butcher's now, where horse meat is sold. And José's wartime madison partner Roger Rioland told me, knowing it was a curiosity, that he was born in the house where he still lives and that, more than that, he is the fourth generation of his family to live there. José was cut from another cloth: the same cloth, perhaps, that made his paternal grandfather, Evarist Beyaert.

Yet something in his story called to mind the striking description by Amitav Ghosh of his experiences as a fieldworker in an Egyptian village where he was expecting to find a settled, restful people. 'I couldn't have been more wrong,' he wrote:

> The men of the village had all the busy restlessness of airline passengers in a transit lounge. Many of them had worked and travelled in the shiekdoms of the Persian Gulf, others had been in Libya and Jordan and Syria, some had been to the Yemen as soldiers, others to Saudi Arabia as pilgrims, a few had visited Europe: some of them had passports so thick they opened out like ink-blackened concertinas. And none of this was new: their grandparents and ancestors and relatives had travelled and migrated too . . . The wanderlust of its founders had been ploughed into the soil of the village . . .

In José's story, as in Ghosh's rural Egypt, Frenchmen and Corsicans, Italians and Belgians, Germans and Spaniards, Argentines and Armenians, Englishmen, indeed, crossed borders, pushed back frontiers and discovered homes away from homes away from homes.

In his book *Les bourlingueurs*, Auguste le Breton says to José:

> 'You're the sort of man who doesn't think a lot. Deep down you're a happy man. You're afraid of nothing, not even death.'
>
> 'Yes, but I'm still afraid of making cock-ups and getting an earful from my wife.'
>
> 'Do you believe in life after death?'
>
> 'You're having me on.'

'You don't believe in Heaven, Paradise?'
'Not even in Father Christmas, no. Nothing.'
'You don't believe in anything? Not even in yourself?'
'Yes, but that's all.'

I was told José's atheism had relented towards the end. He had admitted there might be something more. I hoped it wasn't so. I hoped it was a consideration shown for the believers in his extended family. I wanted to think that the courage to face a meaningless, hostile universe without faintness of heart, devising his own rules of life and persisting in being only what he was, had not failed him and that he had faced death as he had faced life, depleted of all the traditional religious comforts.

'In Colombia people pray,' José had said. 'That's what they do.'

Esperanza Vallecilla does. In September 2008 two friends visited her in Bogotá to chant the rosary. As they did so one of her friends fell into a trance. He told her someone wanted to speak to her. He wanted to ask her forgiveness.

'For the children. His name's José.'

'José Beyaert?'

'Yes.'

'I forgive him.'

'He says he loves you very much.'

Then the trance passed.

REFERENCES

INTERVIEWS

'Big Blond',10/10/2008 by telephone and then 4/1/2009 and 9/1/2009 by text messaging

Bob Maitland, 17/6/2008, Sutton Coldfield

Charles Laurent Fiocconi, 21/10/2008 and 22/10/2008, Pietralba, Corsica

Carlos Morales, aka 'Tachuela', 23/5/2008, Barrancabermeja

Dulce María Veleño, 18/12/2008, Barrancabermeja

Elizabeth Martínez Martínez, 18/5/2008, San Andrés

Esperanza Vallecilla Guevara, 10/12/2008, Bogotá

Francisco 'Pacho' Rodríguez, 12/12/2008, Bogotá

Fanny Tolosa, 15/5/2008, Yarima

Georges Beyaert, repeated conversations between October 2004 and April 2009

Georges Bougaud, 13/11/2008, by telephone

Giovanni Corrieri, 18/9/2008, by telephone

Gabriel Chávez Veleño, aka 'Cochise', 14/5/2008 and 17/12/2008, Barrancabermeja

Guillermo García Jaramillo, 27/10/2008, Cali

Gonzalo Perilla, 13/12/2008, Bogotá

Guillermo Robayo, 13/12/2008, Bogotá

Gil Roberto Garzón Pineda, 24/5/2008, Barrancabermeja

Humberto Vallecilla and Flor Leticia Guevara Gómez, 11/5/2008 and 19/12/2008, Barrancabermeja

Humberto Uribe, 12/5/2008, Barrancabermeja

Javier Buitrago Rodríguez, 11/11/2008, by telephone

Jose Beyaert, 9–10/11/2004 and 12–13/11/2004, Mignon-les-Greves

Javier Buitrago Rodríguez, 11/11/2008, by telephone

Jean-Claude Kella, 23/10/2008, Nice

José Duarte, 11/12/2008, Bogotá

Jacques Marchand, email communications

Jacques Marinelli, October 2008, Melun

'Lola', 10/12/2008, Bogotá

León Velásquez, 10/5/2008, Barrancabermeja

Mario Arroyo Caamaño, 13/5/2008 and 19/12/2008, Barrancabermeja

Mayerly Carolina Beyaert Vallecilla, 15/5/2008, Bucaramanga

Miguel Martínez Rivera, 12/5/2008, Barrancabermeja

Michel Paret, 25/2/2009, by telephone

Marcel Plazz-Lartigau, 28/5/2008, Bogotá

Olga Cecilia Rangel, 10/5/2008, Barrancabermeja

Pedro Bueno, 17/12/2008, Barrancabermeja

Plácido Rojas Morales, 18/5/2008, San Andrés

Roger Rioland, 13/2/2009, by telephone

Roberto Serafín Guerrero, 8/1/2009, Medellín

Walwin Godfrey Petersen, 18/5/2008, San Andrés.

ABBREVIATIONS

ABAC Antony Beevor and Artemis Cooper, *Paris After the Liberation: 1944–1949* (London: Hamish Hamilton, 1994).

ADIMAD Consulted at the Association pour la défense des intérêts moraux et matérials des anciens détenus de l'Algérie française (ADIMAD) unofficial website for veterans of the OAS.

AG Amitav Ghosh, 'The Imam and the Indian', *Granta*, 20 (Winter 1986), pp. 135–46

AGR Alberto Galvis Ramírez, *Cien años de Fútbol en Colombia* (Bogotá: Planeta, 2008).

AHS Alfonso Hilarión Sánchez, *Los Esmeralderos* (Bogotá: Carlos Valencia Editores, 1980).

AL Albert Londres, *Au bagne* (Paris: Privat/Le Rocher, 2007).

AlB 'Bour' Auguste le Breton, *Les Bourlingueurs* (Paris: Plon, 1972).

AlB 'Rififi' Auguste le Breton, *Ils ont dansé le rififi: mémoires* (Le Rocher: Éditions du Rocher, 1991).

AlB 'Rouges' Auguste le Breton, *Rouges étaient les émeraudes* (Paris: Plon, 1971).

AP Anthony Pagden, *European Encounters with the New World: From Renaissance to Romanticism* (New Haven and London: Yale University Press, 1993).

AS Albert Spaggiari, *The Sewers of Gold*, tr. Martin Sokolinsky (London: Granada, 1979).

BMA Cuttings from *News Chronicle*, *The Bicycle* and other periodicals, often with no date or page number, in Bob Maitland's personal archive.

BoxRec Boxing records and statistics consulted at BoxRec.com

Byc *The Bicycle* (UK).

Cali Alejandro Ulloa, *La salsa en Cali* (Cali: Ediciones Universidad del Valle, 1992).

CLFvUS(1) 462 F.2d 475, 24 A.L.R.Fed. 930, Charles Laurent FIOCCONI and Jean Claude Kella, Petitioners-Appellants, v. ATTORNEY GENERAL of the UNITED STATES et al., Respondents-Appellees. No. 833, Docket 72-1425. United States Court of Appeals, Second Circuit. Argued May 12, 1972. Decided

June 12, 1972. Consulted at openjurist.org.

CLFvUS(2) 490 F.2d 1095, UNITED STATES of America, Appellee, v. Jean Claude KELLA and Laurent Fiocconi, Appellants. Nos. 423, 809, Dockets 73-2212, 73-2213. United States Court of Appeals, Second Circuit. Argued Nov. 20, 1973. Decided Jan. 16, 1974. Consulted at justia.com.

CP William McBrien, *Cole Porter: The Definitive Biography* (London: HarperCollins, 1998).

DM David Miller, *Athens to Athens: The Official History of the Olympic Games and the IOC, 1894–2004* (Edinburgh and London: Mainstream Publishing, 2003).

Écho *L'Écho d'Algers* (Morocco).

EGOJ Estefanía González Vélez and Orlán Jiménez Menesis, *Las guerras del Magndalena medio* (Bogotá: Intermedio Editores, 2008).

EH 'MF' Ernest Hemingway, *A Moveable Feast* (London: Grafton, 1977).

EH 'Stories' Ernest Hemingway, *The First Forty-Nine Stories* (London: Arrow Books, 2004).

Esp *El Espectador* (Colombia).

FC Fabio Castillo, *Los Jinetes de la Cocaina* (Bogotá: Editorial Documentos Periodísticos, 1987).

Fig *Le Figaro* (France).

FG 'Picasso' Françoise Gilot and Carlton Lake, *Life with Picasso* (London: Virago, 2007).

FRdN Flor Romero de Nohra, *3 Kilates, 8 Puntos* (Bogotá: Jorge Plazas Editor, 1966).

GC Television documentary, *Albert Spaggiari, Gentleman-Cambrioleur*, Sécrets d'Actualité, INA.

GdV Gérard de Villiers, *Papillon épinglé: la vérité sur le bagne et sur le Vénézuela* (Paris: Presses de la Cité, 1970).

GGM Journalism Gabriel García Márquez, *Obra Periodística 2: Entre Cachacos*, ed. Jacques Gilard (Bogotá: Norma, 1997).

GM Georges Ménager, *Les quatre vérités de Papillon* (Paris: La Table Ronde, 1970).

GSDN Gonzalo Sánchez and Donny Neertens, *Bandoleros, Gamonales y Campesinos: El Caso de la Violencia en Colombia* (Bogotá: Aguilar, 2006).

Haÿ Ginette Haÿ, 'Le fabuleux destin du Lensois José Beyaert', *Gauheria: l epassé de la Gohelle*, 53 (November 2003), pp. 49–54.

HB Herbert Braun, *Mataron a Gaitán* (Bogotá: Norma, 1998).

HVC Heino Von Christen, 'Informe sobre las actividades silviculturales en los tres ultimos anos y el plan de trabajo para 1971: Proyecto Carare-opon, Oct. 1970', in *1 Seminario Nacional de Investigaciones Forestales (Bogotá)* (12–15 October 1970), pp. 121–38.

JAG Jacques Aprile-Gniset, *Génesis de Barrancabermeja* (Cali: Instituto Universitario de la Paz Departamento de Ciencias Sociales, 1997).

JB Jean Bobet, *Le vélo à l'heure allemande* (Paris: La Table Ronde, 2007).

JBA Cuttings from *El Tiempo*, *El Espectador* and other periodicals, often with no date or page number, in José Beyaert's personal archive.

JCK Jean-Claude Kella, *L'Affranchi* (Paris: Éditions du Toucan, 2009).

JJ James Joyce, *Dubliners*, (London: Penguin, 1992).

JLC James Logan Chappell, 'Heroin threat from Colombia', MA thesis, Fort Leavenworth, Kansas, 1996.

JM Jacques Marchand, *Jacques Goddet: Journaliste d'abord* . . . (Anglet: Atlantica, 2002).

JRJ Jean-Roland Julliard, *Mütti . . . ! (Oh! petite maman . . .)* (Paris: Collection Les Manuscrits de lecteur, 1975).

JS Juana Salabert, *Velódromo de Invierno* (Barcelona: Editorial Seix Barral, 2001).

KL Kenneth S. Lynn, *Hemingway* (Cambridge, MA and London: Harvard University Press, 1995).

Kundera Milan Kundera, *Testaments Betrayed: An Essay in Nine Parts* (London: Faber and Faber, 1995).

L'Éq *L'Équipe* (France).

Marchesini Daniele Marchesini, *L'Italia del Giro d'Italia* (Bologna: Il Mulino, 1996).

Mémoire Consulted at Mémoire du cyclisme website.

MG Marion F. Godfroy, *Bagnards* (Paris: Tallandier, 2008).

MR 'Kings' Matt Rendell, *Kings of the Mountains: How Colombia's Cycling Heroes Changed their Nation's History* (London: Aurum Press, 2002).

MVUA María Victoria Uribe Alarcón, *Limpiar la tierra: Guerra y poder entre esmeralderos* (Bogotá: CINEP, 1992).

NC *News Chronicle* (UK).

NHC2 *Historia Política 1946–1986* [vol. ii of *Nueva Historia de Colombia*] (Bogotá: Planeta, 1989).

NJBM Norman Mailer and John Buffalo Mailer, *The Big Empty: Dialogues on Politics, Sex, God, Boxing, Morality, Myth, Poker and Bad Conscience in America* (New York: Nation Books, 2006).

NYPL New York Passenger Lists, 1820–1957. Consulted at http://www.ancestry.com/.

Obit Matt Rendell, 'José Beyaert', *The Guardian* 23/7/05.

OR1948 The Official Report of the Organising Committee for the XIV Olympiad, (London: The Organising Committee for the XIV Olympiad, 1948).

P-R Philippe Conrate and Pascal Sergent, *Entre Paris et Roubaix: Petites histoires d'une grande classique* (Saint Cyr: Alan Sutton, 2006).

Papillon Henri Charrière, *Papillon* (Paris: Robert Laffont, 1969).

Papillon (film) *Papillon*, Feature Film DVD, Sony Pictures Home Entertainment, Catalogue no. CDR 10049.

PCLV Passenger and Crew Lists of Vessels Arriving at New York, New York, 1897–1957; (National Archives Microfilm Publication T715, 8892 rolls); Records of the Immigration and Naturalization Service; National Archives, Washington, DC. Consulted at http://www.ancestry.com/. New York Passenger Lists, 1820–1957 [database online]. Provo, UT, USA: The Generations Network, Inc., 2006.

PL *Le Parisien Libéré* (France).

P-P *Paris-Presse* (France).

RB Richard Berdin, *Code Name Richard,* tr. and eds Jeannette Seaver and Richard Seaver (London: New English Library, 1977).

RC Regards croisés. L'immigration dans le Nord/Pas de Calais. (Béthune, 2002).

RD *'Hut'* René Delpêche, *Parmi les fauves et les requins: Ou la confession de M. Charles Hut, ancien forçat* (Paris: Éditions du Scorpion, 1955).

Rép TdF Jean-Luc Bœuf and Yves Léonard, *La République du Tour de France 1903–2003* (Paris: Éditions du Seuil, 2003).

RH Richard Holmes, *Sidetracks: Explorations of a Romantic Biographer* (London: HarperPerennial, 2005).

RHol Roger Holeindre, 'Les aventuriers de l'émeraude,' *Paris-Match,* no. 1615 (9 May 1980), pp. 3–26.

Rififi Rififi [Fr. *Du rififi chez les hommes*], Feature Film DVD, Arrow Films, Catalogue no. FCD127. Includes Q&A with Jules Dassin, and Jules Dassin at the NFT.

RK Rémi Kauffer, *OAS: histoire de la guerre franco-française* (Paris: Éditions du Seuil, 2002).

RLM René Louis Maurice with Ken Follett, *The Heist of the Century* (London: Fontana/Collins, 1978).

RMFC Robin Moore, *The French Connection* (London: Bloomsbury, 2005).

RP Robert Pollock, *Loophole, or How to Rob a Bank* (London: Coronet, 1974).

RSGA Cuttings from Argentine and Colombian newspapers, often with no date or page number, in Roberto Serafín Guerrero's personal archive.

Sig *El Siglo* (Colombia).

SS Susan Sontag, *Where the Stress Falls* (London: Farrar Straus Giroux, 2001).

TdF Gérard Ejnès and Gérard Schaller, dir., *Tour de France 100 ans, Tome II, 1947–1977* (Paris: L'Équipe, 2002).

TdF Enc Joël Godaert, Robert Janssens and Guido Cammaert, *Tour Encyclopedie Vol. 2, 1930–1953* (Gent: Uitgeverij Worldstrips, 1998).

TdF Presse Robert Ménard, dir., and Sylvie Devilette, ed., *Le Tour de France pour la liberté de presse 1903–2005: Le Tour de France par les journalistes et photographes qui ont écrit sa légende* (Paris: Reporteurs sans frontiers, 2005).

TH Tim Hilton, *One More Kilometre and We're in the Showers: Memoir of a Cyclist* (London: HarperCollins, 2004).

Tmp *El Tiempo* (Colombia).

ToC Rafael Duque, *Los escarabajos de la Vuelta a Colombia* (Bogotá: Oveja Negra, 1984).

VL *Vanguardia Liberal* (Colombia).

VTE Olle Söderström's website.

WGP Walwin G. Peterson, *The Province of Providence* (San Andrés Island: The Christian University of San Andrés, Providence and Catalina, 2002).

XL Xavier Louy, *Un nouveau cyclisme avec Greg, Lucho et Wang* (Monte Carlo: Éditions de Radio-Monte-Carlo, 1986).

ENDNOTES

INTRODUCTION

10 Jean Maréchal . . . Jean Coussy:
identifications are thanks to
Jacques Marchand.

11 rules of fiction: *SS*, p. 15.

11 fictional character: Mr Duffy in
JJ, 'A Painful Case'.

12 MANUAL OF THE
PERFECT ROAD RACER:
L'Éq, 24/2/1949, p. 2.

13 Rider to Watch in 1949: *L'Éq*,
5/1/1949, p. 4.

13 first major race: *L'Éq*, 7/3/1949,
p. 3.

17 Jacques Goddet, who fumed:
TdF, p. 303.

1

21 changed beyond all recognition:
Nord/Pas de Calais and
immigration history from *RC*;
ABAC, pp. 171–2; *KL*, p. 148.

23 a very good regional: *P-P*,
15–16/8/1948, p. 2, cols 1–2.

24 a haven for refugees: *RC*; *ABAC*
pp. 171–2.

25 eve of the Second World War:
KL, pp. 148–9.

25 Evarist Beyaert: *NYPL*, Year:

1912, Microfilm serial: T715,
Microfilm roll: T715 1850,
Line: 25.

2

28 Stade Anastasie: *EHMF*, p. 9.

29 Théo Medina and Emmanuel
'Titi' Clavel: records consulted
at *BoxRec*.

29 a former boxer: *L'Éq*, 11/3/1948,
p. 2, col. 8.

30 imposed restrictions: *NJBM*,
pp. 173–93.

31 ride on the flat: *L'Éq*,
10/6/1949, p. 1.

32 950 professional racing licences:
JB.

33 five thousand young men: *JB*,
p. 27.

34 two versions of the Critérium
National: *JB*, p. 71.

34 Flèche du Rhône: *JB*, pp. 77–8.

38 Charles Berty: *JB*, p. 138.

38 208 killings by members of the
Resistance: *ABAC*, p. 99.

40 16 July 1942: *JB*, pp. 115–6; *JM*,
p. 63; *JS*.

40 survivors began to return:
ABAC, pp. 165–6.

41 Tour de la Haute-Vienne: *JB*,
  p. 197.

3

43 It was 22 August 1944: *ABAC*,
  pp. 88, 94–5, 88–101.
44 General von Choltitz: *ABAC*,
  p. 45.
44 STO: *JB*, p. 144; *ABAC*, p. 26.
45 Artioli and Usotti: *L'Éq*,
  4–5/5/1946, p. 2, col. 5.
48 Olympic Committee not
  decided: *DM*, p. 118.
48 Bitter institutional feuds: *TH*,
  pp. 49–54.
48 Bill Mills: this and many other
  extracts in this chapter are
  undated excerpts from *NC* and
  Byc in *BMA*.
48 Mayor of Folkestone: *BMA*.
51 The autograph: *BMA*.
52 contender for the world: *L'Éq*,
  21/7/1947, p. 3, col. 2.
52 great enthusiasm: *L'Eq*,
  30/7/1947, p. 2.
52 José's fantasy: race description
  in *Byc*, *BMA*.
53 The victim of an accident: *L'Éq*,
  5/8/1947, p. 1.
54 The finish line: *L'Éq*, 10/6/1948,
  p. 4, col. 5.
54 pre-selection for the Games:
  L'Éq, 13/1/1948, p. 2, col. 5.
55 he hadn't been consulted: *L'Éq*,
  16/2/1948.
55 To tell the truth: *L'Éq*,
  8–9/5/1948, p. 3, col. 3.
55 bicycle manufacturer Helyett:
  L'Éq, 11/3/1948, p. 2, col. 8.
55 Matteotti Trophy: *L'Éq*,
  3/5/1948, p. 6, col. 3.
56 stage to Le Mans: *L'Éq*,

22/5/1948, p. 1, col. 5.
57 Folkestone at 7 a.m.: *Byc* and
  NC reports, *BMA*.
58 permission of his Majesty:
  OR1948, p. 44.
58 one mile shorter: *Byc* report,
  BMA.
58 José, acutely aware: detailed race
  report in *Byc*, *BMA*.
59 ham in the sandwich: *L'Éq*,
  7/6/1948, p. 2, col. 2.
59 fifty-five-kilometre breakaway:
  L'Éq, 23/6/1948, p. 1, cols 4–5.
59 winning break: *L'Éq*, 29/6/1948,
  p. 2, col. 6.
59 The day was gruelling: *L'Éq*,
  2/7/1948, p. 3.
59 Monsieur Abadie: *L'Éq*,
  13/7/1948, p. 3, col. 2.
60 READY FOR LONDON:
  L'Éq, 19/7/1948, p. 3, col 3.
60 Beyaert rode: *L'Éq*, 19/7/1948,
  p. 3, col 3.

4

61 would travel on Monday: *L'Éq*,
  5/8/1948, p. 2, col. 6.
61 went for a medical: *L'Éq*,
  7/8/1948, p. 3, col. 8.
61 Rouchet had to join: *L'Éq*,
  8/8/1948, p. 3, col. 8.
62 French riders: *L'Éq*, 12/8/1948,
  p. 3, col. 8.
63 Speicher went to Herne Hill:
  L'Éq, *Ibid*.
63 On the basis of rumours: *Ibid*.
63 The Windsor circuit: *OR1948*,
  p. 332.
64 LAST BIG DAY: *L'Éq*,
  13/8/1948.
64 The circuit was closed: *OR1948*,
  p. 331.

64 Wazir Ali: *Byc* report, *BMA*.

65 Then at 11.24 a.m.: *Byc* report, *BMA*.

65 the safest place: detailed race reports in *Byc*, *BMA*, and *L'Éq*, 14–15/8/1948, p. 2, col. 3.

67 looking over his shoulder: *L'Éq*, 14–15/8/1948, p. 1, col. 1.

67 *The Bicycle* says Rouffeteau: *Byc* report, *BMA*.

68 the wound was closed: *Ibid*.

68 José who led: *OR1948*, p. 335.

68 a good five lengths: *Byc* report, *BMA*.

69 Beyaert's gamble: *Ibid*.

69 But it was useless: *Ibid*.

69 3.6 seconds: *OR1948*, p. 333.

70 WEE JOSE: *Daily Mirror*, 14/8/1948, p. 11, cols 5–7.

71 BEYAERT, THE ROAD MAN: *L'Éq*, 14–15/8/1948, p. 1.

71 little Parisian: *P-P*, 15–16/8/1948, p. 2, cols 1–2.

72 By 1 p.m.: *Ibid*.

73 José left Paris: *L'Éq*, 19/8/1948, p. 2, col. 5.

74 organising the chase: *Byc* report, *BMA*.

74 You know how I beat them?: *EH 'Stories'*, p. 124.

5

76 I'm not twenty-three: *P-P*, 15–16/8/1948, p. 2, cols 1–2.

76 In the 1930s: *Mémoire*, 'Équipes/Maillots'.

76 *L'Espoir* 1949: *L'Éq*, 5/1/1949, p. 4.

76 three thousand kilometers: *L'Éq*, 24/2/1949, p. 2.

76 fizzling, sharp, fired-up: *L'Éq*, 1/3/1949.

76 Aïn Témouchent: *L'Éq*, 28/2/1949, p. 3.

77 pugnaciously: *L'Éq*, 7/3/1949, p. 3; *Écho*, 6–7/3/1949, pp. 1, 3 and 6.

77 his rival conceded defeat: *Écho*, 6–7/3/1949, p. 6.

77 FIRST MAJOR RACE: *L'Éq*, 7/3/1949, p. 3.

77 ride your own race: *L'Éq*, 8/3/1949, p. 1.

77 trained like a pro: *Ibid*.

78 AT THE 'HET VOLK': *L'Éq*, 12–13/3/1949, p. 1.

78 Only echoes: *Ibid*.

78 Beyaert, ill: *L'Éq*, 14/3/1949, p. 2.

78 What we won't see: *L'Éq*, 2–3/4/1949, p. 4.

78 for a long period excellent: *L'Éq*, 4/4/1949, p. 2.

79 EIGHT DAYS: *L'Éq*, 7/4/1949, p. 3

79 Flèche Wallonne: *L'Éq*, 14/4/1949.

79 most notorious finish: *P-R*, p. 94.

79 The press reports: *L'Éq*, 18/4/1949.

79 Look out: *L'Éq*, 22/4/1949, p. 2.

79 *Voilà un brillant tandem!*: *L'Éq*, 29/4/1949, p. 3.

79 surprise no one: *Ibid*.

80 snow, water and mud: *L'Éq*, 30/4/1949, p. 3.

80 hardest, longest day: *L'Éq*, 3/5/1949.

80 despite taking third place: *L'Éq*, 11/5/1949, p. 2.

81 Don't let us forget: *Ibid*.

81 earned him selection: *Ibid*.

81 José's name: *L'Éq*, 14–15/5/1949.

81 After the rigours: *L'Éq*,
17/5/1949.

81 Beyaert wants to show: *Ibid.*

81 But José doesn't appear: *L'Éq*,
23/5/1949.

81 Boucles de la Seine: *L'Éq*,
26/5/1949.

81 Two hundred kilomètres!: *L'Éq*,
10/6/1949, p. 1.

82 By fine-tuning his condition:
Ibid.

82 thick of the race: *L'Éq*,
13/6/1949.

82 Beyaert, despite his class: *L'Éq*,
15/6/1949.

82 a little disappointed: *L'Éq*,
17/6/1949, p. 4.

83 in French national
championships: *L'Éq*,
20/6/1949.

83 Sunday races in Switzerland:
L'Éq, 24/6/1949, p. 2.

83 at his home track: *L'Éq*,
2/9/1949, p. 2.

83 he invited José: *L'Éq*, 5/9/1949.

83 José signed a new contract:
L'Éq, 6/9/1949, p. 2.

84 He went to Italy: *L'Éq*,
21/9/1949, p. 2.

84 Vienna: *L'Éq*, 5/10/1949, p. 3,
col. 1.

85 Bartali was the winner: *Ibid.*

85 I felt the effects: *L'Éq*,
21/9/1949, p. 2.

85 Instead José rode anonymously:
L'Éq, 24/10/1949.

85 he was in Algiers: *L'Éq*,
19/10/1949, p. 2.

85 France was shocked: *L'Éq*,
29–30/10/1949, p. 1.

86 René Vietto left: *L'Éq*,
20/10/1949, p. 3.

86 Many fans have: *L'Éq*,
1–2/7/1950, p. 4.

86 astonishing athletic gifts: MS
of Vietto biography for *La
France Cycliste* kindly sent by
Christophe Pénot.

87 were invited to meet: *L'Éq*,
28/10/1949, p. 3.

87 José was flying: *L'Éq*,
29–30/10/1949.

87 Vietto arrived late: *L'Éq*,
5–6/11/1949, p. 3.

87 Vietto began to sack riders:
L'Éq, 29–30/10/1949.

88 Without him: *L'Éq*, 7/11/1949,
p. 3.

88 no more mysteries: *L'Éq*,
19–20/11/1949, p. 3.

89 *Pas question d'abandons!*: *L'Éq*,
8/12/1949, p. 2.

89 Cauvin the hotelier: *L'Éq*,
29/12/1949, pp. 1–2.

89 Bernard Nehr: *Ibid.*

89 They'll have to train hard: *L'Éq*,
8/12/1949, p. 2.

90 The Teisseire brothers: *L'Éq*,
30/11/1949, p. 3.

90 The Communist newspaper: *Rép
TdF*, p. 137.

90 I was soaked through: *L'Éq*,
22/12/1949, p. 1.

91 Picasso's mansion: *FG 'Picasso'*,
p. 177 and *passim*.

91 Paris was liberated: Pablo
Picasso, quoted in *ABAC*, p. 81.

92 Right-wingers: *ABAC*, p. 81.

92 Hotel Moderne: *L'Éq*,
29/12/1949, pp. 1–2.

92 I'm getting younger: *L'Éq*,
1/2/1950, p. 1.

93 I owe everything: *L'Éq*,
4–5/2/1950, p. 1.

6

95 Avignon Grand Prix: race description in *L'Éq*, 27/2/1950, p. 2.

95 start list for Algiers Grand Prix: *L'Éq*, 2/3/1950, p. 1.

95 notified the race organisers: *L'Éq*, 4–5/3/1950, p. 3.

95 went to Bordighera: *L'Éq*, 6/3/1950.

96 out of gas: *L'Éq*, 21/3/1950, p. 3.

96 José rode poorly: *L'Éq*, 27/3/1950.

96 led the chase: *L'Éq*, 3/4/1950.

96 I escaped alone: *L'Éq*, 17/4/1950.

97 Apart from Beyaert: *L'Éq*, 20/4/1950, p. 1.

97 discipline René requires: *Ibid*.

97 with irony: *Ibid*.

97 exception of Lauredi: *L'Éq*, 11/5/1950, p. 8.

97 Émile and Lucien: *Ibid*.

97 Lauredi and Géminiani: *L'Éq*, 11/5/1950, p. 3.

98 The 1950 Tour: *L'Éq*, 22/5/1950, p. 8.

98 a revolutionary Tour of Italy: *Ibid*.

99 a very good first day: *L'Éq*, 25/5/1950.

99 not José Beyaert: *Ibid*.

99 the famous Raticosa: *L'Éq*, 26/5/1950.

99 only really interested: *L'Éq*, 31/5/1950, p. 3.

99 selling their services: *L'Éq*, 6/6/1950, p. 5.

99 their contribution: *Ibid*.

99 example of André Brulé: *L'Éq*, 5/6/1950.

100 joined each time: *L'Éq*, 6/6/1950, p. 5.

100 difficult for the French: *L'Éq*, 16/6/1950.

101 did not name Corrieri: *Ibid*.

102 not on stage thirteen: *L'Éq*, 8/6/1950, p. 3.

102 in Naples: *L'Éq*, 13/6/1950.

102 the best paid-cyclists: *L'Éq*, 21/6/1950, p. 8.

103 But we all tried: *L'Éq*, 21/6/1950, p. 5.

103 riding another: *L'Éq*, 20/6/1950, p. 3.

103 We're doing Paris–Boulogne-sur-Mer: *L'Éq*, 19/6/1950, p. 7.

103 joint favourite: *L'Éq*, 17–18/6/1950, p. 5.

103 almost didn't take part: *L'Éq*, 19/6/1950, p. 7 (with race report).

104 breathing health: *Ibid*.

104 three-way struggle: *L'Éq*, 27/6/1950, p. 1.

104 forced to abandon: *L'Éq*, 27/6/1950.

104 unheralded dominance: *L'Éq*, 1–2/7/1950, p. 4.

105 not exceptionally good: *L'Éq*, 23/6/1950, p. 4.

105 *La gaité personnifiée*: *Ibid*.

105 the bespectacled rider: *L'Éq*, 6/7/1950, p. 3.

105 a tough morsel: *L'Éq*, 12/7/1950, p. 3.

106 a swashbuckling stage: *L'Éq*, 21/7/1950, p. 2.

107 between *bidons*: *L'Éq*, 21/7/1950, p. 6.

107 I've removed a doubt: *L'Éq*, 21/7/1950, p. 2.

107 I suffered for him: *Ibid*.

107 Raoul Rémy tried: *L'Éq*, 22–23/7/1950, p. 4.

107 The doctor told me: *AlB 'Bour'*, p. 100.

108 His open knee: *L'Éq*, 22–23/7/1950, p. 4.

108 Despite his pain: *Ibid.*

108 astride the guardrail: *L'Éq*, 27/7/1950, p. 6.

108 nine and a half hours: *TdF Enc*, pp. 182–4. José completed stage 19 (Briançon to Saint-Étienne) in 9 hours 18 minutes 19 seconds, and stage 22 (Dijon to Paris) in 9 hours 38 minutes 6 seconds.

7

110 I'm in some pain: *L'Éq*, 7/8/1950, p. 3.

110 Where do we sign on: *L'Éq*, 8/8/1950, p. 8.

110 Tour de France Oscars: *L'Éq*, 9/8/1950, p. 3.

110 José was mentioned: *L'Éq*, 11/8/1950, p. 3.

111 José finished thirteenth: *L'Éq*, 19–20/8/1950, p. 3; *L'Éq*, 20/8/1950.

111 Grand Prix des Cycles Helyett: *L'Éq*, 18/9/1950, p. 5.

111 revival of the legendary: *L'Éq*, 25–26/10/1950, p. 1.

111 The first Bol d'Or: *L'Éq*, 25–26/10/1950, p. 1.

111 first to sign up: *L'Éq*, 1/11/1950, p. 3.

111 I want to ride: *L'Éq*, 3/11/1950, p. 3.

112 news came through: *L'Éq*, 14/11/1950, p. 1.

112 The prize for winning: *L'Éq*, 24/11/1950.

112 THE FEATHERWEIGHT:

L'Éq, 25–26/11/1950, p. 1.

112 The entrants included: *Ibid.*

112 His optimism, his morale: *L'Éq*, Saturday 25–26/11/1950, p. 3.

112 At 11 p.m.: *L'Éq*, 27/11/1950 (full report and timings on p. 3).

115 Rest of the World: *L'Éq*, 8/12/1950, p. 4.

115 fifty thousand francs a month: *L'Éq*, 21/9/1950, p. 3.

116 Lazaridès rejoined: *L'Éq*, 10/10/1950.

116 ride Milan–San Remo: *L'Éq*, 30/11/1950, p. 3.

116 His riders now included: *L'Éq*, 13/2/1950, p. 2.

116 José failed to start: *L'Éq*, 19/1/1951.

116 failed to finish: *L'Éq*, 26/2/1951.

116 Rouen Grand Prix: *L'Éq*, 17/4/1951, p. 3.

116 Circuit du Morbihan: *L'Éq*, 23/4/1951.

116 Tour de l'Est: *L'Éq*, 26/4/1951, p. 3.

116 Noveltex Grand Prix: *L'Éq*, 27/4/1951, p. 3.

116 Tour de l'Oise: *L'Éq*, 14/5/1951.

116 after Crévecoeur: *L'Éq*, 15/5/1951, p. 4.

116 On stage three: *Ibid.*

116 I got off on the wrong foot: *L'Éq*, 15/6/1951, p. 3.

117 José's inclusion: *L'Éq*, 27/6/1951, p. 6.

117 killed in a crash: *L'Éq*, 30/6/1951, p. 1.

117 1951 Tour de France started: *L'Éq*, 5/7/1951, p. 1.

117 Protecting Redolfi's breakaway: *Ibid.*

117 Soon after Somme-Suippes: *Ibid.*

117 José chasing hard: *L'Éq,*
5/7/1951, p. 3, bottom.

118 It has been some time: *L'Éq,*
6/7/1951, p. 6.

118 I attacked: *AlB 'Bour'*, p. 98–9.

8

120 three Italian riders: *L'Éq,*
18/8/1950, p. 3.

120 a rider named Paul Neri: *L'Éq,*
19/7/1947, p. 3, col. 1.

120 foreign names: *L'Éq.*
29–30/7/1950, p. 6.

122 invitation: *L'Éq,* 3/10/1951,
p. 4, col. 4.

122 José Beyaert and B. Loatti: *PL,*
25/9/1951, p. 7, col. 4.

123 I'm in talks: *L'Éq,* 28/9/1951,
p. 3, col 1.

123 leave my family in France: *L'Éq,*
3/10/1951, p. 4, col. 4.

123 Olympic road champion in
1948: *Ibid.*

128 not the only celebrity: *NYPL.*

128 Cole Porter Nights: *CP,*
pp. 328–32.

129 IN THE JUNGLE: *PL,*
27/9/1951, p. 8.

9

This chapter draws extensively on
RD 'Hut', MG, AL and *HB.*

134 the front page: *L'Éq,* 5/4/1950,
p. 1.

134 no FIFA wage cap: the following
is drawn from *AGR,* pp. 41–54,
the best available summary of
football's 'El Dorado'.

136 Our first cycling deserters:
Unidentified Argentine
newspaper in *RSGA,* May 1951.

136 ROME: We learn: *L'Éq,*
11/11/1949.

137 sixteen Italian riders: *L'Éq,*
26–27/11/1949, p. 3.

137 *Vous êtes sur la mauvaise pente*:
MG, p. 77.

138 *Si tu continues*: *AL,* p. 30.

138 Prisoner 27307, Henry
Marcheras: *AL,* p. 131.

138 theatre of audacious robberies:
MG, p. 160.

139 months of sensual bliss: *GdV,*
pp. 101–2; *Papillon,* p. 161.

139 Prisoner 46635, René
Belbenoît: *GdV,* p. 103; *MG,*
p. 212; *Papillon,* p. 149.

139 The very existence: *MG,* p. 214.

139 The decree-law: *MG,* p. 215.

139 Corsicans and Frenchmen:
GdV, p. 271.

139 LES FORÇATS DE LA
ROUTE: reproduced in *TdF
Presse,* p. 45.

141 I felt my legs itch: *RD 'Hut',*
p. 13.

142 introduced me as a future world
champion: *RD 'Hut',* p. 14.

142 stay in this hellhole: *RD 'Hut',*
p. 53.

143 rare butterflies: *RD 'Hut',* p. 65.

144 never saw him again: *RD 'Hut',*
p. 234.

144 But Al Brown was ill: *RD 'Hut',*
pp. 247–8.

145 What made him crazy?: *EH,*
p. 128.

145 I pulled the cord: *RD 'Hut',*
pp. 222–3.

146 Each time the Master: *RD
'Hut',* p. 223.

146 My great sadness today: *RD
'Hut',* pp. 9–10.

147 landed in Bogota: *Sig*,
5/10/1951, p. 6.

147 The people of Bogota: *Ibid.*

147 I'm not a man: *HB*, p. 205. On
Gaitán, I have drawn especially
on *HB*, *passim*.

149 Tour of Colombia: *MR 'Kings'*,
pp. 7–24.

149 Confusion reigned: *Sig*,
5/10/1951, p. 6.

149 The inauguration: *Sig*, 8/12/1951.

149 city-centre races: *Sig*, 2/11/1951,
p. 6.

10

151 stretching their faces: *AlB
'Bour'*, p. 30.

151 He groomed the author
Colette: *AlB 'Bour'*, p. 17.

151 Alric grew restless: *AlB 'Bour'*,
p. 16.

153 Antonio Bertola: *L'Éq*,
26/9/1951, p. 3, col. 1.

153 INTO THE JUNGLE: *L'Éq*,
8/1/1952, p. 3, col. 5.

156 an old friend: *AlB 'Rififi'*,
pp. 287–95.

156 had travelled there in 1951 as
José's soigneur: *AlB 'Rififi'*,
p. 293.

157 climbing with the aid of a wire:
AlB 'Rififi', p. 294.

157 Back in reality: *Tmp*,
28/1/1952, p. 1.

157 in the form of a letter: *L'Éq*,
18/1/1952, p. 3.

158 Colombia's absence: *Sig*,
8/6/1952, p. 10, cols 4–5.
The other absentees were
Bolivia, El Salvador, Paraguay,
Afghanistan, Iraq, Malta and
Syria.

160 *El Siglo*'s offices: *Sig*, 2/2/1952,
p. 6, cols 3–5.

160 Make Yourself a Champion:
series in *Sig*, 26/2/1952 to
1/3/1952.

160 training is beginning to show:
Sig, 18/7/1952, p. 6, cols 4–6.

161 he flew away alone: *Sig*,
16/6/1952, p. 9, cols 4–6.

161 sporadic stage results: *L'Éq*,
2/3/1953, p. 5, col. 4

161 After the twelfth stage: *L'Éq*,
6/3/1951, p. 4, col. 8

161 Four days later: *L'Éq*,
10/3/1953, p. 4, col. 6.

162 overall victory: *Ibid.*

162 first true cycling talent: *GGM
Journalism'*, pp. 476–553; *MR
'Kings'*, pp. 37–48.

162 the hairdressing business: *L'Éq*,
10/3/1953, p. 4, col. 6.

162 take Hoyos to compete: *L'Eq*,
16/3/1953, p. 4. col. 4.

162 Without doubting: *Ibid.*

163 Colombian national team: *L'Éq*,
23/4/1953, p. 4, col. 7.

163 He flew to Paris: *L'Éq*,
8/5/1953, p. 5, col. 1.

163 *un solide pilier*: *L'Éq*, 11/5/1953, p. 5.

163 Two of them fell: *Sig*,
15/5/1953, p. 14, cols 7–8.

163 lowered his straw hat: *L'Éq*,
14/5/1953, p. 5, col. 6.

164 crashed out of the race: *Sig*,
15/5/1953, p. 14, cols 1–2; *L'Éq*,
15/5/1953, p. 5, col 7.

164 Mario Montaño: *Sig*,
16/5/1953, p. 13, cols 3–5.

164 The rest left: *Sig*, 18/5/1953,
p. 14, col. 3.

164 if they could earn enough: *Sig*,
18/5/1953, p. 14, cols 4–5.

164 Mesa was invited: *Sig*,
3/6/1953, p. 8, cols 7–8.

165 crashed in training: *Sig*,
6/6/1953, p. 11, cols 4–5.

165 an amateur event: *L'Éq*,
29/5/1953, p. 4, col 7, bottom.

165 United Press: *Sig*, 11/6/1953,
p. 11, cols 3–6; *L'Éq*, 12/6/1953,
p. 4, col. 3.

165 they were tired: *Sig*, 13/6/1953,
p. 11, cols 6–7.

165 Fabio León Calle: *Sig*,
22/6/1953, p. 12.

165 due in Cannes: *Sig*, 13/6/1953,
p. 11, cols 6–7.

165 abstain from voting: *NHC2*,
pp. 105–26.

165 Technical change in agriculture:
Sig, 14/7/1952, pp. 10–11.

165 a study of rubber: *Sig*,
21/7/1953, pp. 10–11.

165 Colombian cacao varieties: *Sig*,
28/7/1952, p. 10.

166 Franco–Colombian: *Sig*,
1/8/1952, pp. 1 and 14.

167 The race regulations: *Tmp*,
22/1/1954, p. 16, cols 6–7.

167 spontaneously converted: *Tmp*,
22/1/1954, p. 16, col. 6.

167 Santiago to Medellín: *Tmp*,
21/1/1954, p. 12, cols 6–8.

169 José and the other protesters:
Tmp, 22/1/1954, p. 16, cols 7–8.

169 three Tours of Colombia: *Tmp*,
26/1/1954, p. 16, cols 1–2.

169 At Caramanta: *Ibid*.

11

177 Fausto Coppi and Hugo
Koblet: *MR 'Kings'*, pp. 53–70.

178 rebel elements: *RK*, pp. 12, 73
and 147.

179 de Gaulle became premier: *RK*,
p. 75.

179 a stage win in Bogotá: *ToC*, p. 104.

12

This chapter draws extensively on *RK*.

183 fastest urban growth on earth:
Cali, pp. 269 and 309.

183 free black peasantry: *Cali*, p. 200.

183 even they brought rhythms and
dances: *Cali*, p. 265 and *passim*.

186 Massu had led calls: *RK*, p. 74.
For the OAS, see *RK, passim*.

189 more than a hundred
Frenchmen: *Fig*, 23/9/1964, p. 4.

189 Iván Edelény: *Tmp*, 22/9/1964,
p. 11.

189 former members of the FLN:
Tmp, 22/9/1964, p. 1, cols 1–2.

189 Pierre Château-Jobert: *RK*,
pp. 284 and 420.

190 portrait of Château-Jobert:
Tmp, 22/9/1964, p. 1, cols 4–5.

190 The only shadow: *Fig*,
23/9/1964, p. 4.

190 first European head of state:
Tmp, 22/9/1964, p. 1.

190 roads from the airport: *Tmp*,
23/9/1964; *France-Soir*,
24/9/1964, p. 2.

191 residing in Bogotá: *Tmp*,
23/9/1964.

191 no longer in the capital: *Tmp*,
24/9/1964.

191 presidential Caravelle: *Tmp*,
24/9/1964; *Fig*, 23/9/1964, p. 4.

191 José Beyaert (road, 1948):
France-Soir, 24/9/1964, p. 2.

13

This chapter draws extensively on
GSDN.

196 a fabulous restaurant: unidentified cutting, *JBA.*

198 2.5 carat emerald ring: *France-Soir*, 24/9/1964.

199 Emerald trafficking: *Sig*, 28/5/1952, p. 13, cols 3–5.

200 According to information: *Tmp*, 13/5/1965, p. 3, cols 3–4.

200 bandoleros: *GSDN*, p. 10 and *passim.*

200 invariably violent deaths: *Tmp*, 12/6/1965, p. 30, cols 5–8.

201 murder of his father: *MVUA*, pp. 95–7; *GSDN*, pp. 103.

201 Seventy thousand rounds were unleashed: *GSDN*, p. 172.

201 condemned *in absentia*: *Tmp*, 11/6/1965, p. 27, cols 1–2.

201 live on national radio: *GSDN*, p. 172.

201 Fura and Tena: *AHS*, p. 99.

201 use hand tools: *RHol*, p. 11.

204 a priest who deals in emeralds: *FrdN*, p. 61.

206 REVENGE KILLINGS: *Tmp*, 1/6/1973, p. 5A, cols 1–4.

206 world's wealthiest village: *Tmp*, 2/9/1965, p. 4B, cols 1–6.

208 MUSICIAN KILLED: unidentified cutting, *JBA.*

208 he recalls coining the word: *AlB* '*Rififi*', p. 58.

209 Enough raw sex: *Rififi* (the newspaper headline is shown in the DVD extras).

210 I got the screenplay done: *Rififi*.

210 Milo barely touched: *AlB* '*Rififi*', p. 23.

211 the king: *AlB* '*Rififi*', p. 24.

211 longtime Montmartre buddies was Didi: *AlB* '*Rififi*', p. 287–95.

211 met him at the airport: *AlB* '*Bour*', p. 13.

212 religious and provincial: *AlB* '*Rouges*', p. 10.

212 bewitching extensions: *AlB* '*Rouges*', p. 14.

213 canvas, para-style trousers: *AlB* '*Rouges*', p. 207.

213 He pulled her: *AlB* '*Rouges*', p. 18.

213 world titles: *AlB* '*Rouges*', p. 15.

213 to add colour: *AlB* '*Rouges*', p. 33.

214 first Europeans: *AlB* '*Rififi*', p. 296.

214 Muzo village: *AlB* '*Rififi*' p. 297.

215 I'd have shot him: *AlB* '*Rififi*', p. 298.

215 Le Breton fictionalised: *AlB* '*Rouges*', pp. 52–7.

216 It's *bella*: *AlB* '*Rififi*', p. 299.

216 dreams and ambitions: *AlB* '*Rouges*', p. 25.

216 contemptuous of death: *AlB* '*Rouges*', p. 88.

216 Murders happen: *AlB* '*Rouges*', p. 186.

216 You see I've got balls: *AlB* '*Rouges*', p. 180.

217 Monsieur: *AlB* '*Rififi*', p. 299.

218 Cadaver: unidentified cutting, *JBA.*

218 EMERALD MINE IN COLOMBIA: unidentified cutting, dated 16/4/1971 in José's hand.

218 Bernhard Moser: *AlB* '*Bour*', pp. 233–44.

220 plans and deeds: *AlB* '*Bour*', pp. 107–8.

220 In the emerald milieu: *AlB* '*Bour*', p. 108.

220 Shame the same principles: *AlB* '*Bour*', pp. 108–9.

220 Furatena café: *AlB* '*Bour*', p. 109.

221 too easy to pull out a tool: *AlB
'Bour'*, p. 109.

221 I was an emerald trader: *Tmp*,
19/6/1975.

14

This chapter draws extensively on
JRJ, JAG and *EGOJ*.

222 *Mauretania*: *PCLV*, Year:
1950, Microfilm serial: T715,
Microfilm roll: T715 7839,
Line: 2.

222 Eugénie J. Lecussan: *PCLV*, Year:
1952, Microfilm serial: T715,
Microfilm roll: T715 8116,
Line: 9.

223 only ever glimpsed: *JRJ*, p. 39.

223 1870 war: *JRJ*, p. 27.

223 his dying brother: *JRJ*, p. 355.

223 he escaped: *JRJ*, p. 50.

223 Georges's gun: *JRJ*, pp. 194, 259
and *passim*.

224 Ubangi-Shari Infantry
Battalion: *JRJ*, pp. 259–63.

224 As soon as I was capable of
forming an opinion: *JRJ*, p. 15.

228 Gonzalo Jiménez de Quesada:
JAG, passim.

228 Road-builders: *JAG*, p. 16.

228 rubber tappers: *JAG*, p. 21.

228 land of the Yareguí: *JAG*, p. 10.

229 forty savages: *JAG*, p. 43.

229 On 7 November 1918: *JAG*,
p. 95.

229 twice the national rate: *JAG*,
p. 184.

229 fifty-four brothels: *JAG*, p. 219.

229 the girls charged: *JAG*, p. 222.

229 a mayor and a priest: *JAG*, p. 216.

229 use the heat as a pretext: *Ibid*.

229 the town expanded: *JAG*,
p. 212.

230 Campo Capote: *HVC, passim*.

230 the defeated and the deserting:
JAG, p. 56.

231 paramilitary sweep: *EGOJ*,
p. 119.

231 Murder rates soared: *EGOJ*,
p. 100.

238 the plant was in crisis: 'Campo
Capote en peligro', *VL*,
18–20/6/1975, p. 2.

247 A well-known French
businessman: unidentified
cutting, *circa* January 1975.

249 found guilty: *Tmp*, 11/6/1975.

256 Prices ping-pong so sweetly:
The Paper, October 1974, p. 15.

15

This chapter draws extensively on
JCK, RB, GdV and *AlB 'Bour'*.

258 I'll never forget: *Tmp*,
2/11/1977, pp. 1 and 6.

259 Charlot was waiting: *JCK*, p. 21.

259 liked my frankness: *JCK*, p. 22.

259 nice, quiet hold-ups: *JCK*, p. 23.

260 If you were French: *RB*, p.199.

261 I was curious: *RB*, p. 114.

263 subjected to judgment:
CLFvUS(1), para. 2.

263 While his petition:
CLFvUS(1), para. 3.

264 we do not believe: *CLFvUS(1)*,
para. 10.

266 At the Police office: *JCK*, p. 80.

266 false passport: *Tmp*, 4/11/1977,
pp. 1–6.

267 Swedish coffee entrepreneur:
VTE.

267 warrant for Fiocconi's arrest:
FC, p. 33.

267 I've always preferred tennis:
Tmp, 4/11/1977, p. 6.

268 gone into hiding: *Tmp*,
19/9/1978, p. 6A.
270 a rabble of Papillons: *GdV*,
pp. 14–16.
271 the old, pre-1926 regime: *GdV*,
pp. 53–4 and 112.
271 oral and written stock: *MG*,
p. 208.
271 a claim by Charles Hut: *GdV*,
p. 141.
271 The truth emerges: *Papillon*,
pp. 261–6; *RD 'Hut'*, pp. 85–92.
271 Marius de La Ciotat: *Papillon*,
p. 261.
271 Georges Ménager: *GM*, *passim*.
271 thirty thousand kilometers:
GdV, p. 11.
272 Steve McQueen: *Papillon (film)*.
A YouTube contribution points
out that a scuba diver is clearly
visible under the raft.
272 shark-infested waters: *GdV*,
pp. 190 and 202.
272 'S' built a raft: *MG*, pp. 151–2.
272 Émile Renard: *AlB 'Bour'*,
pp. 19–30.
272 Émile escaped: *AlB 'Bour'*,
pp. 19–20.
273 It's a shame: *AlB 'Bour'*, p. 24.
273 died three years: *AlB 'Bour'*, p. 20.
273 St Paul les Dax: *AlB 'Bour'*, p. 349.
273 whose manuscript: *AlB 'Bour'*,
p. 19.
277 Humberto Barrera Domínguez:
Tmp, 5/11/1977, p. 1A.
277 Hernando Rojas Gooding:
Tmp, 15/11/1977, p. 8C.
277 they married: *Tmp*, 4/11/1977,
p. 6A.
277 I asked him: *Ibid*.
277 he was guilty of betrayal: *Tmp*,
2/11/1977, p. 6A.

278 Laurent Fioconi [*sic*]: *Tmp*,
1/9/1978, p. 1.
278 improvised bridge: *Tmp*,
19/9/1978, pp. 1A–6A.
279 walked out of Atlanta Federal
Penitentiary: *JCK*, p. 131.

16

This chapter draws extensively on
RHol.
280 'Green Fever': *RHol*, p. 3.
280 Holeindre's claim: *Rififi*, p. 296.
280 a son of Pantin: *RHol*, p. 4.
281 a colossus: *RHol*, p. 26.
281 an accurate caricature: *Ibid*.
281 machete fight: *RHol*, p. 23.
282 His sombre, virile looks: *RHol*,
p. 26.
282 Carlos Gardel: *RHol*, p. 6.
282 this immense country: *RHol*,
p. 4.
283 spent a month with José: *Ibid*.
283 One image: *RHol*, p. 23.
284 José's drinking companion: *Esp*,
16–17/12/1989.
284 the Bank of the Republic:
MVUA, p. 98.

17

287 1969 Tour of Colombia: *Tmp*,
28/6/1975; *ToC*, p. 52.
287 José gave him a pill: *Tmp*,
24/6/1973, p. 16A; *ToC*, p. 53.
288 the Inverca Group: *Tmp*,
24/7/1982, p. 2B, cols 5–6.
288 chemical precursors: *FC*, p. 154.
288 issues arising: *Tmp*, 13/7/1982,
p. 4C, cols 1–2.
288 the beefalo: *Tmp*, 24/7/1982,
p. 2B, cols 5–6.
288 Carrillo took on: *ToC*,
pp. 278–9.

289 a long solo attack: *Tmp*,
   20/7/1982, p. 9C, cols 1–2.
289 There were stage wins: *ToC*,
   pp. 282–3.
289 Drug money: *MR 'Kings'*, p. 206.
290 Bogotá anti-narcotics police:
   MR 'Kings', p. 216.
290 Bicicletas Ositto: *MR 'Kings'*,
   pp. 154–62.
292 broken with tradition: *XL*, pp.
   58–9; *MR 'Kings'*, p. 147; *Tmp*,
   10/7/1983, p. 3C, cols 1–3.
292 twenty-three Colombian
   journalists: *Tmp*, 17/7/1983,
   p. 1B, cols 2–6.
293 Tour de France radio tribune:
   Tmp, 7/7/1983, p. 3B, col. 1.
293 an attack by Alfonso Flórez: *Ibid*.
293 incidents in France: *Tmp*,
   8/7/1983, p. 3D, cols 2–5.
294 another mentality: *Tmp*,
   13/7/1983, p. 3C, cols 1–2.
294 reached the mountains: *MR
   'Kings'*, pp. 148–9.
294 BORDEAUX, 9 [July 1983]:
   Tmp, 10/7/1983, p. 3C, cols 1–3.
296 Nobel Prize of mountains:
   Tmp, 12/7/1983, p. 1C.
297 in-depth knowledge of cycling:
   Tmp, 20/7/1983, p. 2C, col. 1.
297 five European riders: *MR
   'Kings'*, pp. 149–50.
298 tangle with Van Impe: *Tmp*,
   21/7/1983, p. 1C, cols 1–6.
298 playing an occasional role: *Ibid*.
298 tenth in a race of heroes: *Tmp*,
   23/7/1983, p. 1B, cols 1–6.

18
301 Georges Alric passed away:
   Obituary in *Tmp*, 8/4/1982,
   p. 6B, cols 1–2.

301 Gay had joined: both Gay and
   Holeindre are mentioned in the
   list of the imprisoned given at
   ADIMAD.
302 US intelligence sources: *JLC*,
   passim.
302 After the OAS: Paret is also
   mentioned in the list of the
   imprisoned given at *ADIMAD*.
305 former wedding photographer:
   GC.
306 dark side of the moon: *AS*,
   p. 226.
306 life imprisonment: *GC*.
307 places him briefly: *RLM*, p. 160.
310 He died on 19 July 2004:
   personal communication from
   ADIMAD.

19
312 Seven and a half miles: *WGP*,
   passim.
318 As José grieved: *MR 'Kings'*,
   pp. 218–23.
319 patience has run out: *Tmp*,
   10/8/2000, Deportes.

20
323 Do not learn: *AP*, pp. 40–1.
325 Death came: *Obit*.
326 FOUR LOST: *Esp*,
   16/11/1965, p. 1.
328 fable of two brothers: *RH*,
   pp. 102–3.
330 busy restlessness: *AG*, p. 135;
   quoted in *JB*, pp. 1–2.
330 You're the sort of man: *AlB
   'Bour'*, pp. 111–2.
331 In Colombia people pray: *AlB*,
   p. 104.

ACKNOWLEDGEMENTS

Thanks to José's brother Georges; José's eldest son, also José; *his* wife María and son, yet another José Beyaert. Also, José's two children in Colombia: Mayerly Carolina Beyaert and José Luis Beyaert.

Thanks also to the following:

the interviewees mentioned in the text and the many individuals who helped me locate them.

the archivists and librarians at the ACBB, Bibliothèque Nationale de France, the Luis Angel Arango library, Calne Library, the DIAN in Bucaramanga, *El Espectador*, *El Nuevo Siglo*, *El Tiempo*, *Vanguardia Liberal*, the Industrial University of Santander, the University of Antioquia and the David Lubin Memorial Library in Rome.

Stefano Bonadonna, Ned Boulting, Cristian Chiapponi, Kath Dean, Gilles Durieux, Guillermo Ferreira and family, Luis García, Néstor García, John Gregory, Ginette Haÿ, James and Jill Howard, Gary Imlach, Jean-Claude Kella, Ray Minovi, Gerardo Pedraza and his parents José Orlando and Teresa; Victor Hugo Peña, his parents Hugo Peña and Amalfi Grisales, his brother Ismael and cousin Pedro Julio Peña; Sylvain Piron, Andrew Simms, Aicardo Torres, Mike Watkinson and Donna Zapata.

Graeme Blaikie, Sharon Campbell, Gill McColl, Iain MacGregor and Karyn Millar at Mainstream Publishing.

my father, John Rendell, for tireless proof-reading and copy-editing; my mother Anna Rendell-Knights and stepfather Bryan Knights for support of all kinds; and my stalwart agent, John Pawsey, who kick-started my writing career ten years ago and keeps it spluttering on, and deserves my endless thanks for this and for shielding me from the world on occasion.

the newspaper *L'Équipe*.

my wife Vivi, who transcribed many interviews, especially those with the loggers in Barrancabermeja, read proofs with her remarkable eye for typos and infelicities, and took care of a thousand practical duties while I disappeared beneath a swaying tower of books and papers in the corner.

Matt Rendell
July 2009